TAKING SUPERVISION FORWARD

Enquiries and Trends in Counselling and Psychotherapy

Edited by
Barbara Lawton and Colin Feltham

SAGE Publications
London • Thousand Oaks • New Delhi

Editorial arrangement and Introduction © Barbara Lawton
and Colin Feltham 2000
Chapter 1 © Colin Feltham 2000
Chapter 2 © Barbara Lawton 2000
Chapter 3 © Sue Kaberry 2000
Chapter 4 © Angela Webb 2000
Chapter 5 © Jaquie Daniels 2000
Chapter 6 © Hilde Rapp 2000
Chapter 7 © William West 2000
Chapter 8 © Tom Ricketts and Gill Donohoe 2000
Chapter 9 © Geoff Haines 2000
Chapter 10 © Sue Copeland 2000
Chapter 11 © Stephen Goss 2000
Chapter 12 © Penny Henderson, Steve Page, Elizabeth
Holloway, Alvin R. Mahrer, Jennie McNamara, Michael Jacobs,
Geraldine Shipton, Sue Wheeler, Val Wosket, Brigid Proctor
and Francesca Inskipp 2000

First published 2000

SAGE Publications Ltd
6 Bonhill Street
London EC2A 4PU

SAGE Publications Inc
2455 Teller Road
Thousand Oaks, California 91320

SAGE Publications India Pvt Ltd
32, M-Block Market
Greater Kailash – I
New Delhi 110 048

British Library Cataloguing in Publication data

A catalogue record for this book is
available from the British Library

ISBN 0 7619 6480 0
ISBN 0 7619 6481 9 (pbk)

Library of Congress catalog card number 99 76891

Typeset by Keystroke, Jacaranda Lodge, Wolverhampton
Printed in Great Britain by Athenaeum Press, Gateshead

CONTENTS

CONTRIBUTORS

Sue Copeland is Senior Lecturer in Counselling at the College of Ripon and York where as well as teaching on counselling courses she is co-tutor of the Diploma in Supervision course. She is also a practising counsellor and supervisor, and has many years' experience as a group supervisor in organisational contexts. She is currently completing an M.Phil. researching supervision in organisational contexts.

Jaquie Daniels is Senior Lecturer in Education and Counselling at Sheffield Hallam University, where she teaches on Certificate and Diploma courses in Counselling and the Certificate in Supervision course. She also works as a psychotherapist and supervisor in private practice and is a member of the Independent Practitioner Network. Her most recent publication, co-written with Rosie Bingham, is *Developing Student Support Groups: A Tutor's Guide* (Gower, 1998).

Gill Donohoe is a UKCP registered Cognitive Behavioural Psycho-therapist working within the NHS in Doncaster. She is involved in the training and supervision of cognitive behavioural psychotherapists and has a background in mental health nursing.

Colin Feltham is Senior Lecturer in Counselling at Sheffield Hallam University, a Fellow of the British Association for Counselling and Co-Editor of the *British Journal of Guidance and Counselling*. He has written and edited many books on counselling, psychotherapy and supervision.

Stephen Goss is Honorary Research Fellow at Strathclyde University's Counselling Unit, a counsellor at Napier University and a counselling supervisor. He is Acting Chair of the BAC Research Committee, Chair of the BAC Research Network and sits on the BAC Practice Development Committee. His research interests include tele-counselling and supervision and the evaluation of counselling and psychotherapy. He has recently co-edited with Nancy Rowland a book on *Evidence Based Counselling and Psychological Therapies* (Routledge, 2000) and is currently completing a Ph.D. thesis on pluralist research methodology.

Geoff Haines works with mentally disordered offenders at the John Howard Centre, part of a forensic mental health service managed by City and Hackney NHS Trust. Geoff's role as a lecturer/practitioner has a number of different facets which include providing clinical supervision for nursing staff, teaching, and working with patients within a multidisciplinary team.

Penny Henderson is a counsellor and supervisor with a special interest in primary care. Her other professional interests include organisational consultancy and training about communication, teamwork and team building. She also contributes to the training of doctors in Cambridge, focusing on aspects of personal awareness and doctor–patient communication.

Elizabeth Holloway is Professor and Director of Training in the Department of Counseling Psychology at the University of Wisconsin-Madison, USA. She has conducted several empirical studies of supervision and training in psychotherapy and written many articles and books on the subject including *Clinical Supervision: A Systems Approach* (Sage, 1995) and is co-editor with Michael Carroll of the Counselling Supervision series currently being published by Sage.

Francesca Inskipp is an Accredited Supervisor and Fellow of BAC. Since retiring as Director of Counselling Courses at NE London Polytechnic she has worked as a freelance counsellor, supervisor, trainer and consultant. She founded Cascade with Brigid Proctor, which offers supervisor training, and together they wrote and produced the resource materials *The Art, Craft and Tasks of Counselling Supervision*, parts 1 and 2 (Cascade Publications, 1993 and 1995). Francesca has written extensively on many aspects of counselling and supervision, including *Skills Training for Counselling* (Cassell, 1996).

Michael Jacobs is a Fellow of BAC and a UKCP registered psychotherapist, who is Director of the psychotherapy and counselling programme at the University of Leicester. He is the author of a number of books such as *Psychodynamic Counselling in Action* (Sage, 2nd edition, 1999) and *The Presenting Past* (Open University Press, 2nd edition, 1998).

Sue Kaberry is a BAC Accredited Counsellor and Supervisor and a UKCP registered psychotherapist. She taught for several years on counselling courses at the University of Manchester, where she was Director of the Certificate in Supervision course. Currently she works in the NHS and in independent practice as an analytic psychotherapist and supervisor.

Barbara Lawton is a BAC Accredited Counsellor who works as a counsellor and supervisor at the University of Leeds and in independent practice. She is also a Senior Lecturer in Counselling at University College Bretton Hall where she is Course Leader of the Graduate Diploma in Counselling and Certificate in Counselling Supervision courses.

Jennie McNamara is a Director of the Northern Guild for Psychotherapy. She is Chair of the Professional and Training Committee and Vice-

President of the European Association for Counselling and Chair of the Humanistic and Integrative section of the UKCP. Having worked extensively across Europe she has been involved for the past ten years as co-ordinator of a training programme in Russia.

Alvin R. Mahrer, Ph.D. is Professor Emeritus, School of Psychology, University of Ottawa, Ottawa, Canada KIN 6N5. Email: amahrer@ uottawa.ca. Author of 11 books and approximately 200 publications, recipient of the Distinguished Psychologist Award of the American Psychological Association, Division of Psychotherapy, he is probably best known for his experiential model of human beings and his experiential psychotherapy.

Steve Page is Head of the Counselling Service at the University of Hull. He also acts as a supervisor to a number of counsellors. He is co-author with Val Wosket of *Supervising the Counsellor: A Cyclical Model* (Routledge, 1994) and author of *The Shadow and the Counsellor* (Routledge, 1999).

Brigid Proctor is an Accredited Supervisor and Fellow of BAC. Since retiring as Director of counselling courses at South West London College she has worked as a freelance counsellor, supervisor, supervisor trainer and consultant. She founded Cascade, which offers supervisor training, with Francesca Inskipp, and together they wrote and produced the resource materials, *The Art, Craft and Tasks of Counselling Supervision*, parts 1 and 2 (Cascade Publications, 1993 and 1995). Brigid has written extensively on many aspects of counselling and supervision, most recently *Group Supervision: A Guide to Creative Practice* (Sage, 1999).

Hilde Rapp works as an independent psychotherapist, supervisor and consultant in educational, business, primary care and mental health settings. She is Chair of the British Initiative for Integrative Psycho-therapeutic Practice (BIIP), email: rapp.biip@cableinet.co.uk, and Chair of the Vocational Board of the Counselling and Psychotherapy Central Awarding Body. She serves on a number of national and international editorial boards and professional committees, including the UKCP Training Standards Committee, the Universities Psychotherapy Association and the Society for Psychotherapy Research.

Tom Ricketts is a UKCP registered Cognitive Behavioural Psycho-therapist working within the NHS in Sheffield. He is involved in the training and supervision of cognitive behavioural psychotherapists and has a background in mental health nursing.

Geraldine Shipton is a Psychoanalytic Psychotherapist and course leader for the MA in Psychoanalytic Psychotherapy at the University of Sheffield. She is editor of *Supervision of Psychotherapy and Counselling: Making a Place to Think* (Buckingham and Philadelphia, Open University Press, 1997).

Angela Webb is a BAC Accredited Counsellor who works as a counsellor at Aston University and a Lecturer in Counselling in the School of Continuing Studies at the University of Birmingham. She is currently researching into issues of clinical responsibility in supervision.

William West is a Lecturer in Counselling Studies at the University of Manchester where he is Course Director of the Master's Degree in Counselling Studies and the Advanced Diploma in Counselling. He is also a practising counsellor and counselling supervisor. His Ph.D. study at Keele University was concerned with integrating counselling, psychotherapy and healing and his book *Psychotherapy and Spirituality: Crossing the Line between Religion and Therapy* will be published by Sage Publications in 2000. He is a member of the BAC Research and Evaluation sub-committee.

Sue Wheeler is Senior Lecturer in Counselling in the School of Continuing Studies at the University of Birmingham. She is a Fellow of BAC; a UKCP registered psychotherapist, a BAC Accredited Counsellor and supervisor. She is the Director of a supervision training course and supervises students researching into aspects of counselling and supervision. She is the author of two books and many articles on counselling, counsellor training, professionalism and more recently, supervision.

Val Wosket is a BAC Accredited Counsellor and a Senior Lecturer in Counselling at the College of Ripon and York, where she is co-tutor of the Diploma in Supervision course. She is co-author, with Steve Page, of *Supervising the Counsellor: A Cyclical Model* (Routledge, 1994) and author of *The Therapeutic Use of Self: Counselling Practice Research and Supervision* (Routledge, 1999).

ACKNOWLEDGEMENTS

I would like to thank Julia Tanner, friends, and colleagues at the University of Leeds, Bretton Hall and beyond for providing me with such encouragement and support during this venture.

I would particularly like to thank Nigel Humphrys for use of University Student Counselling Service resources; Mandy Thompson and Lynda Gray for their help with the typing and Carol Dixon for exceptional patience in the face of my technological ineptitude.

Thanks also to Susan Worsey of Sage Publications for her guidance in the early stages of this project, and Melissa Dunlop and Jane Evans for their subsequent involvement.

Above all, I wish to thank my co-editor, Colin Feltham for sharing his editorial experience and expertise so generously, enabling me to translate an idea into reality.

Barbara Lawton, 1999

INTRODUCTION

Barbara Lawton and Colin Feltham

The expansion of counselling and psychotherapy in the past twenty years has led to debate about how those engaged in therapeutic work can best be monitored, supported and facilitated in the ongoing development of their skills, awareness and knowledge. In 1984, the British Association for Counselling (BAC), in its first *Code of Ethics and Practice for Counsellors*, identified regular supervision as the main agent for upholding good standards of practice in counselling and, as a result, much professional attention has been paid to this area in the 1990s.

Key issues debated have included the question of who should act as supervisors and what training should they receive? How should supervision be conducted and how much supervision do counsellors need? What is the role of supervisors and to whom are they accountable? Many books and articles have been published in recent years addressing these concerns. Theoretical models have been developed; creative approaches to the delivery of supervision have been devised, and over forty training courses for supervisors are now in existence across Great Britain. As a result, supervision has become a recognised professional activity with its own *BAC Code of Ethics and Practice for Supervisors of Counsellors* and *BAC Supervisor Accreditation Scheme*, and is also the focus of an increasing amount of research. A number of helping professions such as nursing have reassessed their attitudes towards supervision and are incorporating aspects of it into their own working practices.

With its parameters firmly established, supervision could be said to have reached its first developmental plateau. It is appropriate, therefore, to evaluate the structures and practices we have created in the light of research and of our experiences of engaging in supervision. This book seeks to encourage that process. In selecting the title *Taking Supervision Forward* the editors reflect their belief that the profession's concept of supervision must continue to adjust as new demands are made of it.

In Chapter 1, Colin Feltham, while acknowledging its positive contributions, outlines some of the problems associated with traditional and mandatory supervision and suggests that radical reconsideration and new creative approaches may benefit both counsellors and clients.

Material in subsequent chapters falls into two broad categories: that which illustrates the trend towards more widespread interest and

participation in the supervision process and explores issues arising from
this, and that which identifies concerns relating to current working
practices.

Enquiries

In the past fifteen years BAC has created structures to try to ensure that
counsellors are adequately monitored, helped to develop and supported
throughout their careers. Regular one to one supervision has been seen
as the most effective means of achieving this and while the editors do not
dispute its importance, we have become aware of problems associated with
its delivery.

Four authors, drawing from the findings of their own and others'
research, explore the nature and complexity of the supervision relationship
and highlight difficulties that may jeopardise its effectiveness. Barbara
Lawton illustrates the problematic intensity of the relationship for some
supervisees and considers the implications of this for ethical and effective
practice. Sue Kaberry examines the power imbalance inherent in supervision relationships and considers their potential for abuse. Angela Webb
observes how the supervision process depends on supervisees being honest
and aware enough to bring pertinent material to the attention of their
supervisors, and explores the inhibitory factors that may prevent this.
Jaquie Daniels investigates how supervisors conceptualise and deal with
supervisees' mistakes, and considers the impact of such occurrences on the
supervision relationship, the relationship of the counsellor and client and
the relationship of all three with the counsellor's professional association.

The chapter by Hilde Rapp acknowledges the challenges of working with
difference in supervision triangles, and looks at ways supervisors can
facilitate more sensitive and informed effective practice.

Trends

It is clear that the context in which counsellors work increasingly determines
some of their supervisory needs. The complexity and diversity of settings
where counselling now takes place means that clinical work can no longer
be supervised as if in a vacuum. Supervisors need to develop understandings of the culture of the supervisee's workplace, and of the formal
codes and informal procedures that govern the way they conduct their
therapeutic work. Four chapters address the specific needs of professionals
working in contexts which have only recently begun to utilise clinical
supervision. William West charts the experiences of counsellors operating
within a spiritual dimension who use healing as part of their work, and
draws attention to particular difficulties this group encounter when trying
to access appropriate supervision. Tom Ricketts and Gill Donohoe

demonstrate how cognitive behavioural therapists are developing their own supervision models. Geoff Haines explores the unique position of therapists working in forensic settings or with highly challenging clients and uses case material to highlight issues that are likely to require attention in supervision. Sue Copeland addresses the complexities of supervising in, or for, organisations, considering potential pitfalls relating to boundaries, confidentiality, contracting and accountability.

Finally in Part II, Stephen Goss acknowledges the impact of new technology and explores the trend towards and potential for incorporating aspects of this into supervisory work.

Roundtable

Mindful that this book is published at the cusp of the millennium, the editors asked key figures in the field of counselling and psycho-therapy supervision to contribute short pieces outlining what they feel will be significant issues for supervisory practice in the second phase of its development. Three authors cite the continuing trend towards more diverse methods of delivering counselling and consider the implications of this for supervisory practice. Penny Henderson, responding to the increase of counselling in primary health care provision, reviews the specific supervisory needs of counsellors working in the health service. Steve Page looks at the issues facing counsellors who work in college and university settings and those who supervise them in the light of widening access to higher and further education. Elizabeth Holloway, drawing on experience in the USA, explores the complex roles of those working therapeutically within corporate situations and the implications of this for their supervision. Looking further at what we can learn about supervisory practice from other countries, Alvin Mahrer celebrates the opportunities for better therapy afforded by improved technology, while Jennie McNamara provides an overview of attitudes to supervision across Europe. Four contributors chose to question aspects of hitherto accepted practice relating to the supervision of experienced counsellors: Michael Jacobs, Sue Wheeler and Geraldine Shipton reflect on the mandatory supervision requirement, while Val Wosket focuses on the interface between supervision and therapy. Finally, Brigid Proctor and Francesca Inskipp draw on a wealth of experience as supervisors, trainers of super-visors and founder members of BAC to review where supervision stands at this stage in its development and suggest possible ways forward for supervisors and the process of supervision.

In compiling this book we acknowledge the work done by BAC and other bodies to try to ensure that counselling and psychotherapy have developed in a professional, ethical and appropriately monitored way. Supervision has been a major element of this. It is hoped that the ideas, research findings and information presented here will add to our knowledge about the supervisory process, stimulate further debate about how it can continue to be an effective container for counselling and therapy work in the new century and, where necessary, examine how aspects of supervision may benefit from critical analysis and reform.

1

COUNSELLING SUPERVISION: BASELINES, PROBLEMS AND POSSIBILITIES

Colin Feltham

The desirability of supervision seems to be universally attested to throughout the counselling profession. Indeed within the British context it is mandatory for all BAC-affiliated practising counsellors, however experienced. However much confusion surrounds the identity of counselling (Feltham, 1995), all counsellors observe confidentiality, are prohibited from sexual contact with clients and are regularly supervised. We might almost say, then, that if it isn't supervised, it isn't counselling! Enthusiastic and mandated support for supervision may, however, subtly inhibit exploration of the actual purposes and limits of supervision as currently practised. In this chapter I aim to set out, first, what seem well established and uncontentious supervision baselines; secondly, what appear to be little commented upon problems associated with supervision; and thirdly, some possibilities generated by this discussion.

Baselines

There is little if any disagreement on the need for a certain amount of supervision input for trainees in the various clinical professions. Perhaps one reason for this is that because counselling is largely dyadic in nature, it makes sense to balance group training methods with more intensive, one to one support, monitoring and individualised teaching, mentoring or supervision. Remembering that counselling frequently deals with distressed individuals in confidential settings, it follows that counsellors may need access to confidential support and consultation themselves. Since supervision has evolved from psychoanalysis and psychoanalytic models of therapy training, it is understandable that it has contained a special emphasis on therapist–client interaction, particularly transferential and countertransferential features. With the growth of newer models of counselling and therapy, supervision is gradually being adapted to meet the needs of these models.

Despite the anxiety which most supervisees initially seem to experience when exposing their work (Skovholt and Ronnestad, 1992), supervision is often cited as one of the most helpful ingredients of counsellor training and development – above theory, for example (Dryden and Spurling, 1989). Supervision is probably the main place where real, vivid learning and discovery happens for trainees and beginners; where theory and reality meet in the challenge of actual clients and the idiosyncratic demands they make on counsellors. The opportunity and need to debrief, discuss and reflect on and anticipate next steps in clinical work are usually keenly appreciated. Supervision is the logical opportunity for training supervisors to ensure that trainees understand the ethical and effective application of counselling theory. It provides the space for learning to distinguish between beneficial responses and interventions, and unconsciously loaded projections and distortions. It also offers trainees and other practitioners the chance to offload anxieties and stresses associated with the work. Supervision writers differ in their foci but most would agree that supervision is a necessary, supportive and challenging, multipurpose activity. A number of emerging models of supervision argue that supervisees will be at different developmental stages calling for duly tailored supervision but the focus for many writers appears to remain predominantly on generic tasks (Holloway, 1995; Page and Wosket, 1994).

Problems

I now outline various problems in greater depth than these baselines because I believe we have generally neglected many of the problematic aspects of supervision. For counselling and supervision (and indeed all applied psychology) to move towards greater maturity, a certain amount of judicious problem finding (Arlin, 1990) and critical thinking (Fox and Prilleltensky, 1997) must surely be encouraged. When problematising supervision, we might re-open a simple question put some years ago that has still not been convincingly answered: 'Do the present models attempt to challenge assumptions by active research and critical evaluation?' (Leddick and Bernard, 1980: 194).

Tradition

While no single comprehensive history and analysis of supervision yet exists, clues to its evolution are found in Greben and Ruskin (1994), Jacobs et al. (1995) and Leddick and Bernard (1980). Clinical supervision as a training requirement arose from the psychoanalytic context, reportedly ushered in by Max Eitingon in the 1920s. Before that, informal case discussions were probably the norm. The Hungarian School advocated that the trainee analyst free-associate about patients, with supervisor and training analyst being one and the same person. The Vienna faction insisted on separate roles being fulfilled by two distinct analysts, one offering personal analysis, the other an educationally orientated supervision. This disagreement stems from the 1930s but can still be found today and Carroll (1996) suggests that this controversy has remained unresolved. It bears not only on the problem of conflating counselling with supervision, but also on other problems of dual – or even multiple – relationships involving counselling, supervising, managing and training, including the assessment function (Stone, 1994).

The official position – and attempted solution – of the British Association for Counselling is to declare that while these activities may marginally overlap at times, they are best separated or managed contractually (BAC, 1996). These brief historical and professional allusions highlight the fact that there was and still is no consensus about the best ways to supervise in the midst of conflicting demands. We could also infer that many of our problems in supervision stem from unexamined (psychoanalytic) traditions and assumptions which will not necessarily travel well into other theoretical orientations, into non-private practice settings and into the twenty-first century.

Supervision is less well developed than counselling itself in theoretical and skills terms. In some ways supervision practice may have been more shackled to tradition, and suffer more from lack of innovation and relatively limited research input. As Inskipp (1996) suggests, some trainees may be more up to date in their reading and thinking than some of their supervisors, who perhaps trained many years ago. The trainee today may be more exposed to questions of eclecticism and integration, treatment specificity, short-term counselling, accountability, and the impact of feminist, multicultural and postmodern thought generally (Brown and Landrum-Brown, 1995; Russell, 1996; Taylor, 1994; Thompson et al.,1994). Traditional supervision is likely to be based on ethnocentric theory, like counselling itself. Supervision provided by senior practitioners, and in many cases those with academic training affiliations, will often reflect identifiably white, middle-class values. Short term counselling, including single-session therapy, makes supervisory demands that have probably not been addressed at all (Feltham, 1997). Conscientious supervisors, aware of the many growing needs of knowledge updating, are unsurprisingly vulnerable to considerable stress themselves (Carroll, 1995; Dearnley, 1985).

Differing theoretical orientations

Since psychoanalysis is the oldest of therapeutic orientations it is hardly surprising that the counselling profession as a whole has taken much of its supervision template from it. In Britain the psychodynamic and person-centred schools arguably still predominate – in spite of the continuing rise of cognitive behavioural therapy – and accordingly great emphasis is placed within supervision on the importance of the supervisory relationship, on parallel process, core (relationship) conditions and on transferential and countertransferential foci. At the same time BAC stresses the wisdom of trainees especially receiving supervision from supervisors who share or are comfortable with the same theoretical orientation. In other words, in order to avoid unhelpful mismatches, person-centred trainees and beginning counsellors should ideally have person-centred supervisors, Gestalt counsellors Gestalt supervisors and so on. This is confirmed by Steinhelber et al. (1984) and Feltham and Dryden (1994).

The advent of behaviour therapy, cognitive behavioural therapy, the various humanistic and transpersonal models and more recently a host of integrative, eclectic, systemic and narrative models, forces us to reconsider the question of supervisor–supervisee fit in relation to theoretical allegiance. How can a diehard psychodynamic supervisor supervise a committed behaviour therapist, or vice versa? Obviously, in most cases such oppositional extremes will not occur, and may not even be permitted by the specific professional body concerned. However, given the continuing proliferation of theoretical orientations, it seems statistically likely that supervisees – especially those outside large cities – will often face difficulty finding suitably trained and experienced supervisors with matching orientations.

The existence of competing theoretical and clinical models also creates acute problems for supervisory assessment and interpretation. Kottler (1993: 70–74) argues that therapists quite often receive highly contradictory supervisory interpretations of their clients' behaviour. It is not uncommon in group supervision for a supervisee to be bombarded by supervisory feedback and suggestions from a supervisor and from several colleagues, each with their own idiosyncratic perspective, an experience which can prove more perplexing than enlightening. Jacobs (1996a) presents an illustrative array of five different supervisory inputs into the same client material which could either leave one highly stimulated and productively challenged or utterly confused (or convinced that 'epistemic ravages' (Grünbaum, 1984) really are rife in psychotherapy and counselling). Let us also seriously consider that the parallel process so central and obvious to psychodynamic supervisors may well be non-existent from the perspective of supervisors from traditions without concepts of the unconscious and isomorphic processes, for example.

The flip side of this argument should also be considered. It is quite possible that supervisory dyads with too closely matching theoretical orientations and personalities will find themselves at times in a form of theoretical or clinical collusion. Dearnley (1985: 59) observes: 'In my gloomier assessments of successful supervision, I feel that no more is happening than like being matched by like, with similar personalities and defences, so that the "success" might be just a collusive fight.' Davenport (1992) has argued that a person-centred supervisor failing to point out to a supervisee the possible clinical superiority of cognitive behavioural therapy for depression or the need for psychiatric assessment in certain cases, might well be considered to be acting unethically or even negligently in the eyes of the (US) law. We have to ask ourselves whether, in supervision which has the clear potential to reinforce theoretical traditions at the expense of client welfare, we should not in all cases ask if our preferred clinical approach has limited competency which the client should also be alerted to (Roth and Fonagy, 1996). Davenport's warning is stark indeed:

> Client-centered supervision, appealing as it may be, fails to meet the rigorous ethical and legal guidelines now required of counselor supervisors. (Davenport, 1992: 231)

The dynamics of the mandatory

While concern is sometimes expressed by counsellor trainers that ethical problems arise from demanding that trainees have personal therapy (in a profession in which self-determination is probably the highest ideal), I have heard few protests against mandatory supervision, Getzel and Salmon's (1985) and McFadzean's (1997) arguments being exceptional. Many counsellors say that they would opt to have regular supervision even if it were not obligatory, but this is not the same as the insistence that counsellors *must* have regular, ongoing supervision for their professional lifetime (BAC, 1998a). BAC prescriptively calls for all counsellors to receive a minimum of 1.5 hours of supervision a month, and more in relation to higher than minimal caseloads. The most recent BAC document on these issues unfortunately seems to reflect even more prescriptive, non-negotiable and (presumably unintentionally) paternalistic and evidence-ignoring norms (BAC, 1998b). It is of course quite in order for a professional body to stipulate norms of professional behaviour as it sees fit. However, there are problems associated with mandated supervision that should be raised and addressed squarely.

Lifetime supervision of counselling is not a requirement in the USA, for example (although there are signs that this may change, according to Carroll, 1996). It is not a requirement of all other professional bodies overseeing the work of psychotherapists, psychoanalysts and clinical psychologists in Britain. We have to ask exactly why it was made mandatory in Britain, by what committee, on what research, philosophical or other grounds. One commonly reads texts which include phrases like 'supervision is an essential ingredient of effective counselling' but which fail to offer any evidence for such claims. Is the need for regular, lifelong supervision axiomatic? Is it not reasonable to object that some counsellors may need it (or simply enjoy it) more than others, that some may need it only periodically or find it most beneficial when sought voluntarily rather than received without choice? Could it be that the need for supervision expands in proportion to the absence or inadequacy of trainees' personal therapy or training analysis? There must, after all, be some implication that psychoanalysts, having had lengthy analyses themselves, are not required also to have lifelong supervision, perhaps because they are considered to have substantially worked through their own impediments to effective practice.

A growing concern within BAC is that anti-discriminatory practice issues be addressed and promoted by supervision (BAC, 1996). Unfortunately the logic of regular, mandatory supervision is that, along with ever-rising costs of training, personal therapy, membership fees, accreditation, registration, continuing professional development and insurance, the counselling profession closes its doors to all but the relatively affluent. (Supervision costs are likely to be between £500 and £1,000 p.a., plus travel costs and any loss of income incurred during that time.) Not only do the professional bodies indirectly discriminate in this economic way against everyone on a low income, but they also discriminate philosophically against practitioners who sincerely wish to be optimally self-determining, accountable to peers and clients (not primarily to centralised professional bodies) and to convey the values and practice of self-determination and adult negotiation to their clients (Mowbray, 1995).

Lastly consider the problem of the dynamics of the mandatory within supervision itself. The supervisee must attend for regular supervision whether he or she usually finds this useful or not. If the supervisee does not find it always particularly useful, there is an implication that something is wrong with the supervisee, since supervision is apparently found universally and invariably helpful. Furthermore, the supervisee who harbours any doubts but dutifully attends supervision is bound to find her or himself either acting inauthentically or getting into conflict with the supervisor (who, by definition, presumably believes in the universal usefulness of supervision). It could of course be the case that the hypo-thetically perverse, rebellious, exceptionally gifted, critical or anomalous supervisee implied in this example simply needs a change of supervisor. However, it might be that she or he has different needs from other counsellors and would benefit from a different kind of input – perhaps irregular, voluntary (but possibly timely and impactful) supervision or consultation. Pilgrim and Treacher cite the words of a clinical psychologist remembering one of his early supervision experiences:

> Looking back . . . I visualise numerous barren hours with, I think, dissatis-faction on both sides, deteriorating at last into an empty ritual. . . . This happens because of the things that have remained unsaid. (1992: 101)

Mearns (1991) has itemised some of the permutations of what is likely to remain unsaid. But quite probably in a mandated situation where supervisors sometimes have assessment powers, always have a professional responsibility and often have an investment in orthodox professional views, and where supervisees may be reminded of previous learning anxieties, some things will be very difficult to voice. Were social psychologists to analyse the supervisor–supervisee interaction in terms of expectancy, persuasion, obedience and conformity, it would hardly be surprising if they confirmed the suspicion that a good many anxieties, distorted perceptions and inauthentic behaviours were involved. If the experienced supervisor 'sees' evidence of child sexual abuse in the inexperienced supervisee's case report, yet the supervisee does not see it, who is more likely to doubt themselves? Similarly, if, as reported by William West in this book, the supervisee's and supervisor's views on healing and spirituality differ, supervisory problems are likely to arise (or be suppressed).

The position of BAC is that counsellors must have regular, career-long supervision. Within this stipulation there is freedom to try various forms of supervision (one to one, group, peer, etc.). I am unsure whether periodic supervision or supervision by a number of different supervisors on a one-off basis would be deemed legitimate, as has been suggested by Kaslow (1986). As a British counsellor one is not in a position, like the psychoanalyst, to opt for supervision only when a specific need is felt.

An interesting defence of mandatory supervision has been put to me. Where supervision is *not* mandatory it is likely that cavalier, arrogant and dangerous practitioners would be those most likely to choose not to have regular supervision. Hence, if regular supervision is mandatory for all, such practitioners cannot slip through the net. Even if some counsellors do not really *need or benefit from* regular supervision, a universal mandate is still better than free choice. Such an argument is unlikely to convince the very experienced counsellor with a small, part-time caseload who has to pay perhaps £600 or more per annum out of his or her own pocket purely to ensure that rogue counsellors do not escape from being supervised!

Client outcomes

Everything done in the name of counselling and psychotherapy is ultimately directed towards reducing distress and enhancing understanding, well-being and mental health. In other words, the whole enterprise is about the welfare of clients. Supervision is primarily about ensuring that clients are helped and protected. However, this client focus is easily lost. It may be lost because poor supervisors inappropriately counsel rather than supervise supervisees (Carroll, 1996: 28); because often the client is in no real way represented within supervision (Mearns, 1995); because there is disagreement as to whether supervision is conducted primarily in the interests of the counsellor or the client (Jones, 1989); because rather too much emphasis is placed on the supervisor–supervisee relationship; because we tacitly give up on trying to access actual clinical data and settle for its symbolic representation; or because there is little or no actual or necessary correlation between supervision (however regular and skilled) and client outcome. The latter possibility is indeed quite likely:

> The client is always present in the supervision. Indeed, the supervisor's *raison d'être* is to ensure that the trainee can deliver effective service to the client. Yet ironically, *there is little research that examines client change or characteristics as an outcome or in relation to the supervision process.* (Holloway, 1995: 92; emphasis added)

Should we conclude that there is simply little research in this area but surmise that if there were more it would demonstrate strong positive correlations? Should we infer that although research has been conducted, little of it has been directed at the obvious central question ('Does supervision make any difference to client outcomes?'), perhaps because we are afraid of what we might have to face – that it may not in fact make any significant difference? Steinhelber et al.'s (1984) research into client change suggested some relationship between therapist–supervisor congruence and (therapist-rated) client change, but no clear cut cause–effect relationship between supervision and client outcomes. I have raised elsewhere the embarrassing possibility that the clinical work of unsupervised or irregularly supervised practitioners may not necessarily be inferior to or more damaging than that of closely supervised practitioners (Feltham, 1996a). Should we perhaps infer that little research has been conducted in this area because we have succumbed uncritically to the emotional appeal of supervisory support and the aura of professionalism it bestows on a fragilely developing profession?

Suppose we did indeed conduct research using control groups and we discovered that in spite of the comfort supervisees derive from supervision, this does not translate into significantly better client outcomes? Or, we might find that supervised counsellors are on the whole no less abusive towards clients than unsupervised counsellors or therapists? We might still argue that supervision is valuable or even essential to the well-being of counsellors. So, are supervised counsellors in better psychological shape (less stressed, less prone to low morale, etc.) than their unsupervised or irregularly supervised clinical colleagues? Again, research might enlighten us. If we were to discover that the actual primary benefit of supervision is psychological protection, emotional containment, or stress inoculation for counsellors, this would be well worth knowing. Indeed counsellor protection as the primary task of supervision has sometimes been proposed (Loughlin, 1992) or implied (BAC, 1998b).

It is arguable that until we have some clarity and evidence about supervision and client outcomes, we have no right to be so insistent on ongoing mandatory supervision or to promulgate the view to the public that when seeking counselling they should ascertain whether their prospective counsellor is in regular supervision, as if this guarantees quality or protection. Undoubtedly there is widespread passionate conviction that supervision, like personal therapy, is ethically imperative. But if there is even an inkling that our convictions are misguided, it would be unethical to oversell supervision, to seek funding for it or to make it mandatory. This is a point at which an ethic based on faith is in conflict with an ethic based on empiricism (Feltham, 1996b). As one supervisee put it:

> Does my supervision make any difference to my clients? I doubt it. Given that one and a half hour slot each month in my busy schedule (counselling, training, writing, administration, etc.), I think that probably I've already forgotten most of what was said in my supervision session by the time I get back to my office and into my work half an hour afterwards.

Client protection

Clients are entitled to expect professional and ethical behaviour from their counsellors. To my knowledge, all professional codes make it clear that sexual contact, financial, emotional and any other form of abuse or exploitation is prohibited. Part of the function of supervisors is to reinforce these normative elements of counselling. Views on 'clinical responsibility' differ enormously (who is ultimately responsible should something go wrong – counsellor or supervisor, or both?) and this itself is an area for clarification. How exactly can supervisors actually monitor supervisees' work and have any realistic responsibility towards clients? Obviously no counsellor who deliberately exploits or abuses clients will volunteer this information to his or her supervisor. Unknowingly or incompetently, some counsellors do err at times by failing to make clear contracts, set and maintain boundaries, own their own projections and generally fail to work skilfully (Buckley et al., 1979; Robertiello and Schoenewolf, 1987). Much of this abuse by incompetence or inexperience can be picked up by astute supervisors from the manner in which supervisees discuss their clients, by asking relevant questions and closely monitoring case details.

How can the supervisor know or even suspect that the supervisee flirts with or has sexual contact with a particular client, charges too much, speaks demeaningly to the client, or encourages her or him to persist dependently in counselling which may be going nowhere? Audiotapes can sometimes assist supervisors in identifying such phenomena. Even here, however, supervisees have been known to be selective or artful in how they present tapes and which cases they present (Dryden, 1991a: 56–73). Remember too that many counsellors are quite free to select which supervisors they work with, a choice which reinforces self-determination but also may provide *carte blanche* for evasions and mismatches (Perris, 1993).

Certainly an exhaustive checklist of pertinent supervisory queries might be drawn up in relation to client protection, but there is no way in which any supervisor could guarantee to keep track of such issues in relation to every client discussed by every supervisee. (Actually, if *very* high levels of supervision were mandated – towards a one to one practice: supervision ratio – then client protection might be genuinely vouchsafed!) I suspect that we are burdened with the myth that highly skilful supervisors do, in fact, have something approaching X-ray vision, a kind of supervisory intuition which reliably alerts them to abuses or clinical problems not consciously signalled by the supervisee. It is reassuring to believe in or construct an image of the omniscient and omnicompetent supervisor, preferably supervising the conscientious and open counsellor, both committed to the same therapeutic model. In reality, however, there is probably always an area in which a degree of supervisor ignorance and anxiety overlaps with a degree of supervisee ignorance, anxiety and partial (conscious or unconscious) concealment of significant material.

Some writers have suggested that the supervisory process has relatively little to do with the actual client, but is rather a matter of the counsellor's phantasy of the client meeting the supervisor's phantasy (Jacobs, 1996b). For Jacobs et al. (1995), this admittedly 'illusionistic world' must be accepted and worked with in supervision. Based on my own experience of some supervision groups in which phantasies have abounded, I would say that the poor client sometimes does not get a look in at all, never mind *protection* (see Mearns, 1995 on this point).

Supervision from a communicative perspective attempts to focus closely on the ways in which clients unconsciously signal levels of abuse and damage perpetrated by their counsellors (Langs, 1994; Smith, 1996). Rational emotive behaviour therapy lends itself to a form of supervision which focuses clearly on counsellor skill and strategy (and therefore on protecting the client from counsellor ineffectiveness) but also on the ways in which supervisees may be irrationally (e.g. perfectionistically) abusing themselves (Dryden, 1991a). However, to my knowledge there is no existing approach which systematically monitors what actually happens to clients and protects them. Supervision in some family therapy or clinical research settings, where live supervision or one-way mirrors are used or recording of all sessions takes place, is the exception. Extended use of such supervision methods would prove prohibitively expensive, however.

We can argue that regular supervision makes it less likely that clients will be exploited or abused but I know of no hard evidence that this is the case. Systematic supervision might have the effect of exposing some charlatans, perhaps, and headline abuses (e.g. sexual exploitation) may be reducible. But how are clients to be protected against ineffective counselling methods, for example, when our profession is characterised more by conflicting and well defended theories and traditions than by a consensual focus on effectiveness?

Experienced counsellors

There are now many models of counsellor and supervisee development (e.g. Skovholt and Ronnestad, 1992), so much so that a (linear) developmental element in supervision is probably taken as a truism, in spite of warnings from Fisher (1989) and, by analogy, from critiques of developmental psychology (Burman, 1994) and alternative models of lifespan development (Goldberg, 1992; Lichtman, 1987).

The reasonable position is that nobody can ever consider themselves fully and finally trained; we always have something more to learn and we are all prone to countertransferential errors, cognitive distortions, skills deficits, 'waning enthusiasm' (Malan, 1975) and ordinary human failings. Presumably for these reasons the BAC requires highly experienced counsellors to continue to have regular supervision. One could simply accept the case for lifelong supervision, but even so most would agree that the supervisory needs of experienced counsellors may be very different from those of beginners. As far as I know, no one has satisfactorily discovered exactly what these needs are and how they are to be met. (I am ignoring here the different *individual* needs of experienced counsellors working in different settings with different client groups and practising according to different theoretical orientations.) Fisher (1989) has suggested that individual needs and realities may be more important than developmental stages. See also Carroll and Holloway (1998). Furthermore, the logical problem must be faced that the more experienced one is, the fewer will be those practitioners available with similar or greater levels of experience.

It is often agreed that experienced counsellors may benefit from a collegial style of supervision, sometimes referred to as consultation, or indeed from peer supervision dyadically or in a group (Getzel and Salmon, 1985; Goldberg, 1992). Is it possible that at least some experienced practitioners may benefit more from freely chosen personal therapy or programmes of continuing professional development (or from an annual holiday!) than from costly, everlasting supervision, given that financial resources do not always allow for all such inputs simultaneously? Cooper (1998) suggests that supervision is overburdened with the hope that it will provide all or most of what therapists require for professional accountability and that self-evaluation combined with appropriate continuing professional development needs a higher profile. Others have argued that standardised quality evaluation mechanisms should be used by all therapeutic services and that the importance of such measures may have been overshadowed by our fixation on supervision. I have anecdotal reasons to believe that many long-established and reflective practitioners are pondering such matters without, as yet, arriving at answers (see also McFadzean, 1997).

Casement (1985), an eminent psychoanalyst, emphasises the value of self-supervision. Pilgrim and Treacher (1992: 107) cite the case of a clinical psychologist who had to develop robust self-supervisory habits to compensate for the poor supervision on offer. Getzel and Salmon (1985) cite various arguments that mandatory supervision should be limited to a three- or six-year post-qualifying period. Gerard Egan freely admits to never having had any formal supervision at all, although he values an informal 'stop-and-check' process, and believes that his writing is a kind of self-supervision (Coles and Egan, 1996: 196). Garfield (1995), a distinguished psychotherapist, in a masterly summary of the field barely mentions supervision.

Is it conceivable that some experienced counsellors remain highly self-motivated, are effective self-supervisors and might have difficulty finding appropriate supervisors anyway? Arnold Lazarus, a highly experienced American psychotherapist and not a subscriber to regular supervision, crystallises some of these issues:

> I probably ask for help or input from others mainly when I run into barriers or obstacles, or when I feel out of my depth. If things are running along smoothly, *why bother*, but if there are some problems that make you feel lost or bewildered, or when you feel that you are doing OK but could do better, why not bring it to the attention of somebody else, and discuss the issues? (in Dryden, 1991b: 81; emphasis added)

Skovholt and Ronnestad, in their internationally respected text on counsellor development, *The Evolving Professional Self*, infer from their research that practitioners at the 'individuation stage' thrive on 'personally chosen methods' of supervision and continuing development.

> It may mean meeting individually with a colleague for lunch once a week and talking about therapy/counseling cases in a very trusting and open way. It may mean leaving the USA for six months and going to study in Europe with a renowned therapist of some kind. It may mean watching commercial movies or reading novels and looking for psychological themes. (1992: 83–84)

In the British context one writer has made similar observations:

> I don't think that supervision must continue indefinitely. There comes a time, I think, when you aren't gaining any more and the therapist has to go out on their own. Of course there will always be times when you need to speak about a client with someone else and the important thing is to be able to recognise it. (McFadzean, 1997: 22)

One experienced counsellor I interviewed informally said:

> The last two or three supervisors I've had, although experienced and helpful, didn't really add anything to what I already knew myself. I don't think I'm being arrogant but it just feels sometimes that I'm going along with the ritual. It's also not easy to arrange peer supervision because there are very few people locally

with whom I don't already have some existing professional or friendly relationship, and as I understand dual relationships, this means they're excluded.

Sociological suspicions

As counselling in the UK and Europe edges towards professionalisation, we are bound to ask what non-clinical as well as clinical purposes are served by training, supervising, research and accrediting infrastructures. Accepting that supervision has some real training and clinical uses, we might still speculate that it also serves the function of making counselling look like a profession, along with other hierarchical systems of training, accreditation, continuous professional development and accountability mechanisms. The mysterious element in counselling as a profession which separates it from an activity many people engage in (for example, many use counselling skills in their work), is partly supplied by the assurance of supervision – of professional oversight and quality control. The very word 'supervision', disliked by some counsellors (Williams, 1992), carries inescapable connotations of surveillance, of the professional powerful gaze (Macdonald, 1995). Perhaps supervision both keeps counsellors in order and also impresses on the public that serious steps are being taken to monitor and preserve quality. If Frank (1973) is correct in saying that clients perceive themselves as being helped by sanctioned healers in sanctioned settings, perhaps supervisors supply an important sanctioning layer.

Supervisees' first experiences of supervision usually teach them that counselling, however amorphous at times, has its experts: someone somewhere knows better or facilitates enhanced psychic exploration. In spite of the respect accorded to the principle of self-determination and to possibilities for peer supervision, training institutions and professional bodies tend to present supervision as part of a hierarchy of quality control. Supervisors are usually regarded as senior practitioners of some standing. Yet they too must also secure supervision of their own supervision. There are some practitioners who insist that every counsellor involved in individual and couple counselling, group therapy, training and supervision should have regular supervision of each of these activities by *separate* supervisors. Training norms, accreditation criteria, committees and courses for all such functions seem to evolve exponentially. Critics have noted that our profession tends ingeniously to create escalating in-house demands for its own services (Spinelli, 1994).

There must come a point when we concede that there may be some real limits to this supervisory snowballing and that a degree of professional modesty is in order. The pragmatic basics of supervision carried on in any busy practice may not allow us to lay claim to the level of customised supervisory expertise we might like to (Fisher, 1989). We should perhaps welcome, if with some trepidation, sociological (and psychological) critiques of counselling as an emerging profession, and supervision as an emerging specialism, if we are not to succumb to collective hubris and self-deception. As Dryden (1991c: 3) has humorously and rhetorically inquired:

> Are accredited counsellors who have trained on recognised counselling courses and are supervised by recognised supervisors more helpful to their clients than non-accredited counsellors who have trained on non-recognised courses supervised by non-recognised supervisors?

Possibilities

A summary of the above with possible remedies is given in Table 1.1. The need for improvements in supervision has already been identified by others, of course. A popular suggestion is that greater creativity be employed in group supervision, for example (Inskipp, 1996; Wilkins, 1995). Having seen some creative supervision in action, I would want to warn against creativity for its own sake. It is quite a simple matter to inject colourful imagery, role plays and other creative experiments into supervision and it is not uncommon for supervisees to be entertained and to feel momentarily stimulated by them. I am not so sure that this translates reliably into durably better practice and improved outcomes for clients. (Research might enlighten us here too.) Recently there have been many workshops and writings along the lines of 'making the most of supervision'. This could be seen as carrying the negative message 'Since you've got to be in supervision, you'd better get used to it and try to enjoy it!' More positively, suggestions are being made that counsellor trainees be systematically introduced to what supervision is and how it might be prepared for and used (Horton, 1993; Inskipp, 1996). The importance of preparation and mutually clear contracting was perhaps best described by Bordin (1983), who also stressed that reviewing audio- and video recordings was likely to provide the best avenue for professional growth (see also Proctor, 1997).

Russell (1993) has put forward useful guidelines for trainers and supervisors concerned with sexual exploitation in counselling. There is a role for pre-emptive training, probably using role-played scenarios which raise pertinent situational, ethical and personality issues in this area. These might promote an awareness of warning signs, countertransference implications, temptation-prevention, relationship problem-management and best use of supervision. Perhaps even aversive reports of what has happened to exploited clients and counsellors 'found guilty' might have their uses. We also need to remember that supervisors themselves are not immune to indulging in unethical or exploitative behaviour and may benefit from similar training.

Clearly we need more research and enquiry in these areas. Given that in some settings and countries regular supervision is not mandatory, we might have relatively easy access to control groups or clinical comparisons when examining supervisory impacts on actual client outcomes. We also

Table 1.1 *Supervision problems and solutions*

Aspects of supervision	Positive values	Problems	Possible solutions
Tradition	Tried, trusted and respected.	Risk of ritualised process. Resistance to technical innovation and social critiques.	Review practices. Introduce updating modules for supervisors. Consider innovations, including new technology.
Differing theoretical orientations	Healthy diversity.	Different, sometimes conflicting objectives, methods and language. Risk of blind spots in same-orientation supervisory dyads.	Analyse and compare norms, practices and needs. Specific training for supervision within each orientation. Encourage transtheoretical supervisory training. Promote supervision as an integrative mechanism.
The dynamics of the mandatory	Ensures that it happens; that no one is exempt.	Precludes free choice. Risk of empty ritual. Questionable for experienced counsellors. Cost factors.	Solicit views of all counsellors. Invite genuine debate. Extend research. Consider limit to mandatory period. Mandate minimal *continuing professional development* levels instead of supervision.
Client outcomes	Assumption of and belief in clinical usefulness.	No evidence of improved outcomes resulting from supervision.	Research. Consider whether client outcomes *are* in fact a necessary concern in supervision. Accord greater importance to *evaluation* mechanisms.
Client protection	Self-evident.	Little direct evidence of actual counsellor behaviour. Abusive practitioners unlikely to disclose malpractice.	More attention in counsellor and supervisor training. More emphasis on tape recording and monitoring. Require that all work is logged. Consider issuing all clients with standard client advice form.
Experienced counsellors	Ongoing protection for clients and counsellors.	Different and not well understood needs. Difficulty of finding suitable supervisory arrangements.	Research. Experiment with different formats. Consider limit to mandatory period.
Sociological factors	Regulation of profession. Counselling in process of becoming a profession.	Public relations can assume greater significance than truth seeking. Spuriously increasing hierarchies and bureaucracy almost inevitable.	Invite and encourage sociological analysis of supervision. Include critical component in counsellor and supervisor training. Consider implications of critiques.

need greater analytical clarity and honesty, examining closely whether our faith in counselling and supervision is supported or challenged by tests of common sense and logic (Erwin, 1997). At the same time there is no reason why we should not experiment with alternative forms of supervision or supervisory mechanisms, placing our emphasis not on uncritically extending counselling traditions but on actually helping clients. Alternatively, if we conclude that supervision is primarily a case and stress management resource for counsellors, we should devise forms of supervision better suited to this precise purpose.

The rapid pace of developments in information and communications technology suggests that supervision or professional consultation might increasingly and fruitfully take place by post, as it sometimes did by Freud himself (Jacobs et al., 1995; and see Dryden, 1991a); telephone, including group (conference) formats (Rosenfield, 1997); and internet or other technologically mediated possibilities (Casey et al., 1994). These avenues would certainly provide better access to a wide range of supervisors or supervisory resources around the world. We might also explore the possibility of some sort of supervisory headquarters, a facility offering the necessary data bank addressing supervisee needs and perhaps access to help with crisis queries in the form of a hotline or internet facility.

Current supervision theory and practice is in danger of compounding the problems of counselling itself, particularly if its function as a signifier of professionalisation is overemphasised. Supervisors can deny and repeat the absurdities within some counselling theory and practice (Feltham, 1996b) or, potentially, minimise these by becoming proactive critics of the profession. One of the truly positive contributions of supervision might be to keep the focus on clients and their real needs. This would entail a willingness to suspend theoretical allegiances somewhat and to promote flexibility, familiarity with research (including literature on clients' experiences and complaints), and openness to individual client and counsellor needs.

Supervisors might become *supervisors of the profession*, overseeing and keeping in proportion the distortions of a sprawling, all too abusable activity. Samuels (1992), referring to a 'psychopathology of psychotherapy', has argued that our critics might be perceived as therapists of the field itself. Field-critical supervisors might follow suit, partly by seeking to avoid the psychopathology of supervision. Instead of being primarily clinical wizards able to point out mysterious parallel processes that are invisible to the ordinary person and sometimes of limited benefit to clients (Jacobs, 1996b), perhaps our role might be more about (a) keeping counselling grounded, demystified, and focused on actual client needs, goals and effective change, and (b) revisioning supervision and counselling generally.

All such issues can profitably be raised within counsellor and supervisor training. On a final radical note, we could even restore to supervision a primary training function: if counselling is best learned from actual practice, and if a great deal of theory is perhaps redundant or contradictory, training primarily by intensive dyadic or group supervision along apprenticeship lines might be seriously considered. At least one clinical psychologist endorses this: 'Much more emphasis should be placed on the training function of the supervisor and far less on formal teaching' (Pilgrim and Treacher, 1992: 105).

We surely do not have grounds for believing that we have yet understood or optimally organised the training process. In my view there is curiously little evidence, but much emotional rhetoric, supporting the value or clarifying the purposes of supervision. Even Roth and Fonagy (1996: 373) resort to purely *rhetorical* support for supervision in their otherwise evidence-obsessed study. Supervision, I submit, is highly problematic terrain. And any consideration of the problems of supervision implicitly reminds us of the problems simmering throughout the entire counselling and psychotherapy enterprise (Feltham, 1999).

Note

This chapter in its original form was presented as a paper to the Annual Conference of the European Association for Counselling, in Athens, Greece, September 1996.

References

Arlin, P. K. (1990) 'Wisdom: the art of problem finding', in R. J. Sternberg (ed.), *Wisdom: Its Nature, Origins and Development*. Cambridge: Cambridge University Press.

Bordin, E. S. (1983) 'A working alliance based model of supervision', *The Counseling Psychologist*, 11 (1): 35–42.

British Association for Counselling (1996) *Code of Ethics and Practice for Supervisors*. Rugby: BAC.

British Association for Counselling (1998a) *Code of Ethics and Practice for Counsellors*. Rugby: BAC.

British Association for Counselling (1998b) *How Much Supervision Should You Have?* Rugby: BAC.

Brown, M. T. and Landrum-Brown, J. (1995) 'Counselor supervision: cross cultural perspectives', in J. G. Ponterotto, J. M. Casas, L. A. Susuki and C. A. Alexander (eds), *Handbook of Multicultural Counseling*. Thousand Oaks, CA: Sage.

Buckley, P., Toksoz, B., Karasu, M. D. and Charles, M. A. (1979) 'Common mistakes in psychotherapy', *American Journal of Psychiatry*, 136 (12): 1578–80.

Burman, E. (1994) *Deconstructing Developmental Psychology*. London: Routledge.

Carroll, M. (1995) 'The stresses of supervising counsellors', in W. Dryden (ed.), *The Stresses of Counselling in Action*. London: Sage.

Carroll, M. (1996) *Counselling Supervision: Theory, Skills and Practice*. London: Cassell.

Carroll, M. and Holloway, E. (eds) (1998) *Counselling Supervision in Context*. London: Sage.

Casement, P. (1985) *On Learning from the Patient*. London: Tavistock/Routledge.

Casey, J. A., Bloom, J. W. and Moan, E. R. (1994) 'Use of technology in counselor supervision', in L. D. Borders (ed.), *Supervision: Exploring the Effective Components*. ERIC/CASS Digest Series. University of North Carolina at Greenboro.

Coles, A. and Egan, G. (1996) 'From priesthood to management consultancy: Adrian Coles interviews Gerard Egan', *Counselling*, 7 (3): 194–197.

Cooper, C. (1998) 'Envy and gratitude: attitudes to collaboration', in I. Horton and V. Varma (eds), *The Needs of Counsellors and Psychotherapists*. London: Sage.

Davenport, D. S. (1992) 'Ethical and legal problems with client-centered supervision', *Counselor Education and Supervsion*, 31 (4): 227–31.

Dearnley, B. (1985) 'A plain man's guide to supervision – or new clothes for the emperor?', *Journal of Social Work Practice*, 2 (1): 52–65.

Dryden, W. (1991a) *Dryden on Counselling: Vol 3: Training and Supervision*. London: Whurr.

Dryden, W. (1991b) *A Dialogue with Arnold Lazarus: It Depends*. Buckingham: Open University Press.

Dryden, W. (1991c) 'Training for the trainers of trainers of trainers', *Counselling News*, 2: 3.

Dryden, W. and Spurling, L. (eds) (1989) *On Becoming a Psychotherapist*. London: Routledge.

Erwin, E. (1997) *Philosophy and Psychotherapy*. London: Sage.

Feltham, C. (1995) *What Is Counselling? The Promise and Problem of the Talking Therapies*. London: Sage.

Feltham, C. (1996a) 'Beyond denial, myth and superstition in the counselling profession', in R. Bayne, I. Horton and J. Bimrose (eds), *New Directions in Counselling*. London: Routledge.

Feltham, C. (1996b) 'Psychotherapy's staunchest critic: an interview with Hans Eysenck', *British Journal of Guidance and Counselling*, 24 (3): 423–435.

Feltham, C. (1997) *Time-Limited Counselling*. London: Sage.

Feltham, C. (ed.) (1999) *Controversies in Psychotherapy and Counselling*. London: Sage.

Feltham, C. and Dryden, W. (1994) *Developing Counsellor Supervision*. London: Sage.

Fisher, B. L. (1989) 'Differences between supervision of beginning and advanced therapists: Hogan's hypothesis empirically revisited', *The Clinical Supervisor*, 7 (1): 57–74.

Fox, D. and Prilleltensky, I. (eds) (1997) *Critical Psychology: An Introduction*. London: Sage.

Frank, J. D. (1973) *Persuasion and Healing: A Comparative Study of Psychotherapy*. New York: Schocken.

Garfield, S. L. (1995) *Psychotherapy: An Eclectic-Integrative Approach*, 2nd edition. New York: Wiley.

Getzel, G. S. and Salmon, P. (1985) 'Group supervision: an organisational approach', *The Clinical Supervisor*, 3 (1): 27–40.

Goldberg, C. (1992) *The Seasoned Psychotherapist*. New York: Norton.

Greben, S. E. and Ruskin, R. (eds) (1994) *Clinical Perspectives on Psychotherapy Supervision*. Washington, DC: American Psychiatric Press.

Grünbaum, A. (1984) *The Foundations of Psychoanalysis: A Philosophical Critique*. Berkeley, CA: University of California Press.

Holloway, E. (1995) *Clinical Supervision: A Systems Approach*. Thousand Oaks, CA: Sage.

Horton, I. (1993) 'Supervision', in R. Bayne and P. Nicholson (eds), *Counselling and Psychology for Health Professionals*. London: Chapman and Hall.

Inskipp, F. (1996) 'New directions in supervision', in R. Bayne, I. Horton and J. Bimrose (eds), *New Directions in Counselling*. London: Routledge.

Jacobs, D., David, P. and Meyer, D. J. (1995) *The Supervisory Encounter*. New Haven, CT: Yale University Press.

Jacobs, M. (ed.) (1996a) *In Search of Supervision*. Buckingham: Open University Press.

Jacobs, M. (1996b) 'Parallel process – confirmation and critique', *Psychodynamic Counselling*, 2 (1): 55–66.

Jones, R. (1989) 'Supervision: a choice between equals?', *British Journal of Psychotherapy*, 5: 505–511.

Kaslow, F. W. (1986) 'Supervision, consultation and staff training – creative teaching/learning process in the mental health profession', in F. W. Kaslow (ed.), *Supervision and Training: Models, Dilemmas and Challenges*. New York: Haworth.

Kottler, J. (1993) *On Being a Therapist*. San Francisco, CA: Jossey-Bass.

Langs, R. (1994) *Doing Supervision and Being Supervised*. New York: Aronson.

Leddick, G. R. and Bernard, J. M. (1980) 'The history of supervision: a critical review', *Counselor Education and Supervision*, 20: 186–96.

Lichtman, R. (1987) 'The illusion of maturation in an age of decline', in J. Broughton (ed.), *Critical Theories of Psychological Development*. New York: Plenum.

Loughlin, B. (1992) 'Supervision in the face of no cure – working on the boundary', *Journal of Social Work Practice*, 6 (2): 111–116.

Macdonald, K. M. (1995) *The Sociology of the Professions*. London: Sage.

Malan, D. H. (1975) *A Study of Brief Psychotherapy*. London: Plenum.

McFadzean, D. (1997) 'Supervision: is it time to think again?', *The Therapist*, 4 (4): 19–23.

Mearns, D. (1991) 'On being a supervisor', in W. Dryden and B. Thorne (eds), *Training and Supervision for Counselling in Action*. London: Sage.

Mearns, D. (1995) 'Supervision: a tale of the missing client', *British Journal of Guidance and Counselling*, 23 (3): 421–427.

Mowbray, R. (1995) *The Case against Psychotherapy Registration*. London: TransMarginal Press.

Page, S. and Wosket, V. (1994) *Supervising the Counsellor: A Cyclical Model*. London: Routledge.

Perris, C. (1993) 'Stumbling blocks in the supervision of cognitive psychotherapy', *Clinical Psychology and Psychotherapy*, 1 (1): 29–43.

Pilgrim, D. and Treacher, A. (1992) *Clinical Psychology Observed*. London: Routledge.

Proctor, B. (1997) 'Contracting in supervision', in C. Sills (ed.), *Contracts in Counselling*. London: Sage.

Robertiello, R. C. and Schoenewolf, G. (1987) *101 Common Therapeutic Blunders*. New York: Aronson.

Rosenfield, M. (1997) *Counselling by Telephone*. London: Sage.

Roth, A. and Fonagy, P. (1996) *What Works For Whom?: A Critical Review of Psychotherapy Research*. New York: Guilford.

Russell, J. (1993) *Out of Bounds: Sexual Exploitation in Counselling and Therapy*. London: Sage.

Russell, J. (1996) 'Feminism and counselling', in R. Bayne, I. Horton and J. Bimrose (eds), *New Directions in Counselling*. London: Routledge.

Samuels, A. (1992) 'Foreword', in W. Dryden and C. Feltham (eds), *Psychotherapy and its Discontents*. Buckingham: Open University Press.

Skovholt, T. M. and Ronnestad, M. H. (1992) *The Evolving Professional Self: Stages and Themes in Therapist and Counselor Development*. New York: Wiley.

Smith, D. L. (1996) 'Communicative psychotherapy', in M. Jacobs (ed.), *In Search of Supervision*. Buckingham: Open University Press.

Spinelli, E. (1994) *Demystifying Therapy*. London: Constable.

Steinhelber, J., Patterson, V., Cliffe, K. and LeGoullon, M. (1984) 'An investigation of some relationships between psychotherapy supervision and patient change', *Journal of Clinical Psychology*, 40 (6): 1346–1353.

Stone, A. A. (1994) 'Ethical and legal issues in psychotherapy supervision', in S. E. Greben and R. Ruskin (eds), *Clinical Perspectives on Psychotherapy Supervision*. Washington, DC: American Psychiatric Press.

Taylor, M. (1994) 'Gender and power in counselling and supervision', *British Journal of Guidance and Counselling*, 22 (3): 319–326.

Thompson, J., Proctor, B. and Lago, C. (1994) *Race, Culture and Counselling Supervision: Implications for Training and Practice*. London: British Institute of Integrative Psychotherapy.

Wilkins, P. (1995) 'A creative therapies model for the group supervision counsellors', *British Journal of Guidance and Counselling*, 23 (2): 245–257.

Williams, D. I. (1992) 'Supervision: a new word is desperately needed', *Counselling*, 3 (2): 96.

PART I

ENQUIRIES

2

'A VERY EXPOSING AFFAIR': EXPLORATIONS IN COUNSELLORS' SUPERVISORY RELATIONSHIPS

Barbara Lawton

The motivation for this chapter was a qualitative research study I undertook for a Master's degree in 1995–96. The project sought to explore how a group of established counsellors experienced their supervision relationships and several factors emerged in the findings which may be of interest to supervisors and supervisees when they reflect upon their own working practices.

In this chapter I will present the rationale behind the research project, refer briefly to the methodology used and discuss the findings in the light of current assumptions and directives about supervisory practice. I will also make recommendations which may help to ensure that supervision alliances are negotiated and monitored more carefully, and identify opportunities for further research on supervisory relationships.

Rationale

At the time of devising the research project I had been in practice as a counsellor for nine years and had worked with five different supervisors. The relationship with each was very different, and the nature and effectiveness of the work we undertook together varied considerably too. Many factors could account for this. Two of these supervisors were chosen by me; three were imposed. Two had trained as counsellors and worked from a humanistic/eclectic perspective; three had trained as psychotherapists and worked within a psychodynamic/analytic framework. Two had undertaken specific training in supervision, three had not, inheriting their roles by virtue of their status in their organisations rather than through choice or aptitude. Each of us brought our own needs, assumptions and transference material to these alliances and the relationships I formed with each supervisor were shaped accordingly.

I was aware too that during this time I had moved through the four developmental levels of counsellor competence (Hawkins and Shohet, 1989) and begun to act as a supervisor myself, and that this must have informed the way I presented as a supervisee. I became keen to learn more about the kind of relationships experienced practitioners form with their supervisors, but attempts to read around the subject revealed this was an under-researched area. Most of the research and much of the writing about supervision assumed the supervisee would be a trainee or an inexperienced therapist. This is because traditionally regular supervision has been seen as an important component but not necessarily a regular feature of a qualified practitioner's professional life. Freud (1914) pinpointed 1902 as the year that psychoanalytic training began, although in its early years this consisted of informal meetings at Freud's house where a group of doctors interested in learning more about psychoanalytic theory and techniques gathered to exchange knowledge and discuss their experiences. By the time of the International Psychoanalytic Congress in 1912 Freud was advocating that physicians intending to practise psychoanalysis should undergo an analysis themselves, but until the first training institutes were established in Berlin (1920) and Vienna (1921) there were no formal training programmes. The 9th Congress in 1925 set up the International Training Commission with a brief to standardise psychoanalytic training and it was agreed there should be three components: a training analysis, a theoretical programme of study and supervision of the trainees' work with patients, known as a supervision or control analysis. Debates continued about how this supervision should be carried out (Edwards, 1997; Fleming and Benedek, 1983), but at its inception regular supervision, while equated with learning, was seen as transitional and finite, a view which has persisted in analytic circles (Langs, 1994:195).

In 1984 the British Association for Counselling (BAC) in its first *Code of Ethics and Practice for Counsellors* made regular supervision mandatory for all its members who were practising as counsellors, regardless of their qualifications and experience (3.3). Bond (1993: 156–157) explains the reasons for this decision and observes that it was a departure from the stance taken by counsellors and psychotherapists operating in much of Europe and North America at that time. Although the codes of ethics governing psychotherapy in the UK still vary in their supervision requirements, Holmes and Lindley (1989: 139) are unequivocal in advocating regular consultation for all psychotherapists, while Edwards (1997) and Hughes and Pengelly (1997) illustrate how this trend has spread to professionals in other mental health and social services. As a result, the original concept of supervision as primarily an element of training has altered and its role as a means of providing monitoring, support and education for counsellors throughout their careers has taken on greater significance. This also means that the profile of supervisees has changed considerably. Instead of being inexperienced practitioners, probably still in training, many are long-standing counsellors, perhaps supervisors themselves, and this is likely to affect the dynamics of the supervisory relationship and the way supervision is conducted.

Demand for more supervisors has led to an expansion of supervisor training in Britain during the 1990s and the publication of various books on how the supervision process can most effectively be conducted. For an overview, see Carroll (1996). Research on counselling supervision and supervisory relationships has been slower to appear than in North America, although this book showcases some recent developments. The dearth of material specifically examining what happens in supervision where the parties are more equal in terms of development and experience was the impetus behind this research project.

Nature of the project

The counsellors I studied were working in various further education colleges. Their professional association, the Association of University and College Counsellors (AUCC) stresses the importance of external rather than workplace supervision for its members, so they had all chosen the supervisors they were working with. This, I surmised, would make it less likely that resentment or dissatisfaction would be present in the supervisees (Webb, 1997) and would provide an opportunity to examine what develops when two professionals of similar status and experience engage in super-vision work together. The subjects were all qualified in counselling at least to diploma level and had achieved other significant academic professional qualifications prior to entering the counselling field. Most were employed on lecturers' pay and conditions of service and were also working as trainers in counselling or a related subject within their institutions. Half were designated Head of the Counselling Service. As my intention was to study supervisory relationships where the expertise of the supervisee was considerable, it seemed important to use subjects whose qualifications and professional experiences might be expected to endow them with some authority. While the eight counsellors finally used in the study met my criteria in terms of qualifications and having chosen their supervisor, their experience as practising counsellors was lower than I had hoped, ranging from four to nine years. This reflects the surge in counsellor training at the end of the 1980s and early 1990s and coincides with the increase in counselling provision in further education colleges as a result of changes in funding arrangements.

Face to face interviews were conducted with each subject, lasting an average of fifty minutes. Questions were designed to elicit information about how the subject selected his or her supervisor, how the relationship was formed and how it developed. A fuller explanation of methodology used and the question areas addressed can be found in Lawton (1996).

Findings of the project

Selection of supervisor

Data generated about how the subjects selected their supervisors suggested that convenience and familiarity took precedence over all other considerations. For half, location was a major reason for deciding to work with their supervisor. Even though all the subjects worked in city environments where there was likely to be reasonable public transport and road networks, there was a desire to keep travel to a minimum ('I didn't want to be traipsing off to Manchester') ('I had kids at home and couldn't be going off any old time . . . I couldn't be bothered with the travelling, working full time').

A third respondent was delighted his supervisor was prepared to hold their meetings on the college premises, while a fourth had chosen her supervisor because her offices were situated close to the college. Though supervision was undoubtedly valued by all the respondents, there was, nevertheless, a sense that their time was very pressurised, and while most had permission to attend supervision during working hours, they felt obliged to minimise the amount of time it took up. This seemed partly due to the subjects' perceptions of their own role, responsibilities and workload within the organisation: that they were too busy to justify even legitimate absences, and partly due to their perception of a hostile attitude towards supervision on the part of their managers, who were confused by the label (Williams, 1992) and could not understand why qualified and experienced practitioners needed expensive external consultation.

Half the subjects cited gender as a consideration in their choice. Three female respondents actively sought a female supervisor, having had unsatisfactory experiences with male supervisors in the past, while a male respondent reported that he had always chosen female supervisors as he perceived them as more nurturing. These respondents illustrate tendencies which recur in this research and have been noted by other observers: the desire to stay with the safe and familiar (Feltham and Dryden, 1994: 68–69) and the opportunity the supervisory relationship presents for the acting out of parent/child material (Hughes and Pengelly, 1997: 179–183).

Six of the subjects said the supervisor's orientation or area of expertise was a factor in their choice although not the primary concern. Only two had opted to work with someone whose background was different from their own, despite there being a considerable body of opinion suggesting that experienced practitioners may benefit from the challenge and stimulation of a new approach (Page and Wosket, 1994: 30).

The rest had gravitated towards supervisors whom they perceived as having a similar training or perspective to their own, even when this may not have seemed the most appropriate for the counsellor's current client group. For example, one subject I interviewed whose prior experience and training was in the field of mental health had recently taken up a post in a college environment, a setting in which he had never been employed before. When selecting a new supervisor he again opted for someone from a mental health background, still working in that field ('I thought there would be some kind of shared experience there') when it might have been expected that a supervisor with experience of working in educational settings would be of more help to him in his new post.

This tendency to gravitate towards the familiar was particularly evident in the high level of importance subjects gave to prior knowledge of the supervisor. Only one had made a choice based solely on printed material available. He worked in a college which ran a Diploma in Counselling course and tutors had compiled a file containing the CVs of approved supervisors in the region, from whom the trainees could make their choice. Two other subjects had approached BAC for similar information and been sent the leaflet entitled *Supervisory Services* (now withdrawn), but found it largely unhelpful because it contained no information about the qualifications, orientation and status of those listed, apart from indicating that some were BAC accredited supervisors.

There being little formalised information about supervisors available, most subjects relied heavily on personal knowledge of the supervisor or recommendations from colleagues. Half of them had a previous relationship with their supervisor. One had attended workshops run by the supervisor during her own counsellor training; another had worked alongside his supervisor for a number of years in a previous work setting; a third met hers as the result of a client referral and they had liaised over the case for a period of time, eventually striking up a friendship; a fourth had previously been in therapy with his supervisor. The latter was the only one who displayed any awareness that a prior relationship might be considered detrimental (Langs, 1994:113; Page and Wosket,1994: 58). Three subjects had chosen figures with a high profile in regional and national organisations to act as their supervisor, apparently believing this was likely to guarantee some level of competence in the supervisory role in the absence of personal contact on which to base their decision.

Contracting

When my subjects began working with their supervisors, the original *Code of Ethics and Practice for the Supervision of Counsellors* (BAC, 1988) was still in operation, and this contained a considerable amount of guidance about what needed to be addressed at the contracting stage (C:2). Supervisors were held responsible for informing the supervisee about their own training, philosophy and theoretical approach. They were also expected to ascertain the supervisee's qualifications and methods of working, and personal therapy experiences. Both should make explicit the expectations they have of each other and ensure that regular reviews take place.

When questioned about the rigour of the contracting process they engaged in, only two subjects reported a satisfactory experience, or one which would comply with BAC requirements. Their supervisors were informative about their own background and way of working, and were interested in the counsellor's. Practical issues were systematically addressed and the respondents felt comfortable about questioning the supervisor and negotiating a working alliance that suited their needs. One of the subjects was a supervisor herself and felt that this was significant in her behaviour at the contracting stage ('I think I may have led it quite a bit because I know what I want'). The other six subjects reported a patchy experience, with agreement being reached about duration and frequency of meetings, fees, etc. but little sharing of counselling models and philosophies ('I assumed she worked in the same way as I did. I didn't actually ask her'); ('We just seemed to kind of jump in from the beginning') .Whether the minimal attention to contracting reported by a majority of the subjects is an accurate representation was impossible to gauge. Their supervisors were not interviewed, so could neither confirm nor deny the supervisee's impression of the way the initial session was conducted. The initial session had taken place several years earlier for some subjects, so it is possible they had forgotten or reinterpreted events in that period. The two subjects who reported the clearest contracting were the two who had most recently changed their supervisors, so they were recalling sessions which had taken place only six and twelve months earlier. Neither had any previous contact or relationship with their supervisor, while the four who had a prior relationship with their supervisors reported only a minimal contracting process. Informed opinion indicates that more attention to contracting is needed if dual relationships are involved (Page and Wosket,1994: 57–58), but this research suggested that in practice there may be a tendency to make assumptions and be less careful about observing procedures when the two parties already know each other.

Data about contracting also suggested that several of the subjects felt unable to be assertive during this process, even though they were qualified counsellors when the supervision alliances began and some were holding positions of authority themselves. The subject who voiced most dissatisfaction about the way her supervisor handled the contracting process admitted she felt ill equipped to take the initiative herself, even though at that time she was managing the counselling service in her college:

I can't believe I was let loose on people really. That naivety has gone completely. I know a lot more about what I'm doing, what I want [from supervision].

That several of my subjects seemed accepting of what was presented as quite perfunctory contracting at the start of their supervision alliance bears further consideration. It may indicate that their training courses had not prepared them adequately to take on the role of supervisee and use the process effectively. As most trained during the 1980s when supervision practice was still evolving in Britain, this is possible, and at least one subject admitted it:

> Looking back on it now I think I was incredibly lazy. It was a case of, 'I've got to have a supervisor. This is a supervisor. She seems OK. This will do.'

If so, it is to be hoped that current training programmes have raised trainees' awareness of a supervisee's responsibilities in the supervisory alliance, and that they have made use of materials such as those produced by Inskipp and Proctor (1993).

The practice adopted by many of the early counsellor training courses of allocating trainees to supervisors pre-selected by course tutors may also have contributed to this 'laziness'. Fees, frequency and duration of sessions, theoretical orientation and working practices were often determined in advance, leaving little opportunity for supervisees, or indeed supervisors, to practise their negotiating skills face to face. Perhaps the malaise on both sides reported by some of my subjects is a legacy of that system.

The inhibition mentioned by some subjects at the contracting stage may also be indicative of the power balance in supervisory relationships. Even though the subjects were experienced counsellors and supervisees, it still seemed difficult for some to feel equal in the relationship; indeed several had specifically sought supervisors older than themselves or 'someone smarter than I was' as if it was important to create a fantasy of the supervisor as parent, teacher or guru.

Information gathered about the nature of the relationships which subsequently developed suggested a strong correlation between the rigour of the contracting at the outset and the working practices which then evolved. Langs (1994) stresses the need for a supervisor to establish a fixed frame at the outset within which the supervision can proceed in a boundaried manner. He acknowledges that frame violations may occur but charges the supervisor with the task of ensuring that contamination is kept to a minimum, and working to secure the frame when it is threatened, either by the supervisee's deviant wishes, for example wanting to engage in a social relationship with the supervisor, or by external forces such as the two parties encountering each other at a seminar or meeting. Supervisors must also be aware of their own deviant wishes and resist the temptation to modify the frame to accommodate them.

Subjects in this research who reported tight contracting and a businesslike approach in the first session continued to feel positive about the working alliance. They arrived punctually for sessions, were well prepared, felt the time was focused and productive and the boundaries remained firm.

Others, whose supervisory alliance began in a climate of looser contracting, reported varying degrees of deviance in the frame as the relationship progressed. For some, this involved the sharing of personal material; for another, the introduction of coffee to the sessions. One subject said sessions always ended with an embrace between supervisor and supervisee, while another went out to dinner with the supervisor at the end of the session. All subjects reporting such framebreaks viewed them positively, welcoming it as evidence of the specialness of the relationship. Only one conceded that there might be a professional or ethical conflict in such practices. Even when the parameters of the relationship were so blurred by social contact outside the sessions that the subject was unable to give specific answers to simple questions about how long the supervisory relationship had been in existence ('We're not absolutely sure but it's about four or five years') and the duration of the sessions ('About two hours depending on how many clients we've got'), there was resistance to acknowledging any anomaly, with the subject claiming the dual relationship was 'probably advantageous to me and my practice'.

From this small study it was very evident that a prior relationship meant initial contracting was likely to be less vigorous and the boundaries held less firmly as the supervisory relationship developed. While supervisees welcomed this, as might be expected, if we accept Langs' view that supervisees will inevitably be engaged in 'the relentless human search for opportunities for deviant frame gratification' (1994: 193), the fact that supervisors are not more vigilant highlights how they too may play out unconscious needs and desires in the supervision arena, or perpetuate practices which are no longer acceptable in the current climate. This suggests a need for more rigorous training of supervisors and closer monitoring of their work, issues which have been addressed by BAC through changes to the *Code of Ethics and Practice for Supervisors of Counsellors* in 1996 and in the criteria for supervisor accreditation in 1997.

The supervision relationship

Having ascertained how the subjects selected their supervisors and negotiated a working alliance with them, I was keen to discover what they expected from their supervision. All expected it to be a significant and intimate experience. The extent to which subjects felt this had been achieved varied. Some claimed they already had an intimate relationship with their supervisor; others believed intimacy was growing and cited a perceived relaxation of the supervisor (i.e. more willingness to share personal information, jokes, make coffee) as evidence of this. The two who expressed most dissatisfaction with their supervision lamented the absence of intimacy ('I didn't feel the relationship was complete; there always seemed to be something not quite there').

Most respondents displayed a tendency to view the supervision space as a haven where the counsellor's frustrations, anxieties and shortcomings would be accepted, soothed or resolved. BAC (1988: B1.1) declared that 'the primary purpose of supervision is to ensure the counsellor is addressing the needs of the client', yet only one of my subjects cited this as the most important function of supervision, although several mentioned client protection as an afterthought. The counsellors I interviewed saw supervision primarily as a support for themselves ('It's mine, it's for me'), and it was clearly a much-prized commodity. Most subjects spoke spontaneously about the difficulties they had encountered when trying to secure the kind of supervision recommended by their professional associations (AUCC and BAC). College managers had often questioned the need for any form of supervision, particularly external; some had refused to fund it adequately or even at all, and some were reluctant to allow counsellors to attend in work time. Thus, their institution was often perceived by subjects as withholding, and unsupportive, while the external supervisor tended to be viewed by them as a nurturing ally.

Perhaps the fact that client concerns were not paramount in the subjects' concept of supervision is a reflection of their developmental level. Hawkins and Shohet (1989) building on the ideas of Stoltenberg and Delworth (1987) suggest that supervisees pass through four developmental levels on their journey from novice counsellor to master practitioner and have different supervisory needs at each stage. As experienced counsellors likely to have reached developmental level four, these subjects welcomed the opportunity for consultation when challenging issues arose. Some valued their supervisor's advice on referral options when this became necessary; others said the security of knowing there was someone they could turn to in the event of a crisis was important. Close monitoring of cases did not seem to be what the subjects required from supervision, but more a space to discuss professional issues with an informed colleague. Since half were managing their college's counselling service, they had decisions to make over and above those arising from clinical work, and all were seeing at least ten clients weekly, which meant they had to be selective about what was taken to supervision. Trainees and less experienced counsellors often have a smaller caseload but are likely to be more anxious about their ability to self-monitor it, so may need to feel the supervisor is 'holding' all their client work, i.e. is aware of all their cases and engaging in regular discussion about them in a way that experienced counsellors may not. While in this respect my subjects presented as autonomous and confident practitioners, as befitting their experience and status, further probing into how they related to their superiors revealed their sense of equality was fragile and the potential for transference immense.

The power of the real or imagined relationship was pronounced in several cases. Idealisation of the supervisor was common, although the exact nature of it varied. Very noticeable was the high regard subjects had for their supervisor's knowledge and experience. Most perceived their supervisor as significantly more knowledgeable than themselves and imbued them with a status that was perhaps surprisingly high, given the subject's own considerable levels of training and expertise. One described his supervisor as 'incredibly competent' while another declared his had 'so many letters after his name', was 'such a darned expert' and 'terrifically knowledgeable'. A third admitted she viewed hers as 'a superior knowledge'. All those interviewed had chosen supervisors who had been in practice longer than themselves and who they assumed, therefore, would be better equipped. Professional longevity does not automatically ensure competence or knowledge, however. Indeed, many of the early counsellor training courses were not as rigorously devised or monitored as their recent equivalents, which have benefited from an increased understanding of the needs of trainee counsellors and the findings of research (Wheeler, 1996). The subjects did not appear to have considered that their training might have been more thorough than that of their supervisor, which predated theirs. Indeed several claimed their supervisors had filled gaps in their own knowledge of theory which had not been addressed in their core training. As when speaking of their college managers, the subjects tended to portray their supervisors as rescuing, reparative figures – an empowering and nourishing influence in the face of a limiting and unsatisfactory experience – this time, the subjects' training courses. How accurate their perceptions were of their supervisors' knowledge and competence as therapists was impossible to ascertain from the data collection methods used, but a dogged belief in the supervisor's expertise and superiority was evident in most respondents. One reason might be wish-fulfilment, arising out of the counsellor's need to regard the supervisor as a dependable expert who could contain their anxieties and prove infallible when they felt vulnerable. There may also be a historical component: a counsellor's first experience of supervision is usually during training where there is likely to be a genuine difference in the levels of skill and knowledge between supervisor and supervisee. It is possible that even when counsellors have become accomplished practitioners themselves they retain a distorted perception of that gulf.

Three-quarters of the subjects said they found it difficult to view their supervisors as equals, and half felt, or expected to feel, somewhat intimidated by them. This was evident in the way some subjects were unable to challenge their supervisors or raise contentious issues. The subject who expressed least satisfaction with her supervisor, describing her as 'a bit wishy washy', followed this up by adding, 'I don't feel particularly frightened of her', which implied she thought she should.

Alongside this tendency to see the supervisor as a powerful, even intimidating figure ran a desire in several subjects to align themselves with the expert and form a special relationship with them. For some, the attachment seemed based in parental fantasy. Kadushin (1968) notes the potential for parent/child material to be reactivated in the supervisory relationship, and it may be that the tendency to both idealise and fear the supervisor is part of that dynamic.

While some subjects associated the supervisory relationship with feelings of inferiority and fear, others seized on its potential for a special or erotic friendship. In at least two cases the supervisor was apparently colluding with this: one subject had a social relationship with her supervisor outside the sessions; another always ended supervision sessions by embracing his supervisor, which he described as 'a transmission of love'. Several others perceived their supervisor as someone they might have a relationship with ('He was the type of chap you could have a pint with'), while female subjects felt they had 'similar interests' to their supervisors. In all these cases the supervisees believed their supervisors shared their perceptions of similarity and regard, interpreting developments such as making coffee for them or disclosing personal information as evidence of this.

Kadushin (1968) suggests that unfulfilled desires for nurturing, attachment and specialness can resurface in the supervisory relationship, as can the replaying of anxiety, subordination and disappointment. The potential for transference material (feelings from the supervisee's past being reactivated by conditions encountered in the present) to assert itself in the supervisory relationship has been well documented (Hartung, 1979; Langs, 1994), although usually in relation to a trainee supervisee's experience where there is a clear difference in the levels of status, knowledge and skill of the two parties and the supervisor may be in a formal assessment role.

Although only a small sample was used in this research, there was evidence to suggest that transference issues continue to affect the way some supervisees function in the supervisory relationship long after they have completed their training. One subject, whose mother had died during his childhood, felt his pattern of always seeking female supervisors and the intense relationships he sought to create with them was an attempt to recover the loss. Page and Wosket (1994: 21), using a transactional analysis perspective, note the need for supervision encounters to be predominantly Adult to Adult, but it may be that even supervisees who have reached developmental level four find this difficult. Only two subjects I interviewed identified instances when their own transference material impacted on their supervisory relationship, although several described their orientation as psychodynamic and would, therefore, be familiar with the concept. Some mentioned ways of relating to their supervisor which suggested that transference might be a factor, but did not appear to recognise it as such. One subject seemed in awe of her supervisor and admitted she was 'terrified' of raising a particular issue with her, even though they had worked together for six years. Either the supervisor was unaware that supervisee felt so inhibited or chose not to address it.

Page and Wosket (1994) surmise that supervisors would confront if supervisees were interacting from a Child position in the relationship, but my findings suggested that the dynamics operating in these supervisory relationships were rarely discussed at all, despite a requirement to do so in the BAC Code of Ethics and Practice for Supervision of Counsellors (1988: 2.4, 2.7, 2.8).

The fact that the subjects were experienced practitioners may have contributed to the silence. Perhaps supervisors are more alert to transference material in trainee counsellors and more certain of their authority to challenge it. Perhaps working with supervisees of similar status and developmental level is more gratifying for supervisors and invites more opportunity for collusion (Inskipp and Proctor, 1995: 128). Discovering answers to such questions was beyond the scope of this study, but this highlights other areas of research which might shed light on the dynamics of supervisory relationships.

Termination

The depth of attachment some subjects felt to their supervisors was most vividly illustrated in their attitudes to voluntary termination. BAC (1990) recommends fixed term supervision contracts, although none of my subjects had entered into their supervision arrangements on that basis. Most said the issue of how long they would continue working with their supervisor was never discussed and found it difficult to imagine themselves voluntarily withdrawing from the relationship. Three admitted they knew there was a strong body of opinion against continuing with a supervisor too long, as collusion and staleness might creep in, but most were adamant this did not apply to their relationship. Their reluctance to consider leaving their current supervisory relationship in order to facilitate further professional growth indicated that attachment and comfort are of considerable significance.

Several did not see changing supervisors voluntarily as desirable because they could not believe a new supervisor would be as effective as their present one ('I would be happy to continue for the rest of my career. It's such good quality'), or because they were daunted by the prospect of locating and then relating to somebody new ('It's a risk, isn't it? Are you going to find someone with whom you feel OK?'). Even where subjects had expressed dissatisfaction with their supervisor, there was immense resistance to seeking more effective supervision elsewhere ('You've got to start all over again, building up a relationship, and them understanding you and the way you work. It takes quite a lot of effort'). For some, telling the supervisor they wanted to leave was an unpalatable prospect because they feared the supervisor's wrath ('I'd be terrified of telling my supervisor that I would really like someone else'), or felt their supervisor might be hurt by the implied rejection ('I'd feel quite embarrassed . . . it feels insulting really when we get on OK'). This subject felt it would be acceptable to terminate the supervision arrangement only if her supervisor had failed to provide a competent service. The desire to extend her own experience after six years was not seen as justification for moving on.

Half the subjects could only imagine ending their current supervisory relationship if they or the supervisor moved away from the geographical region. The notion that termination would only occur at the behest of the supervisor surfaced several times, indicating that even experienced counsellors perceive themselves as holding less power in the relationship. Most could not conceive of taking the initiative themselves, even though BAC (1988: 2.8) apportioned joint responsibility for deciding when the relationship should cease.

There was also evidence to suggest that some subjects did not initiate reviews where the viability of the relationship might be discussed because they feared the supervisor might withdraw if given the opportunity. Only one respondent said she had initiated a review and described it as 'very difficult'. Fear of loss, rejection, hurting the supervisor or seeming to be unappreciative led to avoidance of the topic, even though subjects experienced anxiety because they did not know whether their supervisor thought it was time they moved on. Nevertheless, the discomfort of waiting until the supervisor decided or was forced by circumstances to withdraw from the arrangement seemed more desirable to subjects than instigating that process themselves.

Attachment to the supervisor was strong and to voluntarily sever that connection, even for sound professional reasons, was a daunting prospect for most subjects. Responses suggested they would cling on to the safety of the familiar supervision relationship for as long as possible. One subject was about to move to a job in the health service, but had insisted on being allowed to remain with her current supervisor. Another felt her supervisor was no longer fulfilling all her supervisory needs, but could only contemplate supplementing her supervision with input from another practitioner, rather than terminating the long-standing arrangement altogether.

This strong desire to preserve the attachment may be the result of the subjects' childhood experiences (Holmes, 1993), and could lead to counsellors failing to recognise collusive practices in their supervisory relationships. While some of the subjects were aware of the pitfalls associated with long term supervision arrangements (Page and Wosket, 1994: 46), they were reluctant to acknowledge that their own supervision might be adversely affected, even though it was evident in several cases that the tight frame advocated by Langs (1994) had slipped or had never been in place.

Although BAC holds both parties responsible for monitoring the effectiveness of the relationship, data collected indicates that perceptions differ greatly about what constitutes good supervisory practice and neither may be an accurate judge of when effectiveness has dwindled. Supervisees can have strong motives for preserving the relationship beyond that point and it may be that supervisors are also reluctant to terminate relationships that they enjoy. Hawkins and Shohet (1989) observe that acting as a supervisor can provide a welcome respite for some professionals beleaguered by the demands of clinical work, while Stoltenberg and Delworth suggest that supervision of an experienced like-minded practitioner can be 'highly rewarding' for the supervisor (1987: 109). This research suggested that supervisees are unlikely for various reasons to initiate reviews, so perhaps supervisors need to take greater responsibility for monitoring the effectiveness of the supervisory relationship and ensuring that reviews are more structured than the perfunctory 'checking out that we still feel OK' approach which seemed prevalent amongst my subjects.

Conclusions and recommendations

It is clear that more needs to be done to raise the profile of supervision as an inherent and vital part of a counsellor's work, and to ensure its quality. Counsellors, supervisors and their employers would benefit from more information about the process.

Counsellors' needs are twofold. They need practical help to identify good quality supervisors in their local area, and BAC has now recognised this. Since 1996, the *Counselling and Psychotherapy Resources Directory* has been redesigned to give more information about supervisors which should make it easier for counsellors to access appropriate supervision. However, an entry in this directory is not an assurance of quality. There is no requirement for those offering themselves as supervisors to have completed any training in supervision, or undergone any assessment of their competence for the role, and, as there is a fee for inclusion in the directory, practitioners not planning to establish a sizeable private practice tend not to advertise in this publication. Therefore, it seems likely that counsellors will continue to rely on hearsay and prior knowledge when making their choices, even though this may put additional pressure on the supervisory relationship.

Counsellors also need to be educated about their own part in the supervision process. Data collected in this study suggest that even experienced practitioners have difficulty functioning effectively in the role of supervisee, and may collude in sustaining dubious working practices. More attention needs to be paid to supervision on counsellor training courses, with trainees being made aware of the purpose, ethics and potential of supervision, and the counsellor's role and responsibilities within it. Practising counsellors whose training did not provide this focus may benefit from opportunities to reflect upon the effectiveness of their current supervision arrangement, and be introduced to more creative ways of using the supervision space (Inskipp and Proctor, 1993).

While this research project focused on the experiences of one small group of supervisees, results did suggest that further professionalisation of supervisor training might help to promote better supervisory practice. As a lecturer in higher education who has developed a training course for supervisors, I would have welcomed some guidance from BAC about the components they think should be included. While the Association has an exacting set of requirements and standards for its accredited counsellor training courses, it has yet to make similar recommendations for supervision courses, or even state that supervisors should receive specific training. As a result, many practitioners operate as supervisors without ever having to prove their competence in that role, and even those who do obtain what may appear to be credible qualifications in supervision could have very different levels of skill and experience. For example, to gain a certificate in supervision at one Midlands university, a student has to complete a minimum of 120 hours as a supervisor, while to gain a certificate in supervision at another university in the north-west, only about 20 hours of supervision work need to be undertaken.

One development which may help to raise standards is the introduction of a clause (A6) in the 1996 *BAC Code of Ethics and Practice for Supervisors of Counsellors* requiring supervisors to receive supervision of their supervision work. This at least ensures that the work of supervisors will now be monitored by another practitioner, which does not in itself guarantee quality, but acknowledges the increasing complexity of the supervisor's role. The revised BAC accredited supervisor scheme introduced in 1997 makes training in supervision a requirement, although it avoids being specific about how long this training should be, what it should contain and how it should be delivered.

The findings of this study suggest that employers need more education about the nature and necessity of supervision. It may be that the term itself carries unfortunate connotations (Williams, 1992), which contributes to employers' apparent confusion and reluctance to fund it adequately.

Further research opportunities

Apart from suggesting that counsellors would benefit from more information about supervisors available in their geographical area, more education about the supervisory process and a more standardised approach to supervisor training, this project also uncovered opportunities for further research. These pertain to the nature of the relationship that develops between supervisor and supervisee.

My findings indicate a correlation between the initial contracting process and the character of the subsequent supervisory alliance and that clear and comprehensive contracting at the outset, with both parties contributing to the process, sets the tone for an effective and firmly boundaried relationship (Proctor, 1997). There is also evidence to suggest that efficient contracting is less likely to occur if supervisor and supervisee have a previous relationship, and this has implications for the way the supervision work proceeds. If these suppositions are substantiated by further research, it may indicate a need for more specific training for both supervisors and counsellors about their responsibilities at the contracting stage, and clearer guidance on the pitfalls of dual relationships.

The project showed that counsellors experience their supervisors and their supervisory relationships as highly significant and are liable to invest in them fantasies, projections and transferences which may affect their view of the relationship and impede their ability to function in it in a wholly 'adult' and professional way.

Counsellors may have high, often idealised expectations of their supervisory relationships. Issues of attachment, assumptions about power and deep-rooted emotional or sexual longings may be played out in a supervision arena, while dependency and the fear of loss may lead a counsellor to cling on to a supervision relationship even after it has ceased to be effective. This study focused only on how counsellors' needs and assumptions impact on the supervisory process. Obviously the supervisor brings another set of needs and assumptions to the alliance, and further study in the field of supervisory relationships might focus on how these set the tone and influence the interaction.

It was beyond the scope of this investigation to ascertain how accurate the subjects' perceptions of their supervisory relationships actually were. Clearly, there is a need for a future project to study pairs of counsellors and supervisors to assess how far the counsellor's view of the relationship matches the supervisor's. Results may increase our understanding of the significance of the supervisory pact for both parties and of the dynamics that operate within it. Supervision is a complex process and the relationship involves considerable risk. Counsellors are expected to share their vulnerabilities, while supervisors may have the limits of their knowledge and competence tested. Little wonder then that Dearnley, having undertaken research into aspects of supervision, concluded 'That looking in detail at supervisory practice is widely experienced as a very exposing affair' (1985: 54).

References

British Association for Counselling (1984) *Code of Ethics and Practice for Counsellors.* Rugby: BAC.
British Association for Counselling (1988) *Code of Ethics and Practice for the Supervision of Counsellors.* Rugby: BAC.
British Association for Counselling (1990) *Information Sheet 8: Supervision.* Rugby: BAC.
British Association for Counselling (1996) *Code of Ethics and Practice for Supervisors of Counsellors.* Rugby: BAC.
Bond, T. (1993) *Standards and Ethics for Counselling in Action.* London: Sage.
Carroll, M. (1996) *Counselling Supervision: Theory, Skills and Practice.* London: Cassell.
Dearnley, B. (1985) 'A plain man's guide to supervision – or new clothes for the emperor?', *Journal of Social Work Practice*, November: 52–65.
Edwards, D. (1997) 'Supervision today: the psychoanalytic legacy', in G. Shipton (ed.), *Supervision of Psychotherapy and Counselling: Making a Place to Think.* Buckingham: Open University Press.
Feltham, C. and Dryden, W. (1994) *Developing Counsellor Supervision.* London: Sage.

concluded that such figures were 'unworked out' and needed their own therapy. Alonso (1985: 55) considers there to be considerable scope for supervisors to self-idealise and to behave in a grandiose, exhibitionist way to an inexperienced counsellor and comments that 'the supervisor's counter-transference is relatively neglected'.

Pope and Bouhoutsos (1986: 38) in their study of sexual intimacy between therapists and patients considered that the responsibility always lies with the therapist, 'no matter what the behaviour of the patient'. In the parallel relationship of supervision the responsibility always rests with the supervisor, who must be self-aware and developmentally mature enough to contain their countertransference reactions and the supervisee's transference in a way that is helpful and therapeutic to both supervisee and client.

What emerges is that particular dynamics of hope and expectations may be operating right at the beginning of a supervisory arrangement. When supervisee and supervisor have previous knowledge of each other in another role this too is likely to affect the way in which supervision proceeds. To embark on a course of training is a big investment both financially and emotionally. It is reasonable to have hopes of learning, to expect to be treated with respect, and for the environment to be safe and maintained by experienced people who have the best interests of the students at heart. It is the responsibility of those in power to maintain standards and contain the anxieties of those who are less powerful. An understanding and experience of unconscious processes whatever the orientation of the supervisor is crucial, and it is incumbent upon the supervisor to prepare for this.

Breaking boundaries

For five of the supervisees the boundary between counselling and supervision was clearly breached, as well as, in some cases, other boundaries being blurred and unclear. In one case the agency and the supervisor were unboundaried: the supervisor was the manager and offered counselling and socialising as well. The supervisee was also invited to help the supervisor as a trainer in workshops held at the agency. Personal material from the 'counselling' part of the supervision was used in social situations, and as some of this material was to do with confusion over sexual identity the supervisor's flirtatious behaviour towards the supervisee compounded the difficulties. Another supervisee had a similarly unboundaried relationship with a supervisor who was also the chairperson of the voluntary agency where she was a supervisor, and she too offered to be, and subsequently became the supervisee's counsellor. Material from the different aspects of this relationship became muddled and at times the supervisee found herself being given information about the agency and people within it that should have been confidential. Yet another supervisee was involved with a similarly unboundaried agency and supervisor. This supervisor was also her mentor, her teacher, her counsellor, her friend and part of her social network. He ran a counselling agency where most of the people working there were in the same kind of complex and confused relationships with him. Eventually, supervision was non-existent and all the time in the sessions was used for counselling. Others in the study felt invaded when the supervisor probed for intimate details of sexual relationships.

For supervisees whose boundary between counselling and supervision was breached this was a disturbing and distressing experience. The literature review revealed an almost universal agreement amongst authors that supervision is not therapy for the supervisee, and yet it happens. How can this be? Perhaps one of the difficulties is that the interface of therapy and supervision is blurred. Doehrman (1976) points out that supervision is much more than a straightforward didactic process. It is necessary at times to discuss and explore the supervisee's own feelings in regard to their client. Is it the supervisee's own unresolved issues or is the client projecting unbearable aspects of themselves on to the supervisee? Is the parallel process operating here? It may be that the supervisee's personal material can contribute to an understanding of the process and the supervisor has a responsibility to know how far to go with this. Whilst supervisees need to address personal issues that interfere with their performance in counselling, this should properly be done in a personal counselling situation and should not dominate supervision.

All the above-mentioned supervisees had the feeling that the supervisor was using them and their personal material to gratify themselves in some way. In some cases this was sexual with a voyeuristic quality to it, but in one case the boundaries were pushed beyond the voyeuristic and the supervisor attempted to act out sexual desires with the supervisee. In these situations it seemed as if the supervisor was gratifying their need for power and control: assuming many roles with numbers of people over whom they had control, and with whom they assumed a position in which they had power. Pinderhughes (1989) suggests that keeping a supervisee in the one-down position is a way in which supervisors can reinforce their otherwise insecure sense of competence. Jacobs (1991) states unequivocally that students are vulnerable targets for 'dumping' behaviour by 'acting-out supervisors'.

It may be that other personal issues of the supervisor are being played out in supervision too. Kernberg (1987) and Searles (1955) remind us that supervisors may have blind spots and 'non-analysed areas' of their own and Munson (1987) reiterates that it is not safe to assume that a psychotherapy professional is free of conflict. The supervisors may be vulnerable themselves. Butler and Zolen (1977) and D'Addacio (1977) found that sexually-abusing therapists were often in a personal crisis or were vulnerable, needy and alone. Two female supervisees believed that their supervisors had unresolved issues with their daughters, as both supervisors mentioned this. The supervisees thought that these issues were in some way re-enacted or worked out through them (both younger women) in supervision. Two others knew of difficulties in their supervisor's marriage, and one woman perceived her male supervisor as trying to recapture his youth through a sexual relationship with her. Supervisors after all are human and vulnerable, but should excuses be made? They are taking on a position of great trust and special status and agree to an ethic of placing the supervisee's (and client's) interests above all else. A supervisor who gains satisfaction in this way may have considerable difficulty in maintaining the supervisee's (and client's) needs as primary. The kind of behaviour which gratifies the supervisor's needs whether sexual or not can be also seen as deliberate opportunism and poor practice and it is no excuse merely to contend that supervisors may have unresolved areas of psychopathology of their own. It is the responsibility of the supervisor to be adequately trained, supported and supervised themselves so that if difficulties occur they can be worked with in a non-abusive and creative way. Failing that, in training institutes mechanisms should exist which facilitate a change of supervisor if an impasse is reached.

Gender

There was only one male respondent among the fourteen supervisees. It is possible only to speculate upon the reasons for this. It may reflect the greater numbers of women working as counsellors, or it may be that more female counsellors are abused than male counsellors and this would in turn reflect the fact that more women than men are abused in society in general, although this pattern is thought to be changing slightly. A large survey would be needed to begin to see if there is any gender difference in the numbers of counsellors (supervisees) feeling they are abused in supervision and reporting the fact. Reporting and talking about an experience of abuse is not easy, and given the conditioning of men in our society which encourages them to be 'strong', it may be more difficult for men to see themselves as vulnerable, which would make it more difficult still to talk about.

The supervisors were equally split in terms of gender: seven men and seven women. The numbers are again too small for any conclusions to be drawn from this, but it challenges the notion of abusers as predominantly male. However, thirteen out of fourteen supervisees were women in abusive supervisory relationships with both men and women. The one male respondent had a male supervisor.

Features of abuse in a group situation

Five of the supervisees experienced the abuse in a group situation; all of them were part of a training course, so there was the extra anxiety of being assessed by the supervisor, but also perhaps by one's peer group, that is the other group members. Strong feelings existed in the one person in the group who felt left out and abused as if she was carrying all the negative aspects of the group's transference. She felt that the others in the group either idealised the group leader or colluded with what was happening. Three people described feeling scapegoated by the group and as being in the bind of being unable to say or do the right thing. They felt that if they spoke or asked questions they were attacked by the group leader, and if they remained silent that too was a cause for attack. They felt that whatever they said or did was wrong. One person resorted to testing it out like some students in a research study undertaken by Rosenblatt and Mayer (1975). She felt contradicted whatever she said, so she tried to subtly twist her words round to mean the opposite of what she originally said, and was contradicted again.

One supervisee felt left out even though the group she belonged to consisted of only herself, one other supervisee and the group leader. The group leader and the other supervisee discussed clients in an abstract and intellectual way; the supervisor had previously assessed the other supervisee's clients so they had something in common. The supervisee felt excluded and disturbed by this. She had no previous knowledge of supervision and did not know what to expect, but she had thought that her position would be taken into account. Her supervisor forgot to attend supervision when the other group member was absent. Another supervisee too felt that her position was not paid attention to, although it was the opposite of the previous one in that she had a lot of previous training and experience in related fields. Her supervisor did not want to know anything about the supervisee's background and treated the supervisees as beginners. Once the difficulty had arisen it seemed impossible to change and one supervisee noted that she fell into a kind of destructive spiral which paralysed her in a supervision group of six people. The group leader did not pay attention to the group processes, and she felt more and more unable to speak. She was finally failed on the course but there had been no indication that she was not up to standard. On one occasion the supervisor appeared to go to sleep.

In these groups it seems as if one person is carrying the negative feelings that the others, in their idealisation of the group leader, could not bear to own for themselves. These supervisees felt scapegoated by both the group leader and to some extent by their peers who seemed caught up in the whole process themselves and unable to change anything. The supervisors seemed not to realise that issues of sibling rivalry and competitiveness may obtain in a group and that group members will be jostling for attention in their own individual ways. Supervisees unable to participate due to anxiety were not encouraged to join in and the supervisee whose first experience of supervision this was, was barely acknowledged at all. Certainly her naivety and lack of experience seemed to be used against her instead of the supervisor easing her passage into supervision and helping her to use the group. This apparent lack of interest in supervisees seemed to be operating in the case when the supervisee's previous experience was not valued and by implication she felt not valued. Behaviour in which people are forgotten, ignored and not valued for themselves is demonstrating a complete lack of respect for a fellow human being, and no matter how irritating their naivety this is no excuse to abandon patience and behave rudely. It indicates a lack of respect for others on a deep level and raises questions about the supervisor's suitability for this kind of work if this is their fundamental approach.

In a group it would seem obvious and necessary that all members should be allowed some space and time, and that the supervisor should intervene to help this occur when necessary. The basic setting, time, place, etc. need to be kept firmly in place, as in all supervision arrangements.

Some of these supervisors displayed rigid and authoritarian attitudes when questions were asked. This was noted by one supervisee too in individual supervision; her supervisor's attitudes she described as opinionated and doctrinaire. One supervisor even commented that no one had questioned her before. The supervisee found herself in a double bind which was that if she perceived the supervision as persecutory or abusive then she was unable to benefit from the supervision she was offered because of her high levels of persecutory anxiety. This, in effect, puts all the responsibility on to the supervisee and leaves no room for the possibility that the supervisor may in reality be persecutory. Other supervisees found this kind of difficulty, to which there was no satisfactory resolution. Two supervisees found in a group situation that if they spoke they apparently always said the wrong thing – but if they were silent that too was criticised. Another supervisee was caught in the dilemma of wanting to complain about the way the course and the assessment were conducted but feeling that if she complained it would be thought that she couldn't accept failure, and that if she didn't complain then she was 'a wimp'. Another person too felt caught in a similar bind: that because she was unable to work out the problems with her supervisor and left, her credibility as a counsellor was in doubt.

Pedder's (1986) suggestion that groups are less likely to have difficulties with boundaries is not borne out by this study. The difficulties may be different and more surprising because there is a group of people who collude in them, but nevertheless a number of people in the study experienced abuse in a group situation.

The behaviour described above, when good and bad experiences are kept far apart, is known as 'splitting' in psychodynamic parlance. Splitting, provided it is not excessive, is regarded as an important mechanism of defence which is a form of protection from overwhelming anxiety and a normal step in development. Splitting creates larger than life people and larger than life emotions unmodified by their opposites. Perception is distorted so that 'if someone or something is defined as bad, any goodness in them is simply not seen' (Segal,1992: 34). This Kleinian concept is considered a necessary precondition for being able to recognise and react to actual conditions of danger on the one hand (persecutory anxiety) and on the other (idealisation) as a necessary precondition for falling in love, appreciating beauty and forming social and political ideals. In situations of anxiety various splitting mechanisms may become evident: 'feelings of being attacked and under threat may alternate with feelings of euphoria and unrealistic hopes' (Segal, 1992: 35).

It is possible that similar mechanisms may operate in some of these situations both on the part of the supervisor and the supervisee. It is important that this does not blind us to the fact that persecutory behaviour does exist and can be backed up in reality with specific examples. Supervisors need to be aware too of the tendency in supervisees, in a stressful, anxiety-provoking situation, to revert to these primitive methods of defence and not to be seduced or attempt to foster the idealisation of themselves by students. Supervisors need an awareness of their own mechanisms of defence and should consider their own responses to questioning or less compliant behaviour in their supervisees which may appear threatening. 'The test of a good supervisor is how he or she facilitates the student dealing with the primitive feelings that are stirred up both in the work with patients and in the supervision situation' (Crick, 1991: 238). A supervisor needs to make every effort to contain and manage these feelings so that a supervisee may learn and grow and not feel abused or persecuted. An awareness of the dynamics which can operate in situations of anxiety and an understanding of these as normal psychological processes likely to be difficult to manage at times would be helpful to both supervisor and supervisee.

Lack of respect

Under the heading of lack of respect fit many of the features of abuse described by the supervisees: a general demeanour lacking in warmth and politeness, neither listening to, nor including supervisees in a group situation, not answering questions, but behaving defensively or even in an attacking way when questioned. Showing no interest in or regard for previous training and attacking the training and therapy a supervisee is currently engaged in all smack of lack of respect. On further analysis it may be seen as the supervisor not managing their own anxieties, perhaps about their own training, therapy and experience (or lack of it), and perhaps feeling threatened when a supervisee asks questions.

Lack of respect was evident in subtle ways such as recommending individual therapy to a supervisee who was in a group training which necessitated a group therapy for the duration of the training which the supervisor knew made one to one therapy impossible at that time. One supervisee could not get a clear answer to her questions about the contract between her and her supervisor, for example what payment he expected for absences and holidays. She needed and wanted to know, but he was not clear. This is, of course, unethical according to the British Association for Counselling (BAC) *Code of Ethics and Practice for Supervisors of Counsellors* (1996).[2] Not making clear what is required but somehow expecting the supervisee to find out was also common. Part of the work and role of any supervisor is to teach, and although this may diminish as the supervisee becomes more experienced, it is certainly a large part of the role when supervising a beginner (Alonso, 1985; Hawkins and Shohet, 1989; Stoltenberg and Delworth, 1987); and to avoid answering questions clearly and directly is an abuse of the supervisor's role and power. Similarly, not giving clear, straightforward and direct feedback about students' progress and assessment that may be ongoing and part of supervision, is lacking in respect and unhelpful. This can become particularly abusive when feedback is given in a sarcastic way or when 'throwaway', put-down comments are made. If a supervisee is not achieving the required standard, is making mistakes or is not considered suitable, they need, and have a right to know this and the reasons why this is so; if necessary, ways should be found to help them achieve what is required.

As I have mentioned, one supervisor did not turn up on many occasions for supervision, another supervisor forgot, and yet another went to sleep. Certainly mistakes can happen, dates and appointments can be confused or overlooked and people can be tired. When this happens on a number of occasions, and if it is part of behaviour which conveys a general lack of respect or valuing of the supervisee, and if other abusive features prevail, then it is hardly surprising if the supervisee construes this as yet another example of their supervisor's negative attitude towards them.

Effects and endings

Pope and Bouhoutsos (1986) believe, based on their own clinical experience in the USA and a review of the literature, that filing a complaint with either a civil court, a licensing board or a professional ethics committee can be an important and positive way of healing the wound caused by a patient's sexual involvement with their therapist. It can help to counteract the passive feelings of victimisation. They regard this as an act of courage, a refusal to be intimidated into paralysis, and an act of altruism motivated by the desire to prevent the therapist from engaging further in such behaviour with others. The professional in this way is held accountable for their violation of a professional code, and a formal acknowledgement of this can be a significant step along the road to recovery from the trauma.

In a parallel manner it seems likely that to complain about a supervisor would have similar effects. Pope and Bouhoutsos (1986) considered only the type of abuse perpetrated in a sexual way, and although this is a clear violation of many professional codes and constitutes a significant problem in the USA, suits and complaints are filed in only about 4 per cent of cases. In both the USA and Britain sexual contact with clients is regarded as both exploitation and a breach of boundaries amounting to sexual misconduct, and in Britain the BAC *Code of Ethics and Practice for Supervisors of Counsellors* (1996),[3] and many other organisations clearly state that sexual contact is regarded as abusive and exploitative and a breach of professional conduct.

This is now a much more established area of study in the USA than in Britain (Garrett and Davis, 1994).

Nevertheless it obviously is far from easy to complain even about specific behaviour which is a clear violation of the above professional codes. How much more difficult it may be to complain of more subtle forms of abuse which it could be hard to prove took place in supervision.

The BAC *Code of Ethics and Practice for Supervisors of Counsellors* (1996) lists the responsibilities of the supervisor and gives specific information and guidance regarding the implementation of the principles embodied in the *Code*. Member organisations of the United Kingdom Council for Psychotherapy who do not have a code of ethics for supervisors may apply the principles of the *Code of Ethics* to working both with patients and clients and with supervisees. Codes governing professional practice are constantly being reappraised in an attempt to facilitate the process for both parties in a complaints procedure. In spite of this, the low number of complaints demonstrates the difficulties of making a complaint. There are several possible reasons for this. The participants in the study can provide some information as all of them were asked whether or not they had considered making a complaint. Only one person had done this, and her difficulties pursuing it, and the unsatisfactory nature of the outcome may be illuminating when considering ways of improving procedures.

The experience of abuse is a disturbing one and Pope and Bouhoutsos (1986) reflect upon the many profound and sometimes overwhelming and conflicting reactions that a client may have towards an abusing and exploitative therapist. The many similarities between the parallel relationships of counselling and supervision may lead to the conclusion that comparable responses will obtain in an abusive supervisory relationship. To minimise the difficulties caused by these complex reactions it may be of great help to talk to a trusted colleague, friend, or self-help group or to find a counsellor or therapist to explore it with. Many people in the study struggled to make sense of what was happening alone, thinking it was something to be ashamed of, and found themselves in a kind of double bind described by one supervisee; that is, if she could not deal with this in a satisfactory way then her credibility as a therapist was questionable and so leaving the supervisor became difficult. Another supervisee was in the paralysing double bind quoted at the beginning of this section: that appealing against the decision to fail her on her training course would be regarded as her inability to accept failure, whereas not appealing meant she was weak and hopeless. Neither outcome was good and she was left feeling inadequate and open to criticism in her work for quite some time. Another person felt that she would be considered as someone whose psychopathology had caused the problems, rather than it being the supervisor's lack of boundaries (and psychopathology) that was damaging to her and that had resulted in her needing to find a therapist who could help her work through the trauma. Two people felt they needed counselling as a direct result of their experiences. Those who talked about their experience with friends and colleagues, or were able to do some reality checking such as seeing their supervisor in another setting, found this lessened the confusion for them. One person felt herself seemingly compelled to return to her supervisor, perhaps because something was unresolved, until she could no longer tolerate the abuse. In each case, the supervisees felt they were to blame or would be seen as responsible or blameworthy. (Only one person was somewhat of an exception in that she was able to sort this out early on and left the supervisor.) The point was made by one participant, that the researcher was 'brave' to undertake this research, the implication being that 'the establishment' in counselling would be partisan in protecting an established member of the organisation, and that a less well-known or established supervisee would automatically be regarded as in the wrong.

The counselling world is comparatively small and is often regarded as 'incestuous' by counsellors themselves; that is, counsellors often know each other, may have trained together, and in doing so have shared a great deal. Russell (1993) described an occasion when a client made a complaint only to find that the complained-about therapist was on the very committee that dealt with the complaint. Many felt they would experience an 'old boys' network' of this kind, that they would not be taken seriously or paid attention to in opposition to a well-known or highly regarded therapist. Others had not even considered the possibility of complaining; one suggested that it was hard to know exactly what she would complain about or what the procedure was. In the majority of cases it was simply not a serious consideration. Feelings of shame and guilt were experienced by some and these feelings prevented them from telling others. One trainee discussed the matter with her tutor, who urged her to continue trying to work to resolve the problem with the supervisor and when this failed, suggested she train elsewhere.

Only one person seriously pursued a complaint and this was done with the aid of others who had experienced the supervisor in the same way as her. This has proved to be a long and costly business which has taken over her life and has finally resulted in the supervisor being removed from two professional bodies. However, as there is no law in the UK at the present time to stop anyone calling themselves psychotherapist or counsellor and practising in whatever way they wish, this man is still practising.

One person was so frightened of supervision that she delayed finding another supervisor for two years. She could end only by not going to her supervision sessions and making excuses, saying she was ill. Another, compelled by her training to continue in the supervision, found other supervision 'illicitly' elsewhere. Those who were in training or working in voluntary agencies seemed to have no alternative other than to accept the supervisor offered or leave. There was no understanding of problems and no mechanism for change.

Satisfactory endings were not the order of the day – an impasse was reached in which under the prevailing conditions no resolution was possible. The only solution was to leave, or to sit it out until the supervision was no longer required, that is, the training was over. Very few could do this – the problem was so great and so painful that it could not be tolerated. It was particularly difficult to leave in some instances when the supervisor seemed to need to hang on to the supervisee: two of the supervisors finished the arrangement in order to go abroad, but on their return contacted the supervisees to offer more supervision and in one case, therapy. The supervisors seemed to need the relationship themselves.

The themes emerging from this are ones of inability to change the situation by any means – the supervisor will not engage in discussion, using their knowledge of psychological processes to label the supervisee and beat them with it, or their charm and charisma to seduce others into colluding with them against the complaining supervisee. Those who thought they might not be listened to were correct. Many of the reported effects and consequences of abuse are similar to those caused by sexual abuse of clients by counsellors, and of children by adults. There was confusion about who was to blame for what had occurred: the supervisees often blamed themselves, and felt responsible. It took time for them to realise that they were not to blame, and it sometimes took months and even years to identify clearly what was right and what was wrong. Checking out colleagues' reactions to the supervisor and the reporting of boundary breaking to others helped to clear the confusion about who was to blame. Difficulties in trusting others, as in sexual abuse (Jehu, 1994; Pope and Bouhoutsos, 1986; Vinson, 1984), clearly compound this difficulty, as enough of the fear has to be overcome to enable the victim to risk talking about their experience to others. Two people were unable to trust any supervisor for months after and so worked without supervision until they could take the risk.

The feelings reported were of being devastated, overwhelmed, very distressed, confused and angry; and in some cases these feelings were very disturbing and long lasting, as in any experience of abuse. It is particularly difficult and painful to work through and resolve the effects of abuse as victims find themselves disempowered and fearful of not being heard and understood. It is hard to sift through the morass of feelings to gain an understanding of what has happened and to obtain a satisfactory outcome. When abuse is complained about, at the first stage, it needs to be taken seriously otherwise further abuse will be perpetrated.

A typology of an abusive supervisory relationship

One of the main purposes of this study was to produce a typology of an abusive supervisory relationship. Any profile or description needs to be set in context and it became clear that certain features of the context may be important factors which contribute to the development of an abusive supervisory relationship.

The context

A supervisor is likely to be in a position of power over the supervisee, or perceived as such by the supervisee. The supervisor is often connected with training and may be allocated to a trainee who has no choice in the matter. A mechanism for changing this situation or at least a recognition of the difficulties that may occur is not in place. It is likely there will be little or no recognition of the difficulties previous knowledge of, or a previous relationship with the supervisor could engender. There may be involvement of the supervisor and the supervisee in social or other networks. The supervisee may be at a point of transition and/or personal growth and development which renders them vulnerable. The supervisor may be a charismatic, guru type of figure who has a network of people around them in their thrall.

Attitude

The supervisor's attitude summed up in the phrase 'lack of respect' may reveal itself in many ways. There may be a lack of warmth and attention to the supervisee; conversely there may be too much offered in the way of friendship and counselling. In other words a professional attitude or presentation is lacking. The supervisee's previous and possibly different knowledge, training and experience is not valued, and this may be revealed by a complete lack of interest in these areas. Apparently going to sleep during sessions was perceived as gross lack of interest. There may be actual or implied criticisms of the supervisee's training and therapy. Criticism of the supervisee's therapist either directly or indirectly by sarcastic or 'put-down' comments or recommendations for a different kind of therapy may occur. This may include a lack of straightforward feedback and explanations about what is expected or required from the supervisee. There may also be criticism of the supervisee's decisions of a personal nature, for example the amount of time off to have a baby.

Gratification of the supervisor's needs

This may occur in several ways and may be part of a supervisor's own psychopathology and 'unworked problems' which may be relationship/marital problems, sexual identity and life-stage issues which can all lead to areas of need.

The supervisor may be uncertain of their role and may be defensive when questioned. This may lead to a rigid, authoritarian stance and an inability to move freely between didactic and dialectic modes according to the supervisee's needs and stage of development. Narcissistic needs, for example needing to be clever and admired, may cause the supervisor to be unable to hold the boundaries of time and space and basic setting, and may contribute to a blurring or shifting of the boundaries when a supervisor, unable to put aside their own interests, offers or gives therapy and/or friendship. They may use their own knowledge of psychological processes to keep the supervisee in an inferior position while bolstering their own superiority. This may take the form of making intrusive interpretations of the supervisee's unconscious motives, or seemingly labelling the supervisee as someone with unresolved difficulties instead of engaging in a two-person relationship. This notion of unconscious resistance where the supervisor/therapist interprets any difficulties in the relationship as due to the supervisee's unconscious envy or other unconscious feelings can be used as a defence against the supervisor's own unconscious feelings of competitiveness or envy. It effectively stops the supervisor from looking at their part in any difficulties they may encounter together.

Lack of awareness

There was a seeming lack of awareness of both the supervisor's own behaviours and underlying causes, and of the supervisee's anxieties, vulnerabilities, possible lack of knowledge and experience of good and bad practice. In a group there also seemed to be a lack of awareness on the part of the supervisor of the dynamics of small groups. Supervisees were not helped to deal with their lack of ability to find space for themselves in a group, nor were the group dynamics addressed by the supervisor. Lack of awareness of the parallel process may prevent an understanding of either institutional dynamics or the client's/supervisee's difficulties paralleled in the supervisory relationship and setting. Unaddressed, these areas of difficulty are in danger of being acted out in supervision; attended to they can effect growth and change in the supervisor, the supervisee and their client, and even in the institution. Finally, the support which every supervisee needs and wants, the *sine qua non* of supervision, is felt to be lacking when the supervisor is abusive or persecutory.

The role of the supervisee

Emphasis has been laid on the role of the supervisor in determining the characteristics of an abusive supervisory relationship, but consideration should be given also to the part played by the supervisee in the relationship as it is possible that they may be implicated in this.

Supervisees are in the vulnerable position of having to trust the more powerful supervisor. They may be naive, both in counselling and in how to use supervision, and these factors may cause them to experience anxiety at times in their role as supervisee. A certain amount of persecutory anxiety is arguably a normal and healthy protective mechanism but if this anxiety escalates so that everything a supervisor says or does is perceived as persecutory or abusive by a supervisee, then even the mildest or gentlest of feedback given in a supportive way may be perceived otherwise. However, it is the supervisor's responsibility to be alert to this and find ways of dealing with it if it is occurring, including looking at their own practice and altering it if necessary. High levels of persecutory anxiety may explain a supervisee's perception of events but this is not a reason for persecutory behaviour on the part of the supervisor.

In analysing the personal narratives of the respondents in this study there emerged no single defining characteristic which they all shared that would suggest a propensity to being abused. It could be concluded that an abusive supervisory relationship is entirely determined by the character or psyche of the supervisor and by the supervisor's ability to manage a relationship in which it may be considered normal to experience difficulties at times. Many writers have pointed out that no matter what the behaviour of the person in the less powerful role, the more powerful person is responsible for not abusing their power.

Implications and recommendations

Analysis of the data has revealed several areas in which changes could be made in order to prevent abuse occurring. As so many of the supervisees were working in a situation where a supervisor was allocated to them, either in training or in a voluntary agency, and with no possibility of or mechanism for change in place, it would seem of use for the committees of such organisations to consider ways in which a supervisee could be offered an alternative supervisor if problems cannot be worked out. Initially perhaps, help in working out the difficulties would be enough. Certainly, complaints need to be taken seriously in the first instance and some flexibility and openness maintained. Another way is to provide supervision or consultation for the supervisor. In this way, difficulties at an early stage could be aired and dealt with – the supervisor looking at their part in the situation. It seemed as if some of the supervisors were in powerful positions in their agencies, having many roles which made them difficult to challenge. Training for supervisors, in which these issues can be considered and discussed, and even a mandatory register of supervisors who have demonstrated their awareness and capabilities, should hopefully raise standards. The BAC supervisor accreditation procedure is in place, but is purely voluntary at the moment. Certainly the evidence demonstrates that supervisors need to be experienced, highly trained people who are able to look at themselves carefully and thoughtfully. A retraining and reappraisal of standards at regular intervals would maintain the level. Ideally, supervision kept separate from assessment in training would eliminate some anxiety, but if this is idealistic and unrealistic, then some understanding through the training of the supervisor of the high levels of anxiety which are likely to be present in the supervision would help.

As well as the supervisor's preparation, ongoing training and support, it is important to consider how the supervisee may be empowered. This could also be part of training. Areas for consideration would be how to use supervision, what to expect from a supervisor, what the danger signs may be and what questions to ask a supervisor when negotiating a contract.

Supervisees, however inexperienced as counsellors, must be empowered to trust their own feelings and not to lose sight of themselves as a person apart from a counsellor.

Clearly it is in the training of both counsellors and supervisors that these issues can be addressed. The bringing out into the open of these difficult issues, the facing of unpalatable areas of ourselves, is the first step in the move towards stopping abuse. It is hoped that this research will go some way along the road towards achieving this.

Notes

1. The term 'parallel process' refers to the analogy between aspects of the counsellor–client relationship reflected in the counsellor–supervisor relationship. It refers to what is carried over from the immediate past with the client into the adjacent situation of supervision, and may involve the counsellor behaving in some way like the client and the supervisor experiencing what the therapist or the client is experiencing. It may work in reverse, the counsellor treating the client as the supervisor treats them, or as they would like the supervisor to treat them. There are potentially many parallel processes involved in supervision and these processes are unconscious and often occur because the counsellor is unable to articulate the problem with which he/she needs help. This is likely to concern issues which involve conflict and anxiety and as such remain unconscious.

2. This is an update of the 1988 code which was in operation at the time the research was undertaken.

3. At the time this research was conducted the BAC *Code of Ethics and Practice for the Supervision of Counsellors* (1988) was in operation. This code did not specifically mention sexual activity as exploitative but stated that 'supervisors and counsellors are both responsible for setting and maintaining clear boundaries between working relationships and friendships, or other relationships'.

References

Alonso, A. (1985) *The Quiet Profession*. London: Macmillan.

Bond, M. and Holland, S. (1998) *Skills of Clinical Supervision for Nurses*. Buckingham: Open University Press.

British Association for Counselling (1996) *Code of Ethics and Practice for Supervisors of Counsellors*. Rugby: BAC.

Butler, S. and Zolen, S.L. (1977) 'Sexual intimacies between therapists and patients', *Psychotherapy: Theory, Research and Practice*, 14: 139–145.

Crick, P. (1991) 'Good supervision: on the experience of being supervised', *Psychoanalytic Psychotherapy*, 5 (3): 235–245.

D'Addacio, J. L. (1977) 'Sexual relations between female clients and male therapists'. Doctoral dissertation, California School of Professional Psychology, San Francisco.

Doehrman, M.J. (1976) 'Parallel processes in supervision and psychotherapy', *Bulletin of the Menninger Clinic*, 40(1): 104.

Feltham, C. and Dryden, W. (1994) *Developing Counsellor Supervision*. London: Sage Publications.

Garrett, T. and Davis, J. (1994) 'Epidemiology in the UK', in D. Jehu (ed.), *Patients as Victims*. Chichester: John Wiley and Sons.

Halgin, R. P. (1985) 'Pragmatic blending of clinical models in the supervisory relationship', *The Clinical Supervisor*, 3 (4): 23–45.

Hawkins, P. and Shohet, R. (1989) *Supervision in the Helping Professions*. Milton Keynes: Open University Press.

Jacobs, C. (1991) 'Violations of the supervisory relationship: an ethical and educational blind spot', *Social Work*, 36, (2): 130–135.

Jehu, D. (1994) *Patients as Victims*. Chichester: John Wiley and Sons.

Kernberg, O. (1987) 'An ego psychology/object relations theory approach to the transference', *Psychoanalytic Quarterly*, 56: 197–220.

Maclagan, D. (1997) 'Fantasy, play and the image in supervision', in G. Shipton (ed.), *Supervision of Psychotherapy and Counselling: Making a Place to Think*. Buckingham: Open University Press.

Munson, C. E. (1987) 'Sex roles and power relationships in supervision', *Professional Psychotherapy: Research and Practice*, 18: 236–243.

Pedder, J. (1986) 'Reflections on the theory and practice of supervision', *Psychoanalytic Psychotherapy*, 2 (1): 1–12.

Pinderhughes, F. B. (1989) *Understanding Race, Ethnicity and Power*. New York: Free Press.

Pope, K. and Bouhoutsos, J.C. (1986) *Sexual Intimacy between Therapists and Patients*. New York: Praeger.

Pope, K. S., Tabachik, B. T. and Keith-Spiegel, P. (1986) 'Good and poor practices in psychotherapy: national survey of beliefs of psychologists', *Professional Psychology*, 19: 547–552.

Rosenblatt, A. and Mayer, J. E. (1975) 'Objectionable supervisory styles: students' views', *Social Work*, May: 184–188.

Russell, J. (1993) *Out of Bounds: Sexual Exploitation in Counselling and Therapy*. London: Sage.

Searles, H. F. (1955) 'The informational value of the supervisor's emotional experiences', *Psychiatry*, 18: 135–146.

Segal, J. (1992) *Melanie Klein*. London: Sage.

Shipton, G. (ed.) (1997) *Supervision of Psychotherapy and Counselling: Making a Place to Think*. Buckingham: Open University Press.

Stoltenberg, C. D. and Delworth, U. (1987) *Supervising Counsellors and Therapists*. San Francisco: Jossey-Bass.

Vinson, J. S. (1984) 'Sexual contact with psychotherapists: a study of client reactions and complaint procedures'. Doctoral dissertation, California School of Professional Psychology, San Francisco.

Zetzel, E. R. (1953) 'The dynamic basis of supervision', *Social Casework*, 34 (4): 143–149.

4

WHAT MAKES IT DIFFICULT FOR THE SUPERVISEE TO SPEAK?

Angela Webb

Supervision, designed to monitor whether clients are receiving appropriate counselling and assumed to be efficacious, relies upon counsellors having sufficient awareness, confidence and honesty to disclose pertinent issues of concern to their supervisors. However, it is known also to provoke feelings of anxiety and conflict in supervisees. How far are supervisees influenced by such conflicts and what might be the implications for supervision if the conflicts are unduly influential? What are the optimal conditions required for supervisees to feel able to speak openly about those issues which are difficult to address but which may be crucial for understanding the nature of that which happens when they are with the client?

In this chapter the nature of the supervision process will be considered together with some research evidence from an investigation into what it is that the supervisee experiences as difficult to speak about in supervision and why. The research was prompted by the author's own experience as a supervisee in a number of different supervision arrangements which varied greatly in terms of the amount of anxiety and conflict experienced.

Background

What is it to be supervised?

One of the main functions of supervision is the giving of attention to the dynamics at work between client and counsellor. However, an investigation of the literature on supervision provides evidence to suggest a reluctance on the part of both supervisors and supervisees to address feelings in supervision. How, one might ask, is it possible to reflect upon the nature of the therapeutic process without considering the emotional impact which clients have on their counsellors?

In a study carried out in 1976, Goin and Kline discovered that few supervisors working psychodynamically took time to help supervisees consider their countertransference reactions to patients, and attributed this to the belief that such discussions amount to inappropriate therapy for the supervisee. Feelings of love (Celenza, 1995; Searles, 1955), hatred (Mehlman and Glickhauf-Hughes, 1994) and sexual interest (Brodsky, 1980) towards clients are often deemed unacceptable for acknowledgement to oneself as a counsellor and are unlikely therefore to be readily acknowledged in supervision. Reluctance to explore the possible existence of these feelings remains despite such responses having been acknowledged decades ago in psychoanalytic literature (Winnicott, 1949) as legitimate and even necessary.

Although at present there is a widespread conviction that it is most ethical to keep supervision and personal therapy quite separate, this is not a universally held view. In the early days of psychoanalysis it was accepted that during training one's analyst was also the person to whom difficulties experienced in working with patients would be taken. Baudry (1993) speaks for one modern school of supervisory thought which insists that any focus upon the supervisee's pathology is a legitimate and essential part of the supervision process. Similarly, Sarnat (1992) argues that avoidance of the supervisee's feelings, or indeed the supervisor's feelings, allows insufficient exploration of the influences at work in the relationship between therapist and client, and may be due to the supervisor's need to avoid the potential anxiety evoked by being a participant in a two-person supervisory relationship.

However, the supervision phenomenon is a multifaceted activity, charged with all kinds of fantasies, at least for the one being supervised. It is unsurprising that there continues to be confusion over what is and is not acceptable to disclose about the counselling relationship, in supervision. Eckler-Hart (1987) points out that supervision can evoke a fear of being found inadequate not only as a therapist but also in terms of success or failure as a person. Whilst those in training as counsellors have to deal with the anxiety of evaluation as an integral part of supervision (Hassenfeld and Sarris, 1978; Liddle, 1986; Szecsody, 1990), the supervision context *per se* evokes a striving towards perfectionism in a majority of supervisees, which can be a destructive and unhelpful process (Arkowitz, 1990). In disclosing his or her own vulnerability the supervisee fears being considered inadequate as a therapist with 'those particular attitudes or vulnerabilities' (Hawkins and Shohet, 1989)

Olk and Friedlander (1992) undertook research into the extent of role conflict experienced by trainee therapists having to engage simultaneously in a variety of different roles. For example, a trainee might be required to be acquiescent as a student but autonomous as a clinician, to explore issues of professional growth whilst at the same time being evaluated. Evaluation inevitably promotes feelings of anxiety in the supervisee and causes a variety of responses, including a reluctance in some to bring tapes to supervision (Liddle, 1986). The practice of selectively reporting particular therapeutic techniques used in therapy was noted by Sandler (1983) who attributed this to supervisees' fears that these might not be considered 'kosher'. Moreover, Tischler (1968) identified that some supervisees exclude whole cases from consideration in supervision.

Yet more influences have been discovered to affect the level of openness achievable in supervision. Alonso and Rutan (1988) and Mollon (1989) identified shame as a crucial factor when supervisees anticipate the loss of their supervisors' admiration as a result of mistakes made or the potential level of ignorance and confusion displayed. They argue that there is an optimal level of anxiety as a condition of learning and that in order for this not to become excessive supervisors may need to adopt a supportive stance. In many approaches, the practice of therapy involves a process of allowing oneself to be emotionally vulnerable, a vulnerability which is heightened in supervision. As control lessens one may begin to regress and to strive for the supervisor's approval whilst expecting also to be judged (Arkowitz, 1990).

Becoming a supervisee

Developmental theories of supervision acknowledge that to an extent one has to learn how to become a supervisee. Brightman (1984) equates the period of vocational training with the developmental period prior to and into adulthood, characterised both by tasks to be completed in the face of conflict and by the workings of defences. Training supervision, especially in the psychodynamic tradition, needs to be understood as a holding environment throughout a period of extreme narcissistic vulnerability (Brightman, 1984), when the supervisee's self-esteem may be very fragile.

The engagement in supervision as a mode of learning how to become a therapist demands the capacity to re-enter the 'latency-type state' (Hartung, 1979). According to this view, whilst latency in childhood is characterised by a spontaneous move away from sexual interests towards other types of creativity and learning tasks, the learning of therapy in adulthood may evoke earlier Oedipal and pre-Oedipal material which can hinder the process of learning. The working through of such material can be rapid or prolonged and involves the supervisor as the object of the supervisee's transference. Jacobs and Walker (n.d.) interpret Hartung's theory to mean in practice that the supervisee may experience the supervisor as being authoritarian, sexually seductive or sexually inhibiting. Openness and co-operation may become blocked by re-emerging issues of mistrust, shame, separation and rivalry.

The supervisory relationship

Salzberger-Wittenberg et al. (1983) see a complex and ambiguous relationship existing between supervisor and supervisee, with the supervisee fearing judgement, being envious of and competitive with the supervisor, wanting freedom from her and yet needing her admiration; ultimately resisting the process of change.

Book (1973) says that so great is the fear/need conflict in supervision that it distorts the supervisee's recollection of the therapy and he becomes unable to present material which shows himself to be less than perfect.

Just as it is vital for a more complete understanding of the client that the supervisee acknowledge and analyse any negative feelings towards her, so it is necessary also for complete engagement in the supervision process, that the supervisee own any negative feelings he may have about the supervisory relationship, claims Robinson (1949). It is rare to find such a reference to the supervisee's battle with negative feelings about the supervisory relationship. More usually, difficult feelings which are around in supervision are thought of in terms of a manifestation of the parallel process that is stemming from the relationship between client and counsellor rather than that between counsellor and supervisor.

Researching levels of disclosure and factors inhibiting openness in supervision

Most research into supervision has been conducted in the USA where counselling supervision is a component of training only. Of particular importance for consideration of the extent of openness in supervision is a study conducted by Ladany et al. (1996). They discovered that information withheld by supervisees in supervision tends most frequently to comprise negative reactions to their supervisor, where there exists a poor alliance with the supervisor, perceived supervisor incompetence and when consequences of such disclosure are feared.

By contrast, little is known about the British context where supervision of counselling is a career-long requirement (Carroll, 1996). Likewise, most literature on supervision has been written from the point of view of the supervisor (Crick, 1991). A study was conducted (Webb, 1997) therefore, which investigated the supervisee's perspective and, in particular, that which is recognised by supervisees to be blocking openness in the supervision process.

Ninety-six counsellors who work in the UK and who identify themselves as working psychodynamically responded to a postal survey which asked them about their experiences of being supervised. They were instructed to rate their likely ability to talk in supervision about such sensitive issues as their feelings for their client (positive, negative and sexual), their feelings towards their supervisor (negative and sexual) and their feelings about the supervision itself (positive and negative). Openness about instances when they had departed from techniques recognised as legitimate by their theoretical model was another area of investigation.

With a view to discovering more about what would inhibit such disclosure, respondents were also asked to indicate what these influences might typically be. Fears about negative assessment, of being disliked, of revealing personal vulnerability in a sensitive area, feeling ashamed or indeed anticipation of disagreement with the supervisor over the approach to be taken were specific phenomena, the strength of which respondents were asked to rate. Respondents were invited to identify any additional features which might inhibit their ability to disclose.

The quality of the relationship between counsellor and supervisor, namely the supervisory alliance, was a further area of interest. How far would this influence the extent to which supervisees felt able to speak openly about sensitive issues? In order to measure the quality of the supervisory alliance, respondents were asked to rate aspects of the relationship with their supervisor concerning the level of rapport which existed and the extent to which there was a collaborative focus upon the client. These measures were drawn from the Supervisory Working Alliance Inventory (SWAI) designed by Efstation et al. (1990).

Further features of the study were the fact that half of the sample group of counsellors were known to be in training. Supervision experiences included both individual and group, and there was a wide variety of settings in which the respondents counselled. The study was reliant upon self-reporting and so could investigate only conscious experiences of supervision.

The results of the study can be summarised as follows:

1 Counsellors receiving individual supervision were more likely to feel able to disclose sensitive issues regarding their clients than those receiving group supervision.
2 A positive correlation was found between the supervisee's perception of the level of rapport with his supervisor and his ability to disclose sensitive issues relating to his client. Similarly sensitive issues relating to the supervisor and the supervision itself could be discussed with greater openness where there existed a high level of rapport with the supervisor. Inhibitors of disclosure were more apparent where there was less rapport with the supervisor.
3 Counsellors who were receiving supervision while in training as counsellors were found to be significantly less able to disclose sensitive issues relating to their supervisors or their supervision than were counsellors who were not in training. Counsellors who were in training were found also to be more inhibited by the phenomena identified from disclosing sensitive information than were those counsellors who were not in training.
4 Counsellors being supervised independently of their work setting felt significantly more able to disclose sensitive issues relating to their clients and that which occurred in the counselling room than did counsellors receiving supervision at their place of work. They were also significantly

more likely to disclose sensitive issues relating to their supervisor and supervision when being supervised independently of their work settings. Furthermore, counsellors supervised within their work settings were significantly more inhibited by anticipation of disagreement with their supervisors than were counsellors who were supervised independently.

5 Counsellors who had chosen their own supervisors were found to be significantly more able, in supervision, to disclose sensitive issues about their clients, their supervisors and supervision than were counsellors who had been allocated a supervisor.

Implications for the delivery of supervision

INDIVIDUAL VERSUS GROUP SUPERVISION   When considering aspects of the relationship between client and counsellor there was a clear indication that it is easier to be open about this in individual rather than group supervision. This may suggest that there are perceived difficulties in disclosing one's personal feelings in front of a group of people which are not so great in a one to one setting. Given the exposing nature of disclosing one's feelings about a given client, and how one has been influenced by these feelings while with the client, it is unsurprising that anxiety and defensiveness are sometimes evoked by discussion of these. Whilst further investigation is required, there may be a suggestion that a greater number of supervision participants inhibits the supervisee's ability to be open.

The fact that there was no discernible difference between disclosing feelings about supervision and the supervisor in the individual or group settings may have to do with this being seen as less relevant for discussion in supervision. Alternatively, addressing aspects of the supervision may be a greater challenge for the supervisee than discussing the work with the client, regardless of the number of supervision participants.

THE IMPACT OF THE SUPERVISORY ALLIANCE   It was found that those supervisees who experience a high level of rapport with their supervisor feel relaxed and derive enjoyment from their supervision. Similarly they seem more able to disclose sensitive issues and experience fewer inhibitions about doing so. In view of the fact that a good level of rapport between supervisor and supervisee seems related to the ability to disclose sensitive issues there are implications for those supervisees who do not experience a rapport with their supervisors. It is arguable that no longer will it be sufficient to persist with the tasks of supervision if the supervisory relationship is a problematic one by virtue of a lack of rapport. The relationship itself will need to be attended to so that the tasks of supervision are not disrupted (Webb and Wheeler, 1998). Whilst further investigation is needed to establish whether in fact the supervisory relationship itself is given attention and under what conditions, the courage needed for the supervisee to initiate such an exploration must be acknowledged.

THE SIGNIFICANCE OF TRAINEE STATUS   Supervisees in training were found to be less able to disclose sensitive issues, particularly in relation to their supervisors or the supervision process. This particular finding, however, needs to be approached with caution in view of a design error in the study which did not differentiate between trainee 'therapists' and trainee 'counsellors'. In the psychodynamic tradition, with which all respondents identified themselves, the terms 'counsellor' and 'therapist' are not used interchangeably. A respondent may have indicated that they were not a trainee therapist but have had no opportunity, given the format of the questionnaire, to indicate that they were in training as a counsellor. As a result they would have been incorrectly counted as a non-trainee. Further research is needed to substantiate these apparent findings. Nonetheless, a certain amount of reflection upon this theme is possible.

Training to become a proficient clinician necessarily involves a certain amount of evaluation. It is inevitable that this will generate some anxiety about the potential for success or failure. However, if such anxieties contribute to supervisees' difficulties with openness about their feelings and vulnerabilities then these findings may indicate a need for evaluation to be separated from supervision, as proposed by Hassenfeld and Sarris (1978), if supervision is to be effective.

Brightman (1984) suggests that disclosing sensitive issues, including one's own vulnerabilities, demands a certain maturity which takes time to develop and supports the view that people in training have had insufficient time or experience to develop this maturity.

THE SIGNIFICANCE OF THE SUPERVISION SETTING   The research revealed that counsellors feel more able to be open when supervised outside their work setting than when receiving 'in-house' supervision, and several possible meanings could be attributed to this finding. Where supervision is provided in-house there is a potential for it to be contaminated by a supervisee's relationships with her supervisor and/or with fellow supervisees outside the supervision arrangement. Competitiveness and the seeking of approval are universal dynamics of groups, and these have the potential to be magnified by the fact that supervision group participants have to consider different roles beyond the supervision room. Counselling agencies could consider contracting out supervision to avoid this problem.

Some of the respondents in the study were supervised by their line managers despite this being highlighted by BAC as an inadequate arrangement and it could be speculated that in such instances disclosure of sensitive issues would be inhibited particularly by concerns relating to the counsellor's job security.

One of the fundamental principles of supervision, namely the need to own one's vulnerabilities and weaknesses as a practitioner in the service of the client, could be undermined in cases such as these. Not only could the perception of the relationship with a supervisor be influential here but also the reality of that relationship. Perhaps a supervisor from within the same organisation as her supervisee *does* have a different attitude towards the supervisee. Organisational restraints such as lack of resources, high demands for the service, or knowledge of the supervisee outside the supervisory frame *may* influence the supervisor's attitude towards the supervisee or her approach to supervision. Whether or not such factors exist in reality or simply in the supervisee's perception is less important, because both have the potential to inhibit. Perhaps it is simply a matter of safety; how safe the supervisee feels to talk about sensitive issues within the organisation in which she earns her living or is known other than in the role of supervisee.

THE SIGNIFICANCE OF BEING ABLE TO CHOOSE ONE'S OWN SUPERVISOR
Counsellors find supervisors by a variety of means. Some work in independent practice and have the freedom to approach whomever they wish for supervision. Some choose on the basis of recommendation, others choose at random. Those counsellors who work in agencies typically receive supervision from someone to whom they have been allocated, either from within the organisation or externally.

Counsellors in this study who had chosen their own supervisors felt significantly more able to disclose sensitive issues than those who had been allocated supervisors. There could be various interpretations of this finding. It may be to do with the quality of the relationship established between the participants. People who choose their own supervisors presumably choose someone with whom they expect to be able to trust or to have a sense of affinity. Equally, they might choose supervisors whom they perceive as having a certain level of expertise and as able to deal with the disclosure of sensitive issues (Cohen, 1980). These anticipated experiences may be the result of knowing the supervisor personally or through the recommendation of someone else.

The ability to choose one's own supervisor may facilitate a sense of freedom to be open in supervision. In an attempt to understand the reason for this we need to probe further. Whilst this study did not consider the issue of payment it may be that many of the people who are able to choose their own supervisor are paying for private supervision. If the supervisor is being employed or engaged by the supervisee, and can be hired or fired, it may be that the dynamic is changed to an extent which empowers the supervisee to be more open about sensitive issues and more able to take risks in revealing what they really feel. Alternatively, those counsellors who are paying for supervision, possibly themselves in private practice, would probably be more experienced practitioners and consequently able to risk greater levels of disclosure in supervision than less experienced colleagues.

The apparent consequences for disclosure of having chosen one's own supervisor may be a manifestation of the separate finding, namely the level of freedom experienced in being supervised independently of one's own work setting. Biographical data from the study indicated that many of the people who had chosen their own supervisors also received supervision from outside their work setting. The apparent benefits in terms of increased ability to disclose sensitive issues for those counsellors who choose their own supervisors could be most closely related to any one or more of the following: the person of the supervisor, the quality of the supervisory alliance, the discreteness of the supervision arrangement, the empowerment generated by paying for supervision, the level of experience of the supervisee, etc. Further investigation could sharpen our focus upon the influences at work here.

What are the most difficult issues to speak about and why?

The study was based around measuring broad dimensions of sensitivity and inhibiting factors, namely, issues relating to the client and the counselling, issues relating to the supervisor and supervision, feared consequences of disclosure for self and expectation of clashing with one's supervisor. However, in order to determine which particular areas were most sensitive when it came to disclosing them and which specific factors most inhibited disclosure, the endorsement of individual items was considered separately.

Most supervisees reported being likely to feel able to disclose feelings about their clients. However, a degree of reticence existed specifically in relation to being open in supervision about sexual feelings towards their clients. Sexual feelings, considered as personal and private in the widest context of life, nonetheless are considered highly relevant within many theoretical orientations to understanding therapeutic dynamics. Omitting consideration in supervision of these feelings may leave gaps in the ability fully to understand important aspects of our clients. Indeed the capacity to resist acting out sexual responses and thus harming clients may be diminished similarly by the failure to discuss such feelings in supervision.

Patterns of doubt were also discovered relating to the likely ability to disclose feelings about the supervision process itself, both positive and negative. This will have implications for the efficacy of the supervision process. If the supervisee finds herself struggling with negative feelings about her supervision, there is likely to be an impact upon her ability to do the work of supervision and this raises questions about the extent to which her counselling is being adequately attended to.

Similarly apparent from the study was the considerable doubt expressed about the likely ability to disclose personal feelings towards the supervisor. Some respondents felt these were irrelevant for discussion in supervision. However, if negative feelings towards the supervisor are being harboured the implications for the supervision process is a strong argument in favour of their relevance for consideration. This accords with the views of Ladany et al. (1996). Equally, sexual feelings towards the supervisor might well be appropriate for disclosure if they proved troublesome.

Considerable fears about being thought badly of by the supervisor, and of abilities being assessed negatively, were reported as inhibiting disclosure. A picture emerges of the supervisee as caught in a battleground, striving to be open about her feelings in the service of the client whilst fearing being seen as vulnerable, ineffectual or unlikeable. Fears about being considered in a negative light are of course integral to the human condition. However, the capacity to tolerate the fears in order to work therapeutically is crucial. The extent to which supervisees report being inhibited by such fears may indicate the need for further personal development work or indeed the need to alter certain conditions of supervision which contribute to the extent of the perceived threat. Equally, supervisors may need more enlightenment about the potential for such feelings to exist in supervisees and the importance of not avoiding the exploration of them if they occur (Sarnat, 1992).

Reactions to the study

Respondents' reactions to the study ranged from outrage at being asked about such feelings, seeing them as inappropriate for consideration in supervision, to affirmation of their relevance. One respondent stated: 'A lot of these questions are inapplicable. I would freely discuss (in supervision) my sexual feelings towards my client *if* I had them but I don't.' Others, who were noted as having undergone psychoanalytic therapy training, stated that they felt able to talk in supervision about *any* of the sensitive issues identified, with *complete* openness.

All of these responses seem to be characterised by a degree of difficulty in thinking about how far one feels able to disclose sensitive topics in supervision. This is a matter for concern. Are clients getting the best kind of therapeutic intervention where their counsellors struggle to use supervision to look at the most difficult aspects of their work?

Conclusion

Supervision is a dynamic process. It has a variety of tasks as its focus but, significantly, these are undertaken within the context of a relationship, whether one to one or in a group. This phenomenon deserves greater recognition. There has been a partial recognition of the dynamics of supervision in the use of the parallel process to consider the experiences of the counselling room as they are brought into the supervision room. However, there has been insufficient willingness to date to attribute importance to the dynamic processes at work within the psyches of the supervision participants themselves.

This is not to advocate supervision turning into a therapy-like focus upon the supervisee. Rather it is to place greater emphasis upon establishing the conditions under which supervision should take place in order to maximise its effectiveness. If the supervisee feels inhibited from speaking about what they really feel is going on, either with the client or with the supervisor, it is the client ultimately who will suffer.

At present the counselling profession demands that supervision is provided according to a certain minimum ratio of counselling to supervision hours. The quality of the supervision received should be of an adequate standard. The move towards supervision becoming a profession in its own right, with specialist training and an accreditation scheme, is one valuable contribution towards improving the quality of supervision available. However, the ability of the supervisee to make best use of the supervision provided needs to be addressed as a matter of some urgency.

Recommendations for practice

The study outlined above was relatively small-scale and the findings will benefit from being tested in further investigative research. Nevertheless, they do present some issues for consideration when setting up and delivering supervision.

RECOMMENDATION ONE – RECOGNISE THAT SUPERVISEES NEED TO LEARN HOW TO USE SUPERVISION   Proctor (1994) emphasises the need for supervisees to know how to use supervision, so great is the level of performance anxiety/role confusion which is likely to be generated. Supervisees need to know it is acceptable to talk about their mistakes, their feeling responses to clients, however negative or unacceptable these may seem. Indeed it is more than acceptable – it is essential. Proctor draws attention to the particular need to train beginning counsellors in how to use supervision. Still there is a suggestion that even experienced, trained counsellors have some way to go before they can feel fully able to speak openly about what they feel. The owning of vulnerability and not knowing increases the potential for understanding just as much as the owning of competence and knowledge. Encouragement and instruction are needed if supervisees are to see all feelings and experiences as appropriate for discussion in supervision, however unacceptable they may seem. This is a challenge for the training courses in both counselling and supervision.

The leap which must be made away from the prevalent culture of the day which demands demonstrations of accomplishment, and minimisation of areas of vulnerability, should not be underestimated. Unlike the majority of professions, counselling requires that we get tuned in to our sensitivities as a tool for making contact with clients and helping them. This is no excuse for being weak, faint-hearted or incompetent. A balance must be struck between staying in tune with ourselves, and our ability to be sufficiently distanced and skilled to respond appropriately to our clients.

RECOMMENDATION TWO – EQUIP SUPERVISEES TO BE VULNERABLE BY DOING MORE PERSONAL DEVELOPMENT WORK OUTSIDE THE SUPERVISION CONTEXT   Supervision is deemed by BAC to be crucial for monitoring the quality of the relationship between client and counsellor but this is highly dependent upon the counsellor's ability to talk openly about areas of concern. Whilst supervisors can glean much from what is presented and the manner of its presentation, not to mention what appears to be omitted, they cannot do all the knowing, however expert they are.

There may be an argument for further strengthening the focus upon personal development in counsellor training or a greater emphasis upon personal therapy as a component of training if counsellors are to feel more at ease in disclosing to their supervisors mistakes, areas of vulnerability, 'unacceptable' feelings in the counselling room or the supervision room. Indeed the introduction by BAC of personal therapy as a requirement for individual counsellor accreditation (BAC, 1998), although contentious, will be seen by some as a step in the right direction.

RECOMMENDATION THREE – INDIVIDUAL SUPERVISION SHOULD BE A UNIVERSAL REQUIREMENT   The merits of group supervision in terms of shared learning and mutual support are not in doubt. However, the fact that group supervision seems to make it more difficult for sensitive issues to be broached by supervisees suggests the need for it to be complemented by individual supervision, where such inhibitions seem less prevalent.

It is often argued that providing supervision in groups will allow agencies providing counselling to make better use of their scarce resources than by offering one to one supervision. However, if this method of supervision inhibits participants' ability to make the best use of the available resource, then the economies to be made seem counterproductive in terms of the accompanying loss of quality. Indeed many agencies already recognise the value of offering both forms of supervision. The provision of both individual and collective supervision would counterbalance the risk of collusion which has been demonstrated to exist (Lawton, 1996) in some individual supervision arrangements.

RECOMMENDATION FOUR – THE SUPERVISORY RELATIONSHIP ITSELF NEEDS TO BE MONITORED   Just as difficulties in the counselling relationship can be carried over into supervision, so the reverse can occur. In particular, where the supervisory alliance is weak the potential for good supervision work to be done is diminished and the work with the client may suffer. Issues of disclosure and inhibitors thereof are only two areas considered here, but they highlight the struggles supervisees experience in making the best use of supervision.

Given the level of courage required for supervisees to initiate discussion of their experiences of supervision, what they need from supervision and what they feel they are getting, it would seem most desirable for regular joint reviews of the supervision process itself to be built into the contract. In this way, the responsibility for quality control would be shared and, if undertaken at regular intervals, become normalised and imbued with much less apprehension. Whilst it is still potentially daunting for supervisees to identify issues of concern or negotiate changes in the supervision arrangement, the existence of periodic reviews suggests that such matters are legitimate and even necessary for consideration.

References

Alonso, A. and Rutan, J. S. (1988) 'Cross-sex supervision for cross-sex therapy', *American Journal of Psychiatry*, 135: 928–931.

Arkowitz, S. W. (1990) 'Perfectionism in the supervisee', *Psychoanalysis and Psychotherapy*, 8 (1): 51–68.

Baudry, F. D. (1993) 'The personal dimension and management of the supervisory situation with a special note on the parallel process', *Psychoanalytic Quarterly*, 62 (4): 588–614.

Book, H. E. (1973) 'On maybe becoming a psychotherapist, perhaps', *Canadian Psychiatric Association Journal*, 18: 487–493.

Brightman, B. (1984) 'Narcissistic issues in the training experience of the psychotherapist', *International Journal of Psychoanalytic Psychotherapy*, 10: 239–317.

British Association for Counselling (1998) *Criteria for Individual Counsellor Accreditation*. Rugby: BAC.

Brodsky, A. M. (1980) 'Sex roles in the supervision of therapy', in A. Hess (ed.), *Psychotherapy Supervision: Theory, Research and Practice*. New York: Wiley.

Carroll, M. (1996) *Counselling Supervision: Theory, Skills and Practice*. London: Cassell.

Celenza, A. (1995) 'Love and hate in the countertransference: supervisory concerns', *Psychotherapy*, 32 (2): 301–307.

Cohen, L. (1980) 'The new supervisee views supervision', in A. Hess (ed.), *Psychotherapy Supervision: Theory, Research and Practice*. New York: Wiley.

Crick, P. (1991) 'Good supervision: on the experience of being supervised', *Psychoanalytical Psychotherapy*, 5 (3): 235–245.

Eckler-Hart, A. H. (1987) 'True and false self in the development of the psychotherapist', *Psychotherapy*, 24 (4): 683–692.

Efstation, J. F., Patton, M. J. and Kardash, C. A. (1990) 'Measuring the working alliance in counselor supervision', *Journal of Counseling Psychology*, 3: 322–329.

Goin, M. K . and Kline, F. (1976) 'Countertransference: a neglected subject in clinical supervision', *American Journal of Psychiatry*, 133 (1): 41–44.

Hartung, B. M. (1979) 'The capacity to enter latency in learning pastoral psychotherapy', *Journal of Supervision and Training in Ministry (USA)*, 2: 46–59.

Hassenfeld, I. N. and Sarris, J. G. (1978) 'Hazards and horizons of psychotherapy supervision', *American Journal of Psychotherapy*, 32: 393–401.

Hawkins, P. and Shohet, R. (1989) *Supervision in the Helping Professions*. Milton Keynes: Open University Press.

Jacobs, M. and Walker, M. (n.d.) 'Problems in supervision'. Supervision course material, University of Leicester.

Ladany, N., Hill, C. E., Corbett, M. and Nutt, E. A. (1996) 'Nature, extent and importance of what psychotherapy trainees do not disclose to their supervisors', *Journal of Counseling Psychology*, 43 (1): 10–24.

Lawton, B. (1996) '"A very exposing affair". Explorations in counsellors' supervisory relationships'. Unpublished MA thesis, University of Leeds.

Liddle, B. J. (1986) 'Resistance in supervision: a response to perceived threat', *Counselor Education and Supervision*, 26 (2): 117–127.

Mehlman, E. and Glickhauf-Hughes, C. (1994) 'The underside of psychotherapy: confronting hateful feelings towards clients', *Psychotherapy*, 31 (Fall): 434–439.

Mollon, P. (1989) 'Anxiety, supervision and a space for thinking: some narcissistic perils for clinical psychologists in learning psychotherapy', *British Journal of Medical Psychology*, 62: 113–122.

Olk, M. E. and Friedlander, M. L. (1992) 'Trainees' experiences of role conflict and role ambiguity in supervisory relationships', *Journal of Counseling Psychology*, 39 (3): 389–397.

Proctor, B. (1994) 'Supervision – competence, confidence, accountability', *British Journal of Guidance and Counselling*, 22 (3): 309–318.

Robinson, V. (1949) *The Dynamics of Supervision under Functional Controls*. Philadelphia: University of Philadelphia Press.

Salzberger-Wittenberg, I., Henry, G. and Osborne, E. (1983) *The Emotional Experience of Learning and Teaching*. London: Routledge and Kegan Paul.

Sandler, J. (1983) 'Reflections on some relations between psychoanalytic concepts and psychoanalytic practice', *International Journal of Psychoanalysis*, 64: 35–45.

Sarnat, J. E. (1992) 'Supervision in relationship: resolving the teach-treat controversy in psychoanalytic supervision', *Psychoanalytic Psychology*, 9 (3): 387–403.

Searles, H. F. (1955) *Collected Papers on Schizophrenia and Related Subjects*. London: Hogarth.

Szecsody, I. (1990) 'Supervision: a didactic or mutative situation', *Psychoanalytic Psychotherapy*, 4 (3): 245–261.

Tischler, G. L. (1968) 'The beginning resident and supervision', *Archives of General Psychiatry*, 19: 418–422.

Webb, A. (1997) 'The extent of disclosure by psychodynamic counsellors in supervision'. M.Ed. dissertation, School of Education Library, University of Birmingham, UK.

Webb, A. and Wheeler, S. (1998) 'How honest do counsellors dare to be in the supervisory relationship?: an exploratory study', *British Journal of Guidance and Counselling*, 26 (4): 509–524.

Winnicott, D. W. (1949). Hate in the countertransference. *International Journal of Psychoanalysis*, 30: 69–74.

5

WHISPERS IN THE CORRIDOR AND KANGAROO COURTS: THE SUPERVISORY ROLE IN MISTAKES AND COMPLAINTS

Jaquie Daniels

The title of this chapter refers to issues currently adversely affecting the counselling and psychotherapy profession. On the one hand, there are *whispers* throughout the profession about the actions of certain counsellors or therapists that exist only through continued rumour. Therapists can lose clients and even their livelihood through whispers that are never substantiated or openly directed. On the other hand, there are complaints procedures or sanctioning actions that are set in motion either individually or collectively, which can be perceived by the therapist or counsellor involved as a form of *kangaroo court*. A misdemeanour, for example, may be 'confessed' to a supervisor or discovered by a colleague who then informs the organisation or professional body. The therapist is subsequently questioned by a group of people, a judgement is made and the sentence delivered. None of these people appears to support him or her. This is an extreme scenario, but for therapists who do go through a formal procedure, not an unfamiliar picture. Conversely, errant therapists can continue to work unethically for some years because confidentiality, reputation or even the structure of complaints procedures can inhibit action. Without wishing to dramatise, the whole area might be seen to parallel the issue of child abuse, where secrets enable abuse to continue and corrective or educative procedures are slow and complex.

I am an independent therapist, counselling supervisor, teacher, and member of the Independent Practitioners' Network (IPN). I have a concerned interest in this area based on observation and many discussions on the topic with a range of people. My research has included seven semi-structured interviews with supervisors and practitioners from different professional organisations including those linked to the British Association for Counselling (BAC), United Kingdom Council for Psychotherapy

(UKCP) and IPN, who have had a breadth of experience of complaints. The terms 'therapist' and 'counsellor' will be used interchangeably throughout as a reflection of this.

This chapter aims to present some initial thoughts with the intention of provoking further debate. The research process itself has paralleled one of the issues. Some therapists or counsellors who have been through complaints procedures have been left too traumatised to talk to anyone for fear of further reprisals and/or victimisation. Moreover, my interviews and discussions have included 'whispers' that cannot be directly quoted, relating to specific cases of unethical behaviour. Any examples or case studies used in this chapter are based on real events, but in some cases have been substantially changed.

So, what has all this got to do with supervision? There is ambiguity over the role of the supervisor and this ambiguity is accentuated in the light of mistakes and complaints. This raises several questions which will be discussed in this chapter:

1 What is the difference between a relatively minor and a serious mistake?
2 How can minor mistakes be worked with and serious mistakes be avoided through the supervisory relationship?
3 Is it possible for the supervisor to both protect the client and support the supervisee?
4 Likewise for the professional body, is it possible for one organisation to support both the aggrieved client and the accused therapist?
5 Does the supervisor have some responsibility alongside the supervisee when mistakes or complaints are made? This is a question related to the role of the supervisor and the nature of the supervisory relationship rather than a legal issue.[1]
6 There is also a broader question relating to how the supervisor and the profession deal with difficult situations, including mistakes and complaints, and whether mediation or forgiveness has any part in the process. There is little room to explore this explicitly within this chapter but the question does underpin the discussion.

Mistakes will happen

Cases in the media would lead us to believe that there are a number of systematic professional abusers and in this chapter I am not referring to those people who deliberately start working with clients because they intend to abuse. Within the profession there is, I would suggest, a tendency to think of these and of complaints and the resulting 'punishment' as relating predominantly to sexual abuse. This appears not to be the case however (interview with Roger Casemore, Chair of Complaints Committee, BAC, 1998), although it is very hard to obtain specific data because of issues of confidentiality. The majority of counsellors are clear on their boundaries in relation to sexual abuse. Clarity and uniformity on the fine line between relatively minor mistakes and serious mistakes, however, is more difficult than it might at first seem. One of many reasons is that an instance of good practice in one theoretical approach, for example the use of touch, may be considered a mistake in another. It is useful to adopt the image of a continuum as a framework in the discussion of mistakes and unethical behaviour.

There is a trend currently towards the use of legal definition, which, although not ideal, does provide one model for this confusing area. Palmer Barnes (1998) distinguishes between mistakes, poor practice, negligence and malpractice. The continuum here would range from mistakes at the minor end to malpractice at the serious end. Malpractice is defined as 'practice or behaviour that is intentionally, emotionally, financially, physically or sexually abusive' (1998: 51). It usually 'involves a practitioner following a course of action designed to meet his or her own needs' (1998: 52) and is broken down into the following categories: emotional mal-practice, financial malpractice, physical malpractice and sexual malpractice. A mistake is defined by Palmer Barnes as 'an unintended slip in good practice', for example a practitioner forgetting a session.

Robertiello and Schoenewolf (1987) refer to mistakes as 'Common Therapeutic Blunders', which they define as representing: 'all instances in which therapists act out feelings toward patients that are unresolved characterological or cultural conflicts or biases within themselves, whether or not induced by corresponding feelings in the patient' (1987: 3). Counter-transference 'blunders' are divided into erotic, e.g. 'the therapist who fell in love', sadomasochistic e.g. 'the therapist who couldn't say no', and narcissistic, e.g. 'the therapist who feared abandonment'. Counterresistance blunders are divided into characterological, like 'the female therapist and the male chauvinist pig' or 'the therapist who did not want to upset his mother' and also cultural counterresistances like 'the therapist who needed to prove her thesis' and 'the therapist who wanted to reform a call girl'. The titles are humorous but the case studies all too human.

Complaints tend to be heard and mistakes therefore defined by professional bodies in relation to breaches of the *Code of Ethics and Practice for Counsellors* (BAC), the Code of Practice of member organisations of the UKCP, and the Code of Conduct of the British Psychological Society (BPS) (see Jenkins, 1997). Complaints will be discussed more specifically later, but as a backdrop to the discussion it is important to acknowledge that, in theory, any mistake could be the subject of a complaint.

My interviewees, as practitioners and supervisors, not surprisingly, differed when asked to draw a distinction between serious mistakes and minor mistakes. One supervisor defined mistakes as 'failing to act in the client's best interest and those of the profession'. Another started off with discourtesy at the minor end of the continuum, but, in discussion he noted that

Even a discourtesy takes on a greater significance in a counselling relationship because in some sense or another it's a breach of trust. They trust you to be courteous, to be considerate, to be there when you say you'll be there and so on . . .

Most supervisors emphasised the learning process involved:

There are all sorts of our practices where we can always be thinking, 'I could have done that differently. I could have challenged in a less strident way. I could have reflected back more gently, I shouldn't have been quite so quick with that empathic response, too early for the client. All sorts of things. And I think if we're prepared to recognise that, working on it in supervision but also with the client, I think that's really important.

The following examples were provided by interviewed supervisors as minor mistakes which had been successfully worked through within the supervisory relationship:

- Confidentiality issues. Breaching confidentiality through, for example, loose talk in the front office where two counsellors were talking to each other, in front of the receptionist about a client, or even talking to the receptionist about the client; breaching confidentiality when working separately with a couple and not checking out what was and wasn't OK to share;
- Time boundary issues. Counsellors not turning up to appointments. Consistent lateness which meant that clients might have been sitting in the waiting room for half an hour. An increasing sloppiness of time boundaries;
- Issues relating to touch. Hugging a client at a client's request;
- Confusion. Forgetting who said what, mixing something up with what another client had said.

Some supervisors might view these examples as unethical. Others, like one supervisor interviewed, acknowledged mistakes as an integral part of both the therapeutic and the supervisory relationship:

An absolutely perfect mother would probably be the most disheartening carer to have because there was nothing she couldn't cope with . . . you'd feel endlessly incompetent in the face of her. Equally well, a perfect counsellor who gets everything right would be a disempowering influence whereas a counsellor who gets things wrong, makes mistakes, is human, but shows the client how to respond, to acknowledge the mistake . . . and to incorporate the learning from that mistake into future activity . . . it is a very therapeutic process. The same applies across the counsellor–supervisor relationship.

An additional dimension was provided by another supervisor who defined both ends of the continuum in terms of levels of clumsiness:

It's whether the mistake is workable within the therapy relationship and maybe even a mistake might be necessary for the therapy relationship . . . I as a therapist say something that's rather clumsy, and it upsets a client, and the client is able to work through that and to recognise that other people are clumsy. Perhaps other significant people in their life are being clumsy . . . it then ceases to be a mistake and becomes part of the learning process. So there are mistakes all the time . . . but when the clumsiness is inappropriately big and the therapeutic relationship is . . . vulnerable and a fledgling relationship, then that kind of clumsiness would be destructive of the relationship.

Here, then, the continuum is differentiated by contextualising the mistake in relation to the stage of development of the therapeutic relationship.

At the serious mistake end of the continuum were 'categories or acts of commission or omission which can actually do serious harm to someone . . . '. For example, in couple counselling, a counsellor taking sides and setting partners against each other; sexually exploiting the client; violent and emotional abuse of clients, creating hugely dependent relationships; financial extortion from the clients. Also discussed through interview were areas of work that used to be considered 'normal' or permissible practice in therapy that would now be considered 'unethical'. This indicates the dynamic nature of counselling and therapy and its interrelationship within the prevalent culture. Brian Thorne's famous or infamous work with Sally provides one such example of this. It is described in Dryden (1987) and defended by Thorne in Dryden (1993: 111–117).

The following story is an example perceived by the interviewee as a more serious mistake which had the potential to actually harm the client. It is a whisper-type scenario which illustrates one of those situations that cannot be easily addressed. The source of the story is typically confusing. It was brought to the attention of a telephone counsellor by a client who had been counselled by a counsellor from the same organisation. A female client had been talking about her sexuality and her ambivalence about it and her female counsellor, at the end of the session, hugged her. She had never done this before and the client felt very uncomfortable about it. The client didn't want to complain but just wanted a change of counsellor. The interviewee guessed that this was a blind spot for the counsellor and one that she might not have taken to supervision for that very reason.

Although the interviewee who told the story viewed the action as a very serious mistake, because of a mixture of concerns around confidentiality and the complaints procedure's focus on the actions of the client, she felt unable to do anything about it. This scenario could equally be interpreted as an interesting mistake that could be potentially useful for the client and worked through in supervision. Whatever the interpretation, however, the client has now left so there is no possibility of dealing with the issue within the therapeutic relationship. Moreover, there is no way of knowing whether the counsellor did take this to supervision. The therapist's action is left as no more than a whisper and potential rumour.

One supervisor who, as a therapist, had also made a mistake with a client who subsequently left, expressed his regret that the client had not taken her concern or distress to his organisation. A complaints or more likely, mediation process would have given him the opportunity to apologise to the client which he would have liked to have done. Outside of the client taking this action, there was no opportunity for him to apologise. Moreover, in the light of an increasingly legalistic approach to complaints, therapists are advised not to apologise (see Palmer Barnes, 1998).

It is also important to bear in mind that what is perceived as a minor mistake by members of the profession might be devastating to a client. If the client perceives the therapist's behaviour as unacceptable, however it is defined by the therapist, counsellor or the profession, then arguably that client needs support and their grievance needs a place to be heard. Whether that is most appropriately addressed through a mediation process or through a formal complaints procedure is another matter. There is a parallel with harassment cases which are based on the perceptions of the 'victim' rather than the intentions of the perpetrator.

All interviewees were clear on the inevitability of mistakes. This is underlined by Totton (1997: 319):

> Mistakes and failures are integral to the practice of psychotherapy and counselling, because they are integral to life. In both life and therapy, mistakes are invaluable because they bring us up against reality – force us to recognise what is real, rather than what we imagine, fear or hope for.

Mistakes cannot be viewed or judged in isolation nor legislated out of existence. In life, as in therapy, mistakes need to be considered in context to ascertain the meaning and, if necessary, the reason, for the mistake. If mistakes or failures are not used creatively within the therapeutic relationship, for whatever reason, a way has to be found of working with them. The road in between doing nothing and a formal complaints procedure is a dynamic and challenging one.

Working with mistakes within the supervisory relationship

One supervisor noted the importance of exploring, within the supervisory relationship, where the mistake came from, wherever it was on the continuum, in an attempt to prevent repetition. Was it a lack of training or understanding, or the therapist's own issues getting in the way, or feeding inappropriately into the relationship, or a mixture of these? The latter are key sources of mistakes which can lead to a range of actions and touch on the concept of an unconscious.[2]

One source of mistakes and complaints is that of counsellors or therapists trying to get their emotional needs met in various ways by their client. Within supervision, an exploration of the needs of the supervisee may lead to the conclusion that they could be consciously or unconsciously denying their own.

> It is only the denial of needs, shadow, image, power that makes them dangerous. Knowing ourselves, our motives and our needs, makes us more likely to be of real help. In that way we do not use others unawarely for our own ends, or make them carry bits of ourselves we cannot face. (Hawkins and Shohet, 1989: 14)

On a pragmatic level, this could be checked through monitoring the counsellor's emotional and physical resources and support mechanisms. On another level, the counsellor–client relationship can often be explored in the supervisory relationship through some awareness of the parallel process where 'the processes at work currently in the relationship between client and therapist are uncovered through how they are reflected in the relationship between therapist and supervisor' (Hawkins and Shohet, 1989). If the supervisor tries to identify and acknowledge the parallel process, then any issues, including mistakes or failures in the relationship between the client and the counsellor, should in theory arise between the supervisee and the supervisor.

Like a teacher and a therapist, the supervisor has power and the danger is that the supervisor denies that power and the dynamic continues within the therapeutic relationship. Counsellors and therapists can feel incredibly powerless and lose sight of the power they have or are seen to have. This discrepancy demonstrates, as Hawkins and Shohet (1989) suggest, the value of supervision and the constant revisiting of motives. A supervisory relationship is therefore needed that is open to the opportunity to explore issues that may be beneath the surface, reducing as many external barriers as possible, acknowledging the power imbalance that exists in the supervisory relationship and focusing on the 'shadow' side. It is in the nature of the supervisory relationship that this exploration can be either inhibited or encouraged. Hawkins and Shohet (1989: 21) discuss the difficulties inherent in the supervisory relationship. These include the supervisee's issues and anxieties about being judged, or 'put on the spot'.

> Transference difficulties, usually the projecting of critical or uncontaining parental images are often there, just as in therapy, but less easy to recognise. As one worker said in Fineman's study (1985): 'I fear authority and always feel I need to prove to my supervisor that I can do my work.' So supervisors are often not seen for who they are; sometimes they are given too much power, at other times they may be defensively rubbished. Sibling rivalry can also occur in terms of who can manage the client better, and this can come just as much for the supervisor as the supervisee. (Hawkins and Shohet, 1989: 22–23)

In wanting to be a 'good ' supervisee, or even in competition with the supervisor, the supervisee may choose not to take any difficulties or mistakes she or he has in the therapeutic sessions to the supervisor. Supervisee disclosure is discussed by Webb and Wheeler (1998) in some depth. They found a 'positive correlation between the perceived level of rapport in the supervisory alliance and the likelihood of being able to disclose sensitive issues' (1998: 519) and that trainee counsellors were significantly less able to disclose sensitive issues than non-trainees. The importance of the role in this case was emphasised by one of my interviewees:

> As a supervisor . . . it was evident that unless people felt appreciated rather than picked on or picked over in the supervision session, they were going to build a wall and they might not do it deliberately and consciously but they would and I'd get a partial view of their case work.

The supervisor's skills, qualities and approach are paramount in working through sensitive issues including mistakes with the supervisee, before these become serious mistakes or acts of malpractice. The openness and safety of the relationship, however, will also be affected by the definition and context of supervision.

The supervisor – an ambiguous role?

The role of the supervisor in the UK could be perceived organisationally as moving towards the policing of counsellors and therapists on behalf of the profession. This change would parallel both a welcome move towards more accountability across the profession and an increase in public awareness about abuses in counselling and therapy. The effects on the supervisory relationship, however, may not be all positive for the supervisee or for the client (see King and Wheeler, 1999).

Supervision is a requirement in most training organisations and a recommendation, if not a requirement in some UK professional organisations. The BAC *Code of Ethics and Practice for Counsellors* (1998), for example, requires all counsellors throughout their career to engage in supervision for their work and the BPS in 1995 endorsed a requirement that supervisees spend one hour in supervision for every five hours of client work.

Definitions and approaches to supervision appear to differ in their primary focus, which lies between supporting or protecting the client and supporting the supervisee. In some of the literature, the support of the counsellor and the supervisor–supervisee relationship are central to the role, enabling the supervisee to be honest and to take risks:

> Unfortunately the term 'supervision' still carries connotations of managerial oversight and control, mistrust and coercion of the worker by an employer. This is, of course, a long way from its meaning in a counselling context, where

it applies to a professional consultative, supportive aid for counsellors. (Feltham and Dryden, 1994: x)

> Supervision refers to the opportunity for the counsellor or therapist to discuss her or his work with a more experienced colleague . . . this is not the equivalent of line management . . . [it] should therefore provide an opportunity for a counsellor or therapist to talk about patient or client work without any anxiety that she or he will be reprimanded for not working well enough; indeed, it is often the case when starting supervision that counsellors and therapists bring the work that is not going well because they want to learn how to tackle difficult situations, therapy which appears to have got stuck, or clients for whom they feel concern. (Jacobs, 1996: 1)

In other literature, for example that produced by the BAC (1998), the focus leans more towards the counsellor–client relationship.

> B.6.3.1 Counselling supervision refers to a formal arrangement which enables counsellors to discuss their counselling regularly with one or more people who are normally experienced as counselling practitioners and have an understanding of counselling supervision. Its purpose is to ensure the efficacy of the counsellor-client relationship. It is a confidential relationship.

This is underlined in the BAC *Code of Ethics and Practice for Supervisors of Counsellors* (1996):

> 3.1 Counselling supervision is intended to ensure that the needs of the client are being addressed and to monitor the effectiveness of the therapeutic intervention.

It could be argued that here the relationship is one where the supervisee is accountable to the supervisor and as a result, through monitoring practice, the supervisor is expected to bear some responsibility for the supervisee's work. Encompassing both of these approaches, Carroll (1996: 53) suggests a wide-ranging relationship not only based on supporting the counsellor, but also requiring more authority, such as in monitoring ethical issues, teaching and mentoring.

In normal circumstances, this range of tasks and breadth of supervisory role are rarely in question. A continuum can be envisaged, from support at one end to authority at the other with different supervisors at different places on this continuum, depending on their theoretical affiliation, training, personality, setting, etc. When something goes wrong, however, whatever the affiliation of the supervisor, there appears to be a rapid flight towards the authority end of the continuum which can leave the supervisee feeling stranded. One supervisee talked to his supervisor about having broken a boundary. The supervisor later phoned the supervisee and suggested he attend a meeting of the ethics committee. The next and last time he saw the supervisor was at that meeting, where the supervisor appeared to be in attendance as an observer. It could be argued that the supervisor was fearful of the responsibility and passed it on as quickly as he could, leaving the supervisee alone. It might well be that perceptions such as these of supervisor responsibility lead both counsellors and supervisors to work in a more defensive way.

The BAC *Code of Ethics and Practice for Supervisors of Counsellors* (1996) describes counselling supervision as 'a non-exploitative activity. Its basic values are integrity, responsibility, impartiality and respect' (16). Although the statement appears to be clear, the nature and extent of the responsibility are open to question, particularly when problems are identified. King and Wheeler (1999), who conducted a study on supervisor responsibility, noted that skilled and experienced supervisors only took on supervisees that they knew to be competent, as the supervisor is perceived as endorsing a counsellor's practice. What happens then to less competent counsellors, who, if the argument were followed through, are left with less experienced and skilled supervisors?

Difficulties are addressed in the Code (BAC,1996) as follows:

B3.3.9 Supervisors who have concerns about a supervisee's work with clients must be clear how they will pursue this if discussion in counselling supervision fails to resolve the situation.

B3.3.10 Where disagreements cannot be resolved by discussions between the supervisor and supervisee, the supervisor should consult with a fellow professional and, if appropriate, recommend that the supervisee be referred to another supervisor.

In these circumstances, a referral might suggest that it is the supervisee who is in the wrong. One supervisor outlined an example of how he dealt with his concerns and frustration:

I've said to one recently, 'If you're not going to change your way of dealing with this, if you're actually not going to go away and read this up, then I'm not going to supervise you anymore . . . then you won't be able to continue practising.' He replied, – 'Oh well, I'll go to so and so.' I said, 'And I'll be ringing so and so and so and so and saying why I have stopped supervising him.' And I'm prepared to be as tough as that.

On one level, this could be seen as perfectly reasonable; on another it could be seen as the supervisor conducting a form of 'kangaroo court'. Conciliation would be an alternative approach. Another supervisor gave an example of getting into a very difficult victim–persecutor relationship with his supervisee which was eventually resolved through working with an external mediator. It ended with neither being in the wrong but with an acceptance that the supervisory relationship had to end.

The *Code* (BAC, 1996) also charges supervisors with letting the organisation know if there is any unethical practice:

B1.11 Supervisors are responsible for taking action if they are aware that their supervisees' practice is not in accordance with BAC's Codes of Ethics and Practice for Counsellors.

This creates a real tension for the supervisor. Although the action required is not defined, the *Code* would suggest a punitive approach. The consequence is that this may discourage a supervisory relationship that is open and honest enough for the supervisee to explore ethical issues, mistakes and failings and the supervisor to notice initial warning signs. A number of the mistakes discussed earlier could arguably be perceived to be in contravention of aspects of the BAC *Code* (1998) and thus the supervisor could report the supervisee to the organisation. The supervisor's (and the professional body's) approach to the supervisory relationship may well be the deciding factor in whether mistakes are taken to supervision in the first place. The fear and ensuing silence cannot contribute to the protection of the client.

The approach to supervision is further affected by organisational or contextual issues. Some counsellors in colleges do not have supervisors because their managers will not pay for them; others may have a supervisor who doubles as their line manager. This is in spite of the BAC *Code* (1998) and recommendations from the Association of University and College Counsellors (AUCC, 1998) which highlight the need for independent supervision. Similarly, voluntary sector agencies are often unable to afford external supervision for their counsellors. This can lead to difficulties when mistakes occur. In the case of one counselling organisation, for example, the supervisor interviewed was charged with investigating a complaint made against her own supervisee. Rather than being enabled to support him during the investigation, she was required to cross-examine him on behalf of the organisation. This may well have a resonance with the 'kangaroo court' from the perspective of the supervisee.

All of this seems a long way from a supervisor role defined as a 'professional, consultative, supportive aid for counsellors' (Feltham and Dryden, 1994: x). It is clear that the role of the supervisor is a dynamic one that cannot easily be defined and one that is full of contradictions. One supervisor pointed out the difficulties of the supervisor's role in terms of working within an organisation:

Supervisors are fascinating, they hover somewhere between the practitioners and the managers . . . if they go this way, they become a sort of lead counsellor in the counsellor game; if they go that way too far, they become a manager-lackey and alienate themselves from the practitioners so they must inevitably spend their time oscillating and trying to sustain a dialogue in both directions.

At the authority end of the supervisory continuum, whatever the context and professional organisation, the danger is that the balance is lost and mistakes and failings are silenced rather than confronted because the openness can no longer be supported.

From mistakes to complaints

The confusion around the role of the supervisor is accentuated when complaints are made and where supervision is used as a penalty for misconduct. The sanctions page relating to the complaints procedure in the BAC journal, *Counselling* lists errant counsellors, the judgement and the punishment, which is invariably supervision. To cite an example:

> The sanctions are:
> - that the counsellor undertake a period of ongoing supervision of three hours per month for a 2 year period with a supervisor acceptable to BAC
> - supervisor reports are to be submitted to BAC at six-monthly intervals. (*Counselling*, February 1997, 8, no. 1)

As discussed previously, the context of the supervision is central to the supervisory relationship. In this case, with little autonomy in the choice of supervisor and the use of six-monthly reports, it is hard for the supervisee to deal with issues of power within the relationship and to openly and honestly explore professional practice. In another, more recent example where the name and postcode of the guilty counsellor are given, the sanctions were as follows:

> - During the next two years the member's counselling is supervised for at least one hour per week by a supervisor who is agreed by the BAC.
> - Supervision should include the continuous assessment of practice in relation to issues raised at Adjudication and Appeals Panel.
> - Along with the Supervisor's report, the member should submit a case study to the BAC. This should demonstrate the member's philosophy, the theoretical model used and the member's use of supervision. (*Counselling*, May 1998, 2, no. 5)

The supervisor's role here seems to be that of an assessor, very similar to the model used in the USA, where supervisors have an assessment function (see Holloway, 1995: 43).[3] There is some discussion on the use of the naming and shaming 'rogues gallery' as a parallel for the kind of treatment which has been proposed and implemented in some areas for child or sexual abusers who have served their sentence in prison. Given that the process of counselling and therapy involves the client in working through pain, towards responsibility and forgiveness, this punitive action is incongruent with that process.

Mistakes, failings or malpractice in the counselling or therapeutic relationship can lead to three possible actions or non-actions, which parallel the trend in child abuse, as outlined in the following sections.

There is no complaint from the client

Rumours and whispers concerning certain therapists are heard but are not confronted because of fears of litigation or because there is no avenue for addressing them either officially or unofficially. Suspicion of misconduct can be reported by one member against another member and they are advised to 'implement the Complaints Procedure' (Bond, 1993: 148). This is very difficult in relation to rumours or whispers either because they don't fit the procedure, or the procedure, based as it is on a legal approach, isn't the appropriate mechanism. Formal complaints procedures tend to be based on the client's action so therapists are left with encouraging and supporting the client to make a complaint while colleagues and supervisors may feel powerless to act if the therapist's client does not:

> Sometimes things are more than mistakes and yet they don't get complained about. But you can pick them up in some way. And I think you do that more in an organisation than working as an individual supervisor, picking up information from other people. . . . And actually, I think the decision was that nothing could be done unless the client made a complaint about it. . . . And yet you have this information. . . . And it feels like having to work with your hands tied behind your back.

One possibility is to address issues through a third party complaint, for example from the partner or parent of a client. Complaints procedures, however, vary on whether they will hear third party complaints, 'with the problem of confidentiality frequently being cited as a major reason for not considering them' (see Bond, 1993: 260). Another possibility for the BAC, for example, is to raise issues via reference to article 5 of the BAC constitution that refers to serious matters relating to members, clients and counselling in general which would bring the Association into disrepute. This has been used rarely, but most famously against the comedian, Bernard Manning in April 1996 (*Counselling*, August 1996, 7, no. 3).

The client or a practitioner contacts the professional body but the issue is not dealt with

This could be because of lack of proof, because the issue doesn't relate to the appropriate code or because neither wants to put it in writing. Between September 1997 and March 1998 there were 350 phone calls representing initial queries or concerns about counselling practice to the BAC,[4] but in the year up to July 1998, only twenty-two were dealt with through complaints procedures. One explanation may be that on first contacting the BAC, complainants are asked to do their best to work it through with the counsellor concerned and some problems may be resolved in that way. Another explanation relates to the formality of the following stage. The complainant then has to make a written complaint and logically relate it to the appropriate code of ethics and practice. There is nothing in between these two stages. The initial concern or query may well have originated from a situation of emotional distress, and to be required to link this to a code, which is written in unfamiliar language, is hardly likely to be the most supportive or appropriate action. Moreover, the concern or issue may not have involved a breach of the *Code of Ethics*. As Totton (1997: 316) points out:

> Quite frequently someone with a problem is eventually told that the system cannot process their problem at all: it doesn't fall within the terms of the procedure. Rather than the problem determining the procedure, the procedure determines whether it is allowed to count as a problem!

A complaints procedure is instigated

Currently, the supervisor has no specific identified role to play in terms of complaints. In the case of all known BAC complaints up to mid-1998, for example, the supervisor has not been questioned as part of the investigation. If brought to task, the counsellor appears to stand alone with little or no support. None of the supervisors I interviewed or who were discussed in relation to complaints in other professional organisations was asked about their work with the supervisees. There is no suggestion that the supervisor also has a responsibility for the mistake or breach of the *Code of Ethics* and when a complaint is made and upheld, there is unlikely to have been any investigation into the supervision of the accused therapist. Yet in interviews with those who have been involved in complaints procedures and in the literature, it has been suggested that counsellors may well have had inadequate or ineffective supervision. Palmer Barnes (1998: 51) states that:

> It is very rare to have a complaint by a patient against a supervisor though there may be grounds in law since the supervisor could be considered to have sufficient knowledge of the therapy for them to be included in any case of negligence against a practitioner or trainee.

Her view is that supervisors are responsible for the work they supervise and on many occasions mediators and adjudicators of complaints would have liked to discuss with the supervisor 'why the difficulties in the work were not picked up in supervision or managed better between the practitioner and supervisor' (Palmer Barnes, 1998: 51).

Due to the complicated and formal nature of the complaints procedure, the majority of the counsellors involved go straight to their solicitor and not to their apparently immediate form of support, their supervisor. The accused counsellor or therapist, understandably, does not contact their own professional body for support (as in the role of a trade union), because it is the same organisation dealing with the complaint. The roles of the counsellor and the professional organisation hearing the complaint are therefore polarised from the outset. The professional bodies, such as the

BAC and other smaller professional organisations, seem to take on the role of persecutor and the process becomes adversarial. When asked if it was the UKCP's and BAC's function to support the client, one interviewee responded:

> It's not to support the client, it's to hear the client and it's to hear the counsellor, it's to support no one ... it's just to hear the matter is dealt with justly and fairly. And that's very very important: as soon as you start to support one or the other you are effectively discriminating, you're into trouble.

Through interviews with supervisors, there was some recognition that therapists and counsellors might not work as creatively as they did in the 1970s and 1980s because of the increased possibility of complaints and litigation. The latter is borne out by the figures provided by BAC (telephone discussion with BAC Central Office, July 1998) with two complaints in 1995, five in 1996, six in 1997 and twenty-two up to July 1998. Many in the profession had hoped that a complaints procedure would have an educative function. However, as one supervisor said:

> The complaints processes are often not healing for the client or the therapist. ... they have a life of their own which isn't always kind to either, that isn't always healthy to either, they aren't that simple, such as 'I think you've done me wrong', 'yes, I made a mistake' ... it just gets overtaken by a whole bigger process and panic. You get a letter through the door and your heart sinks and you're immediately into defensive behaviour. So you can't talk.

Most agreed that the human cost was high; the view from a member of the complaints committee was:

> It's an unpleasant and stressful process for everyone concerned. . . . I don't think there are ever any winners in it. I think everybody loses to some degree. . . . you've gone through anything up to a three or four year process with a lot of money involved, a lot of pressure, a lot of stress. You will probably have lost work and it's a very painful exercise. And even being exonerated, which you might say is a win, there's a hell of a cost attached to it.

Conclusion

The shadow side of the counselling and therapy profession seems to have become externalised through slow and complex complaints procedures, which can make the therapist the victim, the organisation the persecutor and can leave the client lost in a legal pursuit when all they really wanted was some explanation and apology, perhaps just to have their therapist listen to their grievance. Not only that, but there exists an area of whispers and rumours among clients and practitioners which currently has no voice. The formal process is too unwieldy and legalistic and the only alternative is a continued silence which parallels the issue of child abuse.

In much of the literature, the supervisor appears as a key figure in monitoring the counsellor's practice and in protecting the client, the 'guardian angel' of the counselling world. This raises two unresolved issues which relate to both ends of the authority–support continuum of the supervisor's role. Firstly, in most cases, not only will supervisors know their supervisees' work better than anyone else, but they also have made and are capable of making mistakes alongside their supervisees. If they are not considered in even the most minor way in investigations as part of a complaints procedure, then there seems to be an inconsistency in this approach to the supervisor role. Secondly, the UKCP and the BAC currently are unable to support simultaneously both the aggrieved client and the accused therapist because they are investigating the complaint and cannot be seen to be taking sides. Supervisors can easily find themselves in a similar role, which means they are no longer able to support the accused counsellor. Thus the accused counsellors or therapists can be abandoned not only by their supervisor but also by their professional organisations.

It could be argued that the professional organisations, partly because they have tried valiantly to find definitive solutions, strategies and rules to deal with mistakes and failings, are losing sight of their goals. The profession is getting caught up in a legal framework that becomes more complex as time goes on and doesn't help the client, counsellor or supervisor. Each step I have taken in trying to pin down the issues in this chapter has led me away from the detail towards the context of counselling and therapy and the culture of accountability. The complexity of the various codes of ethics and practice, as Roger Casemore noted (e-mail, March 1999) 'in their fine attention to detail and highly legalistic nature, contribute to lengthy complaints processes and a punitive atmosphere'. It seems, as it stands, that there has to be a victim and persecutor and this contrasts sharply with the work of counselling and therapy itself. The culture of complaints is a culture of blame and the fear it creates can heighten the wall of silence and therefore the problems and abuses within the profession. This leaves the question of how this culture can be changed; and it has to, because it cannot help but affect the therapeutic and supervisory relationships, which in turn will be detrimental to clients. At this stage, there are more questions for discussion and research but with a different emphasis:

- Is there a place for a rehabilitative and healing process to be considered within the current frameworks, or for the concept of forgiveness to be considered?[5]
- How can errant therapists or counsellors, in acknowledging their mistakes or failures, be supported?
- How can clients be encouraged to raise concerns with a third party if they are unable to do so with their counsellor? Moreover, how can this process be encouraged and implemented in a non-threatening way for both parties?

- How can supervisees be encouraged to discuss openly and honestly their vulnerabilities and concerns with their supervisor?
- Can the profession set up structures which promote the development of good practice, provide justice and redress for aggrieved clients and promote wider public confidence without creating scapegoats and victims?

The answer to the final question is positive. There is pressure for reform both from within the established professional bodies such as the BAC and from the initiatives of such organisations as the Independent Practitioners' Network (IPN). Counsellors can, on an ongoing basis, explore and monitor with colleagues and through supervision their own approaches to mistakes, ethical issues and complaints. This is more challenging and time-consuming than it is to be given a set of rules and either to ignore a difficult ethical issue or to direct a complainant immediately to the BAC, for example. The IPN, as a confederation of linked member groups, provides one such model. Each group comprises between five and ten individuals who have agreed to stand by each other's work after a generally painstaking process of checking out through face to face contact. As Totton (1997: 320) writes:

> The really dreadful acts of oppression and exploitation of clients tend to take place in secret, in the closet, in denial. Being part of a peer group at all militates against such acts, though it doesn't prevent them. It is a move in the opposite direction from client abuse to join such a peer group, to expose oneself to colleagues.

It might well be that the IPN and other similar organisations which have or are developing a culture of challenging mutual enquiry and the requirement to stand by each other's work can contribute to a change in perceptions of mistakes and complaints as well as provide support for both the therapist and the client. Moreover, open discussion across a range of contexts such as the media, journals, professional development activity and peer supervision groups will help to continue the debate.

The BAC is now, in 1999, working on developing a system in which support can be provided for members complained against and complainants, through, for example, offering a 'support person' and producing guidelines to complainees (see Casemore, 1998). These changes will, no doubt, be welcomed. Any change in culture, however, would require a re-appraisal of the word 'complaint' and a consideration of other processes such as conflict resolution (see Totton, 1997) or mediation which can provide support and justice for the client and congruence with the traditions of counselling and therapy.

Notes

1 Legally, it is difficult to argue, and I have no intention of attempting it here. There has been a trend in the USA that would suggest that supervisors have vicarious liability (see Palmer Barnes, 1998).

2 For further reference, Langs (1994) clearly articulates the importance of giving attention to transference and countertransference issues in the supervisory relationship, as do Page and Wosket (1994) and Hawkins and Shohet (1989).

3 The BAC is taking this difference into account and the latest proposal is to give this type of supervision a different name (interview with Roger Casemore, July 1998).

4 The exact nature of the concerns are unknown. This is an area which would benefit from further research.

5 The approach to post-complaint supervision with its emphasis on assessment and a fixed term contract adopted by many organisations may or may not allow that development to take place.

References

AUCC (1998) *Guidelines for University and College Counselling Services*. Rugby: British Association for Counselling.

BAC (1996) *Code of Ethics and Practice for Supervisors of Counsellors*. Rugby: British Association for Counselling.

BAC (1998) *Code of Ethics and Practice for Counsellors*. Rugby: British Association for Counselling.

Bond, T. (1993) *Standards and Ethics for Counselling in Action*. London: Sage.

Carroll, M. (1996) *Counselling Supervision: Theory, Skills and Practice*. London: Cassell.

Casemore, R. (1998) 'Support for members complained against' Professional Committee issue paper, British Association for Counselling. Unpublished.

Dryden, W. (1987) *Key Cases in Psychotherapy*. London: Croom Helm.

Dryden, W. (ed.) (1993) *Questions and Answers on Counselling in Action*. London: Sage.

Feltham, C. and Dryden, W. (1994) *Developing Counsellor Supervision*. London: Sage.

Fineman, S. (1985) *Social Work Stress and Intervention*. Aldershot: Gower.

Hawkins, P. and Shohet, R. (1989) *Supervision in the Helping Professions*. Milton Keynes: Open University Press.

Holloway, E. (1995) *Clinical Supervision: A Systems Approach*. Thousand Oaks, CA: Sage.

Jacobs, M. (1996) *In Search of Supervision*. Buckingham: Open University Press.

Jenkins, P. (1997) *Counselling, Psychotherapy and the Law*. London: Sage.

King, D. and Wheeler, S. (1999) 'The responsibilities of counsellor supervisors: a qualitiative study', *British Journal of Guidance and Counselling* 27: (2) 215–229.

Langs, R. (1994) *Doing Supervision and Being Supervised*. London: Karnac.

Page, S. and Wosket, V. (1994) *Supervising the Counsellor: A Cyclical Model*. London: Routledge.

Palmer Barnes, F. (1998) *Complaints and Grievances in Psychotherapy: A Handbook of Ethical Practice*. London: Routledge.

Robertiello, R.C. and Schoenewolf, G.S. (1987) *101 Common Therapeutic Blunders: Countertransference and Counterresistance in Psychotherapy*. Northvale, NJ: Jason Aronson.

Totton, N. (1997) 'Learning by mistake: client practitioner conflict in a self-regulated network', in R. House and N. Totton (eds), *Implausible Professions: Arguments for Pluralism and Autonomy in Psychotherapy and Counselling*. Ross-on-Wye: PCCS.

Webb, A. and Wheeler, S. (1998) 'How honest do counsellors dare to be in the supervisory relationship? An exploratory study', *British Journal of Guidance and Counselling*, 26(4): 509–524.

6

WORKING WITH DIFFERENCE: CULTURALLY COMPETENT SUPERVISION

Hilde Rapp

The personal, professional, educational and political context of supervision: what are the key issues? Closing the gap between principles and practices

As supervisors and supervisees, our immediate concern lies with managing a particular supervisory relationship with an individual or with a group. However, therapy, counselling, and supervision are activities which are tied into social, educational and cultural contexts that influence our values, beliefs and attitudes regarding sexual choice, lifestyle, dress, social customs and ways of relating. We therefore need to place our activities in the wider context of the personal, professional, political and educational dimensions of working with difference.

Increasingly we live in globally connected multi-ethnic, multiracial, and multicultural societies. In expressly democratic societies our political institutions and social and administrative systems are purportedly designed to promote the ethics of equality. Public opinion, whether for moral or for economic reasons, outlaws the unreflecting and dehumanising exploitation of people from a different class, race, gender, culture, religion or country.

We all know that there is a gap between egalitarian principles and actual current practices. Supervision, and the therapeutic work it monitors and reflects, is no exception. It takes time, effort and discernment to detect in practice which bit of process, procedure and day to day behaviour feeds on prejudice, defiantly or unwittingly perpetuating inequalities and human suffering.

How can we develop the kind of supervisory relationship which allows us to open our practice to any kind of scrutiny? How can we define our role and responsibility as supervisors or supervisees so that we can participate productively in the personal, professional, educational and political work that will be required to close this gap between ethical principles and hands on practices? This chapter will explore these questions both conceptually and practically in a variety of ways.

Steer clear of cookbook approaches and culture blindness

Our ideas about health and illness affect our attitudes towards seeking and providing help. We may turn to people inside or outside the family. We may seek out medical, spiritual, professional or lay guidance and support (Helman, 1990). We all have our cultural and political baggage, and we are all prone to ethnocentric bias. Painful past experiences can make us wary and suspicious. While it is part of the vicissitudes of the human condition that all of us are victims and perpetrators of stereo-typing, prejudice and ignorance, we need to remain keenly aware of how this differs from the wholesale exploitation and abuse of men, women and children through institutional racism or oppression. All these factors affect how we think about ourselves and the other person in the room in supervision and any one of them can lead to misunderstandings and misperceptions.

Case example

A white supervisor has a first meeting with a new black supervisee. (I will use the word 'black' in the political sense adopted by the RACE Division of BAC and the Ethics and Equality Group of the 'national organisation for education, training and standard setting in Advice, Advocacy, Counselling, Guidance, Mediation and Psychotherapy (CAMPAG)', the Department for Education and Employment (DfEE) sponsored standard-setting lead body in our vocational sector). The supervisor experiences the supervisee's asking in detail about rights, contracts and values as somewhat aggressive.

On the verge of responding with defensiveness, she hears her internalised supervisor's voice in the back of her mind suggesting that aggressiveness might be a sign of fear. The supervisor decides to test this hypothesis. What is going on for herself and for the supervisee at an emotional level? What prior experiences of supervision has the supervisee had?

It soon transpires that the last supervisory relationship with a female white supervisor was unsatisfactory, and that the supervisee had felt deskilled and rejected. Was this sense of rejection due to racism? What has re-stimulated this fear in the present encounter?

The supervisor empathises with the supervisee's discomfort. She voices her concern that the supervisee seems tense and uncomfortable. She shares that she herself feels anxious about this. This helps both of them to get enough distance from their feelings to be able to share some of their thinking.

They uncover together the supervisee's painful experience of coming up against repeated unthinking traces of heterosexism in the previous supervisory relationship. Rigidly held and unreflected theories about genital maturity, derived from psychoanalytic writings, dating from a time when homosexuality was widely considered pathological, had repeatedly informed the previous supervisor's approach (Haslam, 1997).

What has re-stimulated the fear that the current supervisor might be similarly prejudiced? The supervisor's bookshelf contains a book by Socarides about homosexuality. This had subliminally, unconsciously, caught the supervisee's attention, and brought back memories of unpleasant experiences of being at the receiving end of heterosexist prejudice and 'theoretical abuse' (Basseches, 1997).

The supervisor shared that the book had been bought in order to inform her very active protest against giving a public platform to Socarides' views on homosexuality without any commitment to give space for debate.

The supervisee shared that she had found it hard to end the previous supervisory relationship, as there were very few supervisors to choose from who were acceptable to her training organisation. She could not bear to become trapped in yet another painful relationship. Therefore, she had plucked up all her courage to put to the test whether this supervisor would be willing and able to discuss her values openly and without abusing her power.

Learning from Experience

Had the supervisor in our case example continued to assume that the supervisee was aggressive, or that the discomfort in their relationship arose from a difference in racial origin, she could easily have been caught up in generalisations, stereotyping or labelling. She would certainly have completely missed the real issue. There would have been no chance for a supervisory alliance to form. The supervisee would have had yet another disappointing experience of insensitive supervision, reinforcing her sense of rejection, foreclosing a further opportunity for acknowledging the damaging effect that prejudice has in our professional relationships.

If we can be humble and open-minded, aware of the power relationships which inevitably obtain between any two people from any two races, ethnic groups, cultural backgrounds, classes, genders, sexual orientations and levels of ability, we may be able to avoid getting drawn into 'defensive' practice, which is actually destructive. Another important lesson to be drawn from this example is that we should not presume what is important to people, but we should ask them, and this means that we should not only check things out in our individual encounters with others, but also that, collectively, we should conduct research. In this context, Weinreich (1998) has made available a very user friendly research tool for uncovering and mapping the many complex choices a person makes to put together all their different identifications to arrive at an overarching sense of identity.

An example from research

William Cross, the original author of the well known 'Nigrescence' model, has told a highly relevant cautionary tale against himself. His original model (Cross, 1971) states that if a black person does not strongly identify as 'black', this indicates that they have identified with the cultural oppressor, and that they are in denial about their identity. Twenty-five years on, following a whole spate of research originally inspired by his model, Cross (1995) announced the radical revision of his model, rapidly followed by a second revision (Ffagen-Smith and Cross, 1996). He now maintains that identity is complex. What is salient for one person may not be salient for another. For instance, a person's professional identity may have greater salience than their racial identity.

In fact, increasingly, colleagues who explicitly do multicultural, intercultural or cross-cultural work decry 'cookbook approaches', which advocate global solutions and give general recipes for working with clients labelled as black, Hispanic, African-Caribbean, Bangladeshi and so on (Speight, 1991). At the same time, in our attempts not to stereotype, we need to guard against becoming 'culture-blind', that is, ignoring cultural differences and their political import altogether (Fernando, 1991,1996; Nadirshaw, in press).

Counselling, therapy and supervision are centrally concerned with being open to experience. Supervision gives supervisees space to tell their story about how they help their clients to construct narratives of their life experiences. Supervision is the place where we examine how we can gain another person's confidence, and how we demonstrate that we respect and understand his or her values, norms and meaning systems. As supervisors we model how to encourage another person to tell us what we need to know in order for us to be helpful to them.

Opposing institutional oppression, cultural hegemony, and insensitive practice without shaming individuals for their psychological limitations

Personal challenge and support

In supervision we invite trust, we encourage people to show their limitations, and therefore we must not shame one another for sharing our weak spots, our blinkers and our prejudices. Few people who work in our field actively want to hang on to their prejudices. Most of us, within the limits of our capacity to work through shame and guilt, are genuinely intent on finding more open and acceptable ways of grappling with the difficulties which arise out of experiences of difference. We need to help and encourage one another to let go of our insensitivities, preconceptions, prejudices and our irrational fear of difference. I plead that we should be compassionate at a *personal* level.

Raising political awareness

As soon as we are dealing with organised collectivities of human beings, we move from the personal into the *political* arena. Institutional '–isms' have crept into every nook and cranny of our daily lives, our language, humour and the fine detail of our daily practices, down to what socks we wear and what messages they give. I advocate that we be politically proactive and oppose all forms of 'institutional' racism, sexism, homophobia, and disregard of the needs and rights of disabled people. Here we have a different responsibility, unless we want to become guilty of bystanding (Clarkson, 1996).

Co-constructing guidelines for good enough professional practice

Regarding the *professional* dimension of our work, I urge that we set clear ethical bottom lines regarding what is, and what is not acceptable and that we firmly confront poor practice, remaining understanding of personal struggle, aware of political inertia, and supportive of educational opportunities for further personal and professional development.

When we work as *supervisors* we do need to confront racist beliefs and practices, homophobic and defensive ways of dealing with gay or lesbian fellow citizens, condescending and disregarding ways of talking down to or across a person with learning disabilities, or lack of appreciation of the courage and resourcefulness with which a disabled person lives their life. Likewise, if, as *supervisees*, we find that our supervisor informs their practice predominantly with reference to 'white theory', we will have to address the professional limitations of our supervisor.

Working together to thoroughly revise curricula, theories, techniques and trainings

However we also need to recognise that all our professional frameworks are importantly supported by the beliefs and practices of 'dead white men' (Pedersen, pers. comm.). We are dealing with the influence of professional and academic institutions which regulate our trainings, our accreditation, our personal counselling and therapy, our way of writing case histories and records, the way we arrange our appointments, and even the furniture in our consulting rooms (Lago and Thompson, 1996). We are actually faced with the outcome of *educational* practices.

When it comes to the *educational* context in which therapy, counselling and supervision are taught, we should promote courses as exemplary wherever considerable effort has been made to work through these issues. However, even in educational settings where the multicultural agenda has been taken on board, there is often still a gap between programmatic statements and the way courses walk their talk. Most of us agree by now that we must, and should, and will, take difference into account. Yet, once we get down to the small clinical details, the sophisticated discussions of transferences and parallel process, our trainings and supervisions become whiter and whiter.

Over ten years ago, Paul Pedersen (1987) found fault with much of the literature and thinking in the field of counselling and psychotherapy. He strongly indicted its overemphasis on individualism and independence, accompanied by the neglect of the client's support systems, focusing on changing the individual without changing the family system. He was also highly critical of the fragmentation of knowledge into dissociated academic disciplines, the lack of historical awareness, compounded by ethnocentric assumptions regarding normality, and the attendant dangers of cultural encapsulation, the overuse of abstract language and a bias towards linear rather than systematic thinking.

We are witnessing the pervasive cultural and intellectual hegemony of Western, white, patriarchal, individualistic meaning systems (Lago and Thompson, 1996; Pedersen, 1996), anchored in oppressive academic power structures which have regulated and controlled what may be written about, what will be disseminated through teaching and publication and what will be silenced, hijacked or tokenised (McLeod, in press). Inevitably, these cultural beliefs, habits and practices, and politically and historically derived forms of social organisation impact on how we think and act with clients and in supervision.

I believe that there is an increasing appreciation that all our theories and concepts need to be radically rethought in a very fine-grained way. There have been various collective efforts to define standards for culturally competent counselling, therapy and supervision. (See Sue et al., 1995 for a review of this endeavour and an examplary set of standards of practice adopted by the (American) Association for Multicultural Counseling and Development (AMCD), and Rapp, 1998b for UK-based standards adopted by the British Initiative for Integrative Psychotherapeutic Practice (BIIP)). Below I give an outline of culturally sensitive competencies that can be used to guide supervision.

Thinking about client needs in supervision: what does the other person need from us?

I conceive of culturally competent supervision as a template for all good supervision, since, in practice, we are all always working with difference and diversity. All therapeutic and supervisory work is subject to cultural variability, even if both participants have the same ethnic origin, the same gender, and speak the same language. Both may be English, but one may be Catholic, lesbian and middle class, the other heterosexual, a Jehovah's Witness (and hence possibly homophobic on religious grounds), and working class. There is research to suggest that cultural differences between two people who speak the same language can make for greater misunderstandings than differences where the need to translate from one idiom into another is clearly marked. 'Differences within cultures' are at least as important as 'differences between cultures' and it may, in fact, be more difficult to remain aware that a supervisee or supervisor who has much in common with us is nonetheless an 'other', a unique and different individual. We would be wise to assume as little as possible about another individual's very personal understandings of themselves and their world. This is the heart of good counselling and psychotherapy. Indeed, the whole December 1998 issue of *Anthropology and Medicine* was devoted to this very subject. A number of authors picked out how difficult it is to retain our awareness of the ways in which others are unique and different despite significant surface similarities (Fainzang, 1998; van Dongen, 1998; van Ginkel, 1998).

Competent practice in a multicultural society involves developing a sound awareness of our own assumptions and prejudices. This means that as counsellors and psychotherapists we need to work with tact (empathy, sensitivity) and skill (competence) using different perspectives. We need to create the conditions in which we do not dissemble, but trust each other to look for one another's blind spots. We need to learn how to challenge one another with compassion, firmness and respect, for instance by adopting the perspective of the client, or using our internal supervisor to help us hear with different ears and to see with extra eyes. As supervisors we must also help our supervisees learn to tell the difference between the pain of a victim of personal envy and spite, the pain of a victim of systematic racial or homophobic harassment, and the pain and confusion of a person on the verge of paranoid psychosis.

Monitoring social exclusion

All human beings live and conduct social relationships according to some common guiding principles. We all have prejudices, preferred ways of doing things, routines and behavioural recipes. Not all of these are harmful. Some are more like ready made pre-judgements which are the natural outcomes of learning what works for us, and of doing again what has worked before. To do anything else would be to keep reinventing the wheel. The challenge of supervision in a multicultural context lies in identifying and highlighting when our existing ways of working are productive and when they become harmful and alienate and exclude the very people we are trying to reach.

The person seeking psychotherapy, counselling or supervision may have quite different expectations about what is on offer from the practitioner whose help they are seeking. Supervision should help us to balance ordinary expectations of social relating with what is appropriate to offer in counselling or therapy: whether to shake hands with a new client, wear formal clothes, offer a cup of tea, accept a modest gift, and whether or when to give advice. These decisions need to be taken with tact and sensitivity, putting saving a person's face before blind compliance with a rule or convention, without giving in to genuinely untenable requests and expectations. The 'customer' is not always right: need and demand are not the same thing (Birchwood, 1997).

However, unless we establish culturally relevant and acceptable ground rules, people most in need of help may never wish to enter an official building again, let alone apply for help from what they perceive as a cold and rude stranger. Unfortunately, there is plenty of evidence that both counselling and psychiatric services available through the NHS (for which we have some figures) are underused by young people, ethnic minority groups (Asian women and African Caribbean men especially), and people identifying as working class, because the conditions under which the service is offered are seen as unhelpful or inappropriate (Rapp, 1998a).

Supervision should help us to situate the very personal meanings with which we are working in a culturally reflective professional framework, tracing asymmetries of rights and responsibilities, variations in shared customs and habits, and in the way we use language, and power. It is important for the supervisor as the person with the greater real and perceived power in the situation to take the lead in exploring with a supervisee whether and why certain social expectations should, or should not, be met. She may role-play how to explain to a client how professional 'helping relationships' differ from getting support through a peer friendship, advice from an elder, spiritual guidance from a community healer, and medical treatment from a traditional psychiatrist. The onus is on us to clearly and warmly set the scene about what is and what is not going to happen in this encounter which, in every culture, Western or Eastern, is surrounded by a certain amount of awe and mystery (Helman, 1990).

Individuals, nuclear families, family groups and communities

Individual therapy along Western lines may not only be inappropriate but actually harmful when working with clients from a different cultural group. This is especially true with groups tied into a more traditional social organisation, where the extended family acts as the main source of support. We need to make sure that training adequately deals with redressing this current bias towards equipping trainees to offer only individual adult therapy. Meanwhile the burden of assessing the appropriateness of what is offered in therapy or counselling falls on supervision.

Even where the counsellor is only working with one family member, it is vital that the implications of any changes sought by the counsellor and the client for the whole family system are thoroughly explored in the supervisory dyad. Culturally competent supervision includes the rigorous examination of all our concepts about individual and family mental health; about the roles of significant others within the wider community who are traditionally involved in the mediation of distress or conflict; and the costs, benefits and limitations of using a still predominantly Western, or predominantly middle-class approach to helping people with problems with living (Ariel, 1997, 1999).

It is crucial that we find ways of helping supervisees move between different perspectives and theoretical frameworks, so they get to understand how specific techniques will have different meanings and outcomes when used with different clients, depending on their underlying personal and cultural value systems and beliefs (Messer and Woolfolk, 1998; Safran and Messer, 1997).

Tooling up: attention, attunement, attachment, cultural and perceptual matching, contracting

Supervision provides an opportunity to think, in the presence of a trusted colleague, about the moment to moment relationship between our clients and ourselves. Before supervisor and supervisee can get down to defining tasks, roles and procedures of good enough culturally competent supervision, they need to tune in and adjust to one another's different ways of tackling life and work.

From an integrative and systemic perspective it is clear that individual differences in learning style will affect the relationship between the client and the practitioner, and that this difference will then impact again on the supervisor–supervisee relationship. Such differences may also already have been a contributing factor to interpersonal and relationship difficulties which all three participants in the supervisory matrix may have experienced independently in their respective families of origin or in their significant current relationships. If the supervisory process becomes stuck and uncomfortable, divergences in values and cultural styles need to be sensitively explored.

The first step is to give interest and attention

Much of our work is so subtle, and has so much to do with how genuinely we are interested in the other's story, how well we remember the small details of their lives, how tactful we are in knowing when to pursue a sensitive issue and when to leave well alone, or how courteous we are towards a person who has often been looked down upon or passed over. Without finely tuned attentiveness to the details of intersubjective communication, no amount of book learning will enhance our client work.

The second step is to attune to the other

This is to focus on what we actually perceive and sense in our *own* body as we listen to the other's narrative. The Kagans' technique of Interpersonal Process Recall (IPR) (Kagan and Kagan, 1975), invites us to stay in touch with our bodily felt sense, engage with our thinking and our knowledge of the world, alive to our understanding of our own motives, wishes and impulses to act. We need to keep our focus on the small gestures of human relating which bring us closer together or which drive us further apart. Hesitations and silences, broken eye contact, shifts in posture, changes in the tone of voice and suchlike are in fact the signs which alert us that something has changed in the emotional flow between ourselves and the other, be this friend, client, counsellor, supervisee or supervisor. We need to track how present we are in the session and how present the supervisee is, so that an interpersonal attachment can form between us on which to build a supervisory relationship.

The third step is to match perceptual and cultural styles

Following research in perceptual, cognitive, social and cognitive developmental psychology, Richard Bandler and John Grinder (1975), the founders of neuro-linguistic programming (NLP) looked for systematic differences in the preferred information-processing mode of therapists and clients. Through shadowing and modelling the performance of particularly successful therapists, such as Milton Erickson and Virginia Satir, researchers soon noticed that matches and mismatches between the visual, auditory or kinaesthetic information-processing strategies of participants have profound effects on the relationship between therapist and client as well as on the therapeutic task. This is equally true of supervision.

We need to explore the match between cultural frameworks and political values which inform this shared learning. Identity, modality, agency, timing and context are some of the variables which come into play and determine the level at which any intervention needs to focus, so that we can learn more about how to work with the actual problem the client or the supervisee has brought to the session. We need to discover how values and beliefs affect our preferences, tastes and habits.

The fourth step is to manage complexity and contracting

This means keeping track of all the tasks which need to be performed so that the supervisory space can open up, the supervisory relationship can develop and the learning alliance can be formed, which allows the supervisory work to be done. In good supervision we contract to monitor our felt sense about how closely each is following the other's feelings, thoughts and interpretations. We contract to monitor and discuss mis-perceptions on both sides, what we may wish to call transferences and countertransferences. We contract to listen deeply, reflect accurately, contract clearly, bridge theory and practice in an integrative way, and to review our practice responsibly and responsively (Page and Wosket, 1994). If the principles of good practice truly guide the moment by moment conduct of the counsellor–client dyad as well as its reflection in the supervisor–supervisee dyad, there will be a good balance between challenge and support, giving space and showing respect for the other's meaning systems, leaving little room for the gross abuses of '–isms'.

**Guidelines for culturally competent supervised practice.
Organising the work in context: relationship, authority,
frameworks, experience**

Humility and clarity help to create an environment in which it feels safe
to confront, both in oneself and in the other, inherent racism, sexism, and
any other deeply ingrained barriers to forming close relationships and
to engaging in open and honest communication. Supervision requires
'finding the right balance between challenge and support' (Inskipp and
Proctor, 1993). It is also an opportunity for perspective taking, for 'extra
vision' to be brought to bear on the task (Houston, 1995).

Relationship

Throughout this chapter, we are explicitly or implicitly examining the
quality of the supervisory relationship. The way that the perceptual style,
learning style, temperament and personality adaptation of the supervisee
and supervisor match, mismatch or combine will serve to help or hinder
how the supervisee as therapist or counsellor manages to build rapport
between him or herself and the client. The supervisory relationship models
all the time how two people can work together to choose appropriate
learning strategies which advance the shared task, whether this is supervision, therapy or counselling. The supervisor demonstrates, explicitly or
implicitly, how to make space for cultural variation, how to remain mindful
of the changing developmental needs as they emerge in the relationship
(Carroll, 1996; Holloway and Poulin, 1995).

Most good supervision is emancipatory, encouraging the autonomy of
the supervisee to use their own meaning system, and set their own agenda
by taking responsibility for contracting what work is to be done to ensure
culturally competent ethical practice. It provides permission for equal,
open and collegial sharing of thoughts, feelings and experiences in which
both supervisor and supervisee may find relief in mutual understanding.
Moments like this can be very precious and affirming. I will briefly discuss
below how the supervisor may use a theoretical framework to guide his
or her decisions about what kind of supervisory functions and tasks will
most appropriately support the supervisee's continuing professional
development in tune with variations in experience and expertise regarding
the needs of different client groups.

Authority

Many courses (not only in our own field) have made a firm commitment
to improve the quality of trainings and standards of practice. Modules
intended to raise our awareness about issues of race and culture, gender,
sexuality and disability, have been tacked on and the adequacy of single
orientation, single theory training, has been challenged.

It falls to supervision to clinically work through the implications of this commitment to culturally sensitive practice by monitoring the subtle ways in which we all constantly misuse one another. We must be willing and able to embody our authority to provide a clear framework that guides how we organise our work so as to use our judgement to ensure that ethical principles are upheld, and bottom lines regarding ethical practice are met (Rawls, 1967). As supervisees we will not feel safe unless we can invest our supervisor with the power to robustly challenge harmful or unacceptable behaviour (Kadushin, 1993). Since the dynamics of oppression can be acted out in supervision or in counselling, it falls to supervisors to ensure that all parties are informed about the proper channels and procedures for dealing with any impasses, breakdowns or complaints which may arise.

In order for a person to learn and grow, facilitation, advice, guidance, mentoring and coaching need to be available from someone who has already achieved competence and maturity in the area in question (Inskipp and Proctor, 1993; Raw, 1996; Sexton and Whiston, 1994). Clarifying and discerning feedback which is given in a non-patronising way and which respects our meaning systems is likely to be received as constructive. Especially, as the learner becomes able to plan and execute their skills in an ethical and competent way, the supervisor increasingly needs to move into a partnership model (Rapp, 1996). Pacing and helping need to give way to letting go and supporting. (Most mothers of young infants learning a new skill know how to do this with exquisite tact and timing: Fogel, 1993; Marr, 1982).

Frameworks: functional and developmental models

The task of supervision is to support the supervisee in working safely, competently and with cultural awareness, both in and with the client relationship in order to help the client resolve some difficulty in their lives. Most competence-based approaches, such as the CAMPAG mapping in the UK of counselling, psychotherapy and supervision (consultative workshops were held, but standards are not yet agreed), or the multi-cultural counselling standards in the US, are based on mappings of competence expressed in terms of roles, tasks and functions. While they provide a functional analysis of what we need to know at the point of assessment, for instance about building, maintaining, containing and concluding a professional, yet intimate, relationship, functional models do not address the process of learning how to build and maintain relationships over time. It falls to developmental models to attend to processes of personal and professional growth, and experiential learning. These models, however, can be too rigid and too stage- or phase-oriented, and thus fail to reflect the variety of learning needs supervisees from diverse backgrounds have at different times (Rapp, 1996).

In analogy to the old debates in physics about whether light consists of particles and waves, we might say that there has been a debate about whether supervision should focus on functional competencies or on developmental processes. Physicists have in the main agreed a compromise formulation positing we should think of light as consisting of wavicles: that is light has both wave-like and particle-like properties, depending on the context of our investigation. In this vein, I propose a hybrid model which allows us to define competencies both as endpoints which can be assessed in terms of specific learning outcomes, such as managing endings, and as organising schemata which direct the process of learning itself, as when we assess the supervisees vital capacity for learning to learn.

As supervisees we move through a number of learning positions which reflect the current stand of our expertise, confidence and competence. This varies with the level of experience and familiarity we have in a certain field, with particular client issues and client groups. As supervisors we need to be very responsive to the variability of our supervisees' needs, so that we support, reflect, evaluate, teach, facilitate, counsel, monitor, consult, model, advise, mentor, coach and encourage appropriately.

Experience in context: case example

A young Asian supervisee who has experience in working with alcohol support services for Asian women is ready to critically adapt his theories and ways of working with transactional analysis (TA) to better suit the needs of his client group, even though he is only in the second year of TA training. The supervisor simply needs to encourage and support this work. The supervisee has been referred a young self-harming client from an African-Caribbean background as a private training client. With this client the supervisee feels like a very unskilled and unconfident 'novice', who needs teaching, modelling and guidance, even though he feels, with justification, that he is almost most a 'master' in relation to his alcohol work. Arguably, these very terms – 'novice' and 'master', drawn from the hierarchical organisation of the medieval guild system – may be of questionable usefulness when it comes to thinking about skills which are of vocational value in a flat learning society – i.e. one fostering flexible learning partnerships between peers (Rapp, 1996, 1997a, 1998a).

Once we think of supervisees occupying different positions in the learning cycle, the task of supervision becomes that of putting together ever more complex systems of relationships between the concepts we use to make sense of the world and behaviours that keep us safe and allow us to thrive.

Research into the development of skilled practice (Connor, 1994; Lambert, 1989; Lambert and Arnold, 1987; Norcross,1992; Sexton and Whiston, 1994) suggests that there are higher order competencies, which involve the organisation of skilled, multi-tasked activities over time, integrating conceptual underpinnings with administrative and practice-based knowledge. With greater experience and expertise our horizons expand and we are increasingly able to include more context as we feel better able to manage the complexity of our work overall. This should allow us to develop a more systemic perspective. We track what the client issues are, what our own learning needs are, but also how our therapeutic work enacts and reflects reciprocal relationship patterns. We appreciate the politics of professional organisations, peer accountability and the broader social, political and developmental issues which impact on the setting in which we work.

Each setting is characterised by a particular culture which embodies the history, shared values, vision, mission, goals, and styles of practice of the people who work within it, be this private practice, general practice, hospital settings, educational settings, forensic services, agencies in the community, and so on. In order to facilitate joint learning about how best to serve clients or patients, services are increasingly keen to develop, or draw on, shared guidelines, based on a shared understanding of core competencies. For instance, I am involved in a consultation at present in which MIND, a consortium of Primary Care Groups, a local Health authority, and Social Services want to develop a joint service framework to resource and evaluate counselling in primary care for patients from ethnic minority groups. Guidelines such as the ones below are useful as an initial shared framework around which to develop the specific applications which are most relevant and acceptable to the actual people on the ground. Exactly which specific principles and practices are shared by common consensus may vary both between and within settings, but all settings have in common that all relevant stakeholders do have tacit understandings regarding good practice, and that these centre on basic issues such as equal access and safety, relationship building, the planning, organisation and evaluation of the work, engaging with painful experiences, and respecting cultural differences. It is very important to clarify these issues and to arrive at explicit shared understandings about potential culture clashes regarding fundamental values. Only then can service funders and service managers properly serve the needs of the counsellors and therapists who serve the clients, so that they can get their needs met. By definition, it is the task, role and function of supervision to raise, clarify, and manage all these issues in the interest of the client's welfare.

Guidelines for assessing CORE competencies for culturally competent supervision

I. Working safely within a culturally competent professional framework

Core skill:

Development of an ethical and competent professional framework, exploring our own and the supervisee's understandings about human development, social organisation, beliefs and values, continually developing further theoretical understandings and professional skills.

continued . . .

Key elements: basic competence in working with four aspects of the professional framework

1 working within the supervisor's responsibilities according to a culturally sensitive code of ethics and practice for counselling supervision
2 taking account of issues of ethnicity, race, culture, class, gender, sexual orientation and dis/ability as they relate to the counselling context/setting
3 negotiating and monitoring the business, clinical and learning elements of the supervision contract, mindful of the norms and expectations which may be valued in other cultures
4 arranging supervisor support and development opportunities in accordance with identified strengths and learning needs which reflect the supervisee's cultural style

II. Working sensitively with the supervisory relationship

Core skill:

Therapeutic responding and the capacity to engage emotionally in the depth and breadth of human experience in an open, non-judgmental, culturally sensitive, and non-defensive way, able to keep oneself, the supervisee and the client safe from harm.

Key elements: basic competence in working with four aspects of the supervision relationship

1 the ability to create a warm, professional relationship within which the aims of supervision can be effectively facilitated: supporting, holding, challenging, mentoring, instructing, facilitating, sharing joys and triumphs, fears and worries, and sharing a good belly laugh or cry
2 exercising authority appropriately, mindful of the different power relationships and their potential misuse in the supervisory relationship
3 applying a foundation of identifying, understanding, and working with transference and countertransference, ignorance and prejudice in interpersonal and intercultural perceptions.
4 applying a foundation of understanding and skills in working with small groups

III. Working with the supervisor's and supervisee's personal experience in a cultural context

Core skill:

The ability to provide space for the supervisee to explore their sense of themselves and their own patterns of thinking, feeling and behaving, facilitating the development of their own practice in a coherent way, freed from culturally insensitive and distorted views which may impinge on the supervisee's path to becoming more fully themselves.

continued . . .

Key elements:

1 culturally sensitive and empathic attunement between the learner and the facilitator
2 an awareness of personal, interpersonal and cultural blocks and issues which may impact on the supervisory role, tasks and functions
3 an ability to model culturally sensitive, self-aware thinking, feeling and behaving in the supervisory role
4 monitoring and matching the supervisee's needs regarding perceptual style, learning cycle and cultural expectations

IV. Working creatively and coherently to organise supervision to meet the client's requirements within a cultural, organisational and professional context

Core skill:

Development of a thorough understanding of the context, the setting, and the professional framework in which our practice is grounded, with a shared commitment to ongoing assessment of the conditions for safe, competent and productive work and regular review of the process and outcomes of clinical practice

Key elements:

1 judging wisely the balance between challenge and support needed by the learner, taking account of the effects of cultural and political power imbalances
2 identifying conflicts between individual, institutional and social values and practices and helping the learner to manage these
3 respectful and robust enquiry into the theoretical orientations on which we base our values, concepts, principles, theories, models, techniques and ways of working
4 accurate assessment of the learner's level of tacit and explicit knowledge and skill, reaching into areas in need of further development and modelling; and providing observation and feedback of the learner's skills practice, putting every step in the learning process into cultural context

© Rapp 1999. (These guidelines draw on the competence framework CoDAS (Counsellor Development and Assessment System) developed with Anthony Crouch, Counselling and Psychotherapy Central Awarding Body (CPCAB, 1999)

Eight ways forward: resourcing ourselves to work with difference

In this final section I offer a number of programmatic statements about how we might collectively, in our respective professions, take forward some of the issues raised in this chapter. While I see a great need for a stringent critique of power relations, the forceful indictment of racism, sexism, homophobia, neglect of the needs and rights of disabled people, disregard for spiritual and cultural sensitivities, both in the community and within our professions, I have, in the main, focused on what will take us forward.

We need to search for common ground regarding the training of practitioners and supervisors, as well as shared solutions to the provision of relevant services to problems with living and a sophisticated and keen awareness of how our best efforts continue to leave issues unaddressed. The following remarks are born both of the pessimism of the intellect which allows us to see perpetual conflict, compromise and human misery, and the optimism of the will, which inspires the hope, determination and resourcefulness, at least, to prevail in the face of adversity, and perhaps, on occasion, to triumph over it.

Eight signposts for the new millennium

1 Examine the politics of experiences of difference: become aware of how voices are being silenced, community groups are being marginalised, and how, especially on training courses, individuals from minority groups may be treated as token representatives of their constituencies (Rapp, 1997b).
2 Achieve real and lasting change by putting supervision practice on a firm professional footing, properly integrated into trainings.
3 Construct clear frameworks, concepts and procedures, achieving a balance between macro issues and micro issues in working with difference.
4 Clinically work through our understanding of difference, instead of tacking on programmatic statements. Actively co-construct with the other what is professionally salient, personally important, culturally meaningful and politically acceptable in a way that steers clear both of culture-blindness and a potentially stereotyping cookbook approach.
5 Respect the trainee's or supervisee's meaning systems. Solutions informed by the trainee's full participation are more enduring than solutions which the supervisor attempts to impose (Holloway and Poulin, 1995).
6 Promote realistic social action towards setting up relevant and affordable services for those most socially excluded and oppressed and most troubled by problems with living. Here we might consider intervening in debates about clinical effectiveness, which are driven by considerations of 'value for money'. We might invite policy makers to bear in mind the potentially greater cost-effectiveness of providing appropriately supervised, timely help, which might well prevent people from becoming socially excluded (Rapp, 1998a).
7 Carry out empirical and practical research on how to deliver relevant and integrative services to minority groups who are currently poorly

catered for. Such research should include investigating what contribution appropriate and skilled supervision makes toward improving client outcomes.

8 Build an integrative platform on which to engage in the crucial intellectual and moral enquiry about the boundary of authority. Here we might think about advocating that instead of focusing in a short-sighted manner on 'value for money now', we might invest 'money for values' which will help us to create better, fairer psychological services for the future. Making culturally competent supervision an integral part of any service in our field may be a beginning.

Acknowledgment

I want to express my appreciation to Alexandra Chalfont for her superb editorial assistance.

References

Ariel, S. (1997) 'Strategic family play therapy', in *Play Therapy, Theory and Practice: A Comparative Casebook*. New York: Wiley.

Ariel, S. (1999) *Culturally Competent Family Therapy*. Westport, CT: Greenwood.

Bandler, R. and Grinder, J. (1975) *The Structure of Magic. A Book about Language and Therapy*, Vols. I and II. Palo Alto: Science and Behavior Books.

Basseches, M. (1997) 'A developmental perspective on psychotherapy process, psychotherapists' expertise, and "meaning-making conflict" within therapeutic relationships: a two-part series', *Journal of Adult Development*, 4 (1): 17–33; 4 (2): 85–106.

Birchwood, M. (1997) 'Cognitive theory and therapy of schizophrenia'. Lecture given at 12th International Symposium for the Psychotherapy of Schizophrenia, 'Building Bridges: The Psychotherapies and Psychosis', London, 14 October.

Carroll, M. (1996) *Counselling Supervision: Theory, Skills, and Practice*. London: Cassell.

Clarkson, P. (1996) *The Bystander (An End to Innocence in Human Relationships)*. London: Whurr.

Connor, M.(1994) *Training the Counsellor: An Integrative Model*. London: Routledge.

CPCAB (1999) CoDAS (Counsellor Development and Assessment System). This framework is regularly updated. Information from: CPCAB (Counselling and Psychotherapy Central Awarding Body) e-mail: cpcab@.co.uk website: info@cpcab.co.uk address: P.O. Box 1768, Glastonbury, Somerset BA6 8YP.

Cross, W. E. Jr, (1971) 'The Negro-to-Black conversion experience', *Black World*, 20: 13–27.

Cross, W. E. Jr, (1995) 'The psychology of nigrescence: revising the Cross model', in J.G. Ponterotto (ed.), *Handbook of Multicultural Counseling*. Thousand Oaks, CA: Sage Publications.

Fainzang, S. (1998) 'Anthropology at home via anthropology abroad: the problematic heritage', *Anthropology and Medicine*, 5 (3): 269–278.

Fernando, S. (1991) *Mental Health, Race and Culture*. London: Macmillan in association with Mind.

Fernando, S. (1996) 'Psychiatry, diagnosis and Black oppression', in T. Adams (ed.), *Transcultural Counselling/Therapy Forum Symposium 1994. Psychotherapy and Black Identity: Addressing the Debate*. London: Goldsmiths' College.

Ffagen-Smith, P. and W. E. Cross, Jr (1996) 'Nigrescence and ego identity development', in P. B. Pedersen (ed.), *Counseling across Cultures*. Thousand Oaks, CA: Sage Publications.

Fogel, A. (1993) *Developing through Relationships*. London: Harvester Wheatsheaf.

Haslam, D. E. (1997) 'Psychotherapy and sexual orientation', in H. Rapp (ed.), *New Controversial Discussions: Experiences of Difference*. London: British Institute of Integrative Psychotherapy.

Helman, C. (1990) *Culture, Health and Illness: an Introduction for Health Professionals*, 2nd edn. London: Butterworth-Heinemann.

Holloway, E.L. and Poulin, K. (1995) 'Discourse in supervision', In J. Siegfried (ed.), *Therapeutic and Everyday Discourse as Behaviour Change: Towards a Micro-analysis in Psychotherapy Process Research*, New York: Ablex. pp. 243–273.

Houston, G. (1995) *Supervision and Counselling*. London: Rochester Foundation.

Inskipp, F. and Proctor, B. (1993) *Making the Most of Supervision. Part 1*. Twickenham, Middlesex: Cascade Publications.

Kadushin, A. (1993) 'What's wrong, what's right, with social work supervision', *The Clinical Supervisor*, 10: 3–19.

Kagan, N. L. and Kagan, H. (1975) *Influencing Human Interaction*. Washington: American Personnel and Guidance Association.

Lago, C. and Thompson, J. (1996) *Race, Culture and Counselling*. Buckingham: Open University Press.

Lambert, M. (1989) 'The individual therapist's contribution to psychotherapy process and outcome', *Clinical Psychology Review*, 9: 469–485.

Lambert, M. and Arnold, R. C. (1987) 'Research and the supervisory process', *Professional Psychology: Research and Practice*, 18: 217–224.

Marr, D. (1982) *Vision*. San Francisco: Freeman.

McLeod, J., (in press) 'Human experience on trial: power and exclusion in psycho-therapy'. Research paper given at the Annual Conference of the Universities' Psychotherapy Association, London, 14–15 November 1997.

Messer, S.B. and Woolfolk, R.L. (1998) 'Philosophical issues in psychotherapy', *Clinical Psychology: Science and Practice*, 5 (2): 251–263.

Nadirshaw, Z. (in press) 'Different and equal: an insider's view of working with diversity and difference'. Paper presented at the British Psychological Society Annual Conference, 1997.

Norcross, J. (1992) *Training in Psychotherapy Integration*. New York: Basic Books.

Page, S. and Wosket, V. (1994) *Supervising the Counsellor: A Cyclical Model*. London: Routledge.

Pedersen, P. B. (pers. comm.) Comment made in the context of the talk: 'The upside of culture', given at the Transcultural Counselling/Therapy Forum Symposium, 1997. '"A Safe Haven". Transcultural Counselling and Psychotherapy for the Millennium', 17–19 October, Goldsmiths' College, University of London.

Pedersen, P.B. (1987) 'Ten frequent assumptions of cultural bias in counselling', *Journal of Multicultural Counseling and Development*, January: 16–24.

Pedersen, P.B. (1996) *Counseling across Cultures*. Thousand Oaks, CA: Sage Publications.

Rapp, H. (1996) *Integrative Supervision: Intersubjective Assessment in a Reflective Learning Space*. London: private publication.

Rapp, H. (1997a) *The Assessment of Practitioner Competence*. London: British Institute of Integrative Psychotherapy.

Rapp, H. (ed.), (1997b) *New Controversial Discussions, Experiences of Difference*. London: British Institute of Integrative Psychotherapy.

Rapp, H. (1998a) *Healthy Alliances to Promote Mental Health and Social Inclusion*, a BIIP discussion paper. London: British Initiative for Integrative Psycho-therapeutic Practice.

Rapp, H. (1998b) 'Aims, means and outcomes of integrative psychotherapeutic practice', in H. Rapp (ed.), *Healthy Alliances to Promote Mental Health and Social Inclusion*, a BIIP discussion paper. London: British Initiative for Integrative Psychotherapeutic Practice. pp. 77–84.

Raw, D.S. (1996) 'When (and how) does psychotherapy integration improve clinical effectiveness?' in J.C. Norcross (ed.), When (and how) does psycho-therapy integration improve clinical effectiveness? A roundtable, *Journal of Psychotherapy Integration*, 6: 295–332.

Rawls, J. (1967) 'Two concepts of rules', in P. Foot (ed.), *Theories of Ethics*. Oxford: Oxford University Press.

Safran, J. D. and Messer, S.B. (1997) 'Psychotherapy integration: a postmodern critique', *Clinical Psychology: Science and Practice*, 4 (2): 140–152.

Sexton, T. L. and Whiston, S. C. (1994) 'The status of the counseling relationship: an empirical review, theoretical implications, and research directions', *The Counseling Psychologist*, 22: 6–78.

Speight, S. (1991) 'A redefinition of counselling', *Journal of Counselling and Development*, 70(1): 29–36.

Sue, D., Arredondo, P. and McDavis, R. (1995) 'Multicultural counseling competencies and standards', in J.G. Ponterotto (ed.), *Handbook of Multicultural Counseling*. Thousand Oaks, CA: Sage Publications.

van Dongen, E. (1998) 'Strangers on terra cognita: authors of the other in a mental hospital', *Anthropology and Medicine*, 5 (3): 279–294.

van Ginkel, R. (1998) 'The repatriation of anthropology: some observations on endoethnography', *Anthropology and Medicine*, 5 (3): 251–268.

Weinreich, P. (1998) *Identity Structure Analysis Conceptual Framework and The Identity Exploration*. Computer Software, available from the author, University of Ulster, Jordanstown, UK.

PART II

TRENDS

7

SUPERVISION DIFFICULTIES AND DILEMMAS FOR COUNSELLORS AND PSYCHOTHERAPISTS WHOSE WORK INVOLVES HEALING AND SPIRITUALITY

William West

This chapter draws on the findings of two recent research studies undertaken by the author (West 1995b, 1997a, 1998a) and presented at the BAC Annual Research Conferences in 1995 and 1997 (West, 1995b, 1997b). The first study was into counsellors and psychotherapists whose work includes healing. In this research I found that my respondents were using the word 'healing' in three different ways: as a blanket term for the outcome of any caring activity; as an intentional activity by someone calling themselves a healer, for example laying on of hands; and as unintentional experiences of a healing nature that can occur within the work of counsellors and psychotherapists well described by Rogers' concept of 'presence' (Kirschenbaum and Henderson, 1990) or Buber's (1970) I–Thou relationship. One of the key findings of this research was that eight of the thirty therapists interviewed reported experiences of supervision difficulties.

The second study was into the impact of counsellors' and psychotherapists' spiritual beliefs on their work. For this study I used a definition of spirituality developed within a humanistic-existential framework by Elkins et al. (1988):

Spirituality which comes from the Latin spiritus, meaning 'breath of life', is a way of being and experiencing that comes through awareness of a transcendent dimension and that is characterized by certain identifiable values in regard to self, others, nature, life, and whatever one considers to be the Ultimate. (Elkins et al., 1988: 10)

In this second study five of the eighteen therapists interviewed reported supervision difficulties.

The nature of the supervision difficulties experienced by both sets of respondents, which include issues of trust and supervisor competence, are explored with particular reference to the BAC *Code of Ethics and Practice for the Supervision of Counsellors* (1996). The choices open to the respondents are considered, including: having two supervisors, downplaying or ignoring the healing and spiritual experiences, or accepting the dilemmas involved. Some implications for practice are explored which include: the training of therapists and supervisors; integration issues; and the need for further research.

In October 1992 I began doctoral research into counsellors and psychotherapists whose work includes healing. This was a qualitative study seeking to explore and understand how the respondents made sense of healing within therapy (for further details see West, 1995a, 1997a). The first stage of this research involved interviewing thirty therapists who had replied to letters to the journals *Counselling*, and *Self and Society*. I had a set of questions (see West, 1995a for details) to explore with the respondents in the interviews. However, the main aim was to establish a dialogue with each participant around the whole area of therapy and healing. Curiously, supervision was not an issue in my original set of questions. Three-quarters of the way through my fourth interview with a therapist the following exchange occurred in the context of the therapist discussing her use of healing and transpersonal techniques within her work as a therapist:

> *Therapist*: . . . I can move around in what I've learnt quite easily from one thing to another. I can't do that with my supervisor because he doesn't even like any of this stuff.
> *William*: Yes, this could be a sort of interesting sub-topic, how supervisors cope with . . .
> *Therapist*: Yes. I've never found a supervisor yet who's really seemed to me as somebody I could be entirely open with and I find that very, very, difficult.

The role of a good qualitative researcher is to be open to what those they research are telling them. From that point on supervision issues became a question to raise in the interviews and with previous interviewees. Eight of the people interviewed reported supervision difficulties.

Having completed this first research project I was left wanting to know more about how therapists deal with their own spirituality in their work since this was one of the key issues that arose in the first research. In 1996 I began a study into the impact of therapists' spiritual beliefs on their practice (West, 1998a). During this study I interviewed nineteen members of the Religious Society of Friends (Quakers). This time I asked about supervision from the first and I found that five of the therapists I interviewed had supervision difficulties.

Findings

It might be thought that those with supervision difficulties would tend to be the less experienced therapists. This proved not to be the case. In my first study the mean length of time the thirty respondents had been therapists was 12.5 years; for the nine with supervision difficulties, the figure was 12.0 years. In the second study the mean for all therapists was 11.8 and for those five with supervision issues 12.6 years.

I will present the findings that relate to supervision difficulties from the first study, then those from the second before discussing the issues raised. My interviewee mentioned above, a very seasoned therapist, had plenty more to say about her supervision difficulties:

> Every time I go to supervision they bring in a map. They say 'Next time you want to do this.' I do it and it screws up a session completely.

She later said that her work with clients was not going as well as during the previous year and that:

> I have to move on to a different level of being with clients and I haven't found it yet. And that's not very fair on the client and it's quite difficult for me, and I know that my normal supervision has been totally useless for this. They are not going to help me in that. They're just going to bring me back to the style that they teach.

She seemed to be moving towards an eclectic or integrative style of working that was not valued by her supervisor:

> You go to supervision and you talk about your client and you say you're mixing things and you're bringing in a bit of this and a bit of that, and then the supervisor gets upset. But you have to make your choice. I hope I am choosing for the benefit of the client and for the benefit of myself now, not for the benefit of the supervisor.

Interestingly, this therapist also had difficulties within her group supervision:

> I'd often come out quite angry, because I feel in some way my client has been degraded, by exposing their confidentiality. I don't feel the client has been helped,

and I feel in some way there's some sacred thing that has happened that has been exposed to the group, that has not affirmed the sacredness of what was going on in the counsellor–client relationship.

She is willing to accept her part in the process and has subsequently begun a further training course as a transpersonal psychotherapist, which may well ease some of her supervision dilemmas.

Another therapist, also female, with several years' experience, revealed in a letter:

At a very mutual moment in a counselling session, a client and I worked (as in hand-healing) on her pounding headache. Did I write this up in my case notes? Or mention it in my group supervision, or to my personal supervisor? No!! (What was that all about I wonder?)

After exploring this issue within a research interview this therapist was moved to say:

I can't talk like this where I work. I can't talk like this. I can't there. It would be an insult to all their knowing. They would interpret it as an insult to their knowing.

I asked her why she could not take her use of healing to her supervision group at work and she replied:

I imagine they would think, 'Oh, this young puppy what does she know?' Cos I'm the youngest one there. I think their reaction would be, 'This puppy is bursting into healing. What does she think she is doing? An invasion of boundaries. And has she enough discernment? Does she know what she is doing?' I think the answer is, 'It was good, it was right at the time.' No doubt about that.

Another respondent was wrestling with her experience of group supervision:

They didn't seem to want to draw that part [the healer] out of me, so I didn't give it. They knew the work that I did, but it seemed to me I was continually saying, 'I'll do my healing, but I'll not bring my healing clients to you.' They did not seem to want to help me develop the relationship I have . . . because there must be a certain way I look at all the people I work with, even though I'm separating counselling and healing. They're trying to ask me to look at that, but by the same token they're not helping me and encouraging me. So I felt, 'Okay, it's not being encouraged, it's not being looked at, so I'll just tuck it away.' That's not right. They didn't offer that, so I just shut the bridge off.

This respondent was speaking of group supervision on her counsellor training course. Maybe 'shutting off the bridge' was appropriate but it left her with unresolved dilemmas which unfortunately cannot be taken to healing supervision as it largely does not exist, as will be discussed below.

These conflicts can be painful and poignant, as expressed by one interviewee, a seasoned therapist involved in training, in a letter written to me in response to a report on the first sixteen interviews:

> When I read the part about supervision I cried. This part more than anything else produced my emotional response. The loneliness I feel in respect of the split I have between doing counselling and psychotherapy and doing healing, most especially with my psychotherapy supervision is very painful . . . I cannot be myself as a healer in this professional relationship.

She has been able since then to successfully address these issues through supervision and further training work.

Another very experienced respondent, despairing of ever being able to find the right supervisor, said that she was exhausted with trying to understand what happens in her work:

> I do feel I'm constantly having to turn myself inside out and upside down and back to front, to create it from inside my guts. It feels my very being is the soil from which things are created.

Furthermore she went on to say: 'I think I've given up the fantasy a long time ago that there might be someone who can say, "well this is it, and this is how you do it".'

This desire to be truly understood in supervision was echoed by the experience of another respondent who, because of the difficulties in finding an appropriate supervisor, was not at the time of his interview in supervision for the group ritual work he was doing:

> I'm not proud of that. I'm actually very worried about that. I don't know what to do about that at the moment . . . I know that I have partly a personal, idiosyncratic resistance about that which is just my stuff, and also genuinely don't know anyone who is working in the sort of way I am.

Of course, the fact that there may not be anyone available who works in exactly the same way as this practitioner does not mean that some kind of supervision is impossible:

> That does not mean to say I couldn't get the supervision from someone who's working in a clearer system, but no, I haven't met such a person. . . . It feels like basically I can't continue doing what I'm doing unless I get that sort of system in place.

Other respondents also reported solutions that were less than satisfactory. One seasoned therapist who was also a psychiatrist solved his supervision difficulties by using his wife as his supervisor:

I'm so fortunate to have my wife, who's also a very gifted healer and a psychotherapist, and we give each other peer supervision. It's very rare to find a supervisor who can resonate on all these different levels.

However, not everyone by any means had such supervision difficulties. One very experienced therapist solved his supervision needs by having a supervisor who was both a therapist and a former priest. This was especially helpful when, working with several clients, the therapist found himself addressing the issue of spirit presences in the therapy room:

> Fortunately my supervisor is familiar with these phenomena because he is a priest, or was a priest, and so he's capable of looking at it from a psychological perspective . . . and looking at it from a spiritual, religious perspective. I think he was useful in discouraging me from spending too much energy in trying to define the phenomenon.

Turning now to the second study (of Quaker therapists) we find that although the majority reported no conflicts around supervision, a significant minority of five out of nineteen did. When asked to quantify, three replied that such conflicts were frequent, and the other two replied sometimes. An example:

> I found that when I did have one client for whom the spiritual was very important, it was quite difficult to deal with, being supervised by someone who had no sense of the spiritual . . . either I took what I'd done to supervision and got it rubbished or I left it outside supervision, protected it increasingly by not getting it supervised, being quite sure that with this client that was the right way to go.

This was a therapist working for a voluntary agency who seemed quite content with the unethical choice that she had made.

Another seasoned therapist spoke movingly of an occasional experience in her work:

> There are moments I think when you almost feel a presence . . . I feel most humbled by those experiences, it's almost like, being present to something that's really beyond what you could do, there is a sense of at-oneness. . . . This would not be easy to share with my supervisor.

A different therapist spoke of her work with a voluntary agency and of how she used supervision there:

> The work I do there I'm circumspect in how I work with my supervisor . . . I'm cautious there. It's about wanting to remain credible. . . . I think my supervisor would be right to question if I wanted to spend too much time on what are for me questions about my own practice, contextualising my work within the spiritual dimension.

This therapist had eased this dilemma by having a one-off consultation on spiritual issues with another supervisor.

A further therapist, involved in training counsellors, whilst not acknowledging a current problem, spoke of a possible and difficult scenario: 'I would find it difficult if I had a supervisor who as it were dismissed the spiritual element completely or always wanted to psychologise everything.' Fortunately this therapist works within a transpersonal framework, which seems one clear way of dealing with these dilemmas. She was however cautious with her therapy colleagues:

> Some of my colleagues feel aware of a spiritual dimension in their work, some don't. I am fortunate in having a number of colleagues who are pretty open and receptive, but there are some I don't talk to about spirituality.

Not surprisingly, conflicts were not experienced by those Quaker therapists in this study who had been trained in a transpersonal approach where the spiritual is accepted and worked with. Yet this did not always prove true for those trained by and working for the Westminster Pastoral Foundation, which may reflect its change in orientation towards a more psychodynamic approach.

Discussion

Supervision is now regarded as an essential and routine practice for psychotherapists and counsellors within Britain. Such supervision is concerned with the relationship between counsellor and client; monitoring and supporting the counsellor in the counselling role; the relationship between the counsellor and the supervisor, which should be both critical and supportive; clarifying the relationship between counsellor, client, supervisor, and the organisation the counsellor works for (if any); and ensuring that ethical standards are maintained (BAC, 1996).

Reflecting on the above examples of supervision difficulties experienced by the therapists in these studies, we can see clear examples of breaches of the BAC supervision code. (We could also explore the therapists' actions in relation to other supervision codes; however, the majority of respondents' work would fall under the BAC *Code*.)

Considering the therapists in the first study we find that the first respondent is experiencing difficulties but she is at least staying in group and individual supervision and thereby facing her dilemma. The second therapist in choosing to hide her hand-healing work from her individual and group supervisors and from her case notes is clearly acting unethically. The third therapist is learning a difficult lesson about the boundary between counselling and healing as understood within the supervision group on her counsellor training course. The fourth therapist is experiencing pain around her sense of a split between therapy and healing but she also is staying within therapy supervision. The fifth therapist shared the exhaustion of trying to understand her work and expressed her need for a supervisor who could understand her work. The sixth therapist is taking a huge risk having no supervision at all for his group work based on the use of rituals. Perhaps he has set too high a standard for such a supervision rather than settling for second-best or even 'good enough' supervision (Hawkins and Shohet, 1989). He is clearly acting unethically. The seventh therapist in using his wife as a peer supervisor is evidently unaware of the boundary implications and transferential difficulties that are likely to arise, making his choice inevitably unworkable and thereby unethical.

With regard to the smaller number of Quaker therapists in the second study we find the first therapist acting unethically by not taking one of her clients to supervision. We have to ask how many future clients will she do this with? The second therapist speaks of almost feeling a presence in the therapy room and how this would be difficult to share with her supervisor. As long as she does make the effort her work will remain ethical. Better to really talk this through in supervision before the next example of it arises. The third therapist feels that the background exploring of the spiritual dimension in her work is not appropriate with her voluntary agency supervisor. She has chosen to consult another supervisor, which seems an appropriate short-term solution to her dilemma. The fourth therapist acknowledges a difficulty should her supervisor be dismissive of spirituality, which is clearly not the case for her currently and she is aware of the problem.

Possible solutions

Exploring the possible solutions to these therapists' dilemmas around healing and spirituality, it seems that there are four approaches. The first solution, which is really no solution at all since it is ethically unacceptable, is that of ignoring or playing down the healing and spirituality that occurs. Apart from the risk that this places the client in it also will tend to undermine the supervision relationship relating to the whole of the therapy work supervised and will create incongruence in the supervision relationship.

A second possible solution is that of using two supervisors, one to supervise the counselling/psychotherapy, the other to supervise the healing/spirituality aspect of the work. However, problems immediately arise: how can the therapist deal with what might be conflicting advice from the two supervisors? Does this result in a classic split of good supervisor/bad supervisor? How can the therapy supervisor make sense of the impact of the healing or spiritual intervention on the client? Do we try to break any one therapy session down into parts which are only counselling/psychotherapy and parts which are healing/spirituality? Clearly an unworkable solution.

A third solution would be to confine the therapist within a therapy boundary and limit the healing/spiritual work to other helping relationships with their own forms of supervision and guidance: an apparently neat solution to many dilemmas explored above. However, clients often find or seek out therapists with spiritual or healing gifts and demand both of their therapists. To deny clients what we know in our hearts to be valuable and potentially very healing for them is to my mind unethical. This is not to say that we should routinely offer such possibilities to clients who have not sought them. That is another matter.

A fourth possible solution would be to find a supervisor who has experience of both being a therapist and being a healer. This, however, may not work since we are talking about how to bring healing and spirituality within the therapy frame. This requires supervisor competence in the use of healing and therapy in combination, which is currently largely unavailable. This is an issue that is unlikely to go away. Indeed, I expect it will become even more pressing as more and more therapists begin to use approaches drawn from healing and complementary medicine and practitioners of these disciplines engage in therapy. This problem is being recognised but has been little explored as yet (Michael Carroll, personal communication, 1994).

The Quaker therapists in my study have a somewhat different variation on this dilemma: can they be present as the spiritual being they see themselves as within the therapy framework? Part of the answer to this lies in how the therapy framework is defined. Those therapists working with an approach which takes a positive view of spirituality such as Jungian (Jung, 1967) or transpersonal therapy (Guest, 1989) have fewer dilemmas. What my research did show was that the spiritual faith of my Quaker respondents was impacting on their work in ways that included the use of inspiration, prayer and spiritual preparation before and between sessions, and awareness of the client journey as potentially a spiritual one (West, 1998a). There was no evidence that these therapists sought in any way to evangelise their clients or even to speak about or admit their own faith. Yet conflicts, especially around supervision and with colleagues, remained as discussed earlier.

A fifth possible solution is to accept that these dilemmas have no neat solutions, and to work with the issues within the supervisory relationship as elsewhere, as a number of therapists discussed above have done.

It is also clear the last four ethical solutions to the dilemmas raised above do not always work. When we have such an eminent counsellor as Brian Thorne talking of having to leave his soul outside of the counselling room door (Thorne, 1991) then perhaps we are dealing with something that does not always permit an easy solution. If a therapist is experiencing spiritual and healing phenomena or feels that their own sense of spirituality sits uncomfortably with their therapy work then this is a matter for supervision and possibly for personal therapy or further training.

One of the difficulties involved is that healing, therapy and forms of spiritual counsel, whilst sharing some common features and ancestry, have evolved separately (West, 1995a). Healers do not as a rule have supervision of their work. If they choose to join a healing organisation they will receive support and guidance especially whilst they are probationers. This will often come from an experienced healer, either individually or in a group setting. Such support will tend to focus on how to heal, how to look after oneself as a healer, how to evaluate the progress of the healing, etc. The healer–client relationship is not likely to receive much attention, in contrast to therapeutic supervision, in which the therapist–client relationship is usually central.

There is the beginning of a move towards supervision among healers, which has been pioneered in Britain by the Association of Therapeutic Healers. This has led to some debate within the spiritual healing world on the need for supervision (McNeill and Williams, 1993). However, at present, therapists who become healers and healers who become therapists tend to lack supervision for the healing side of their work.

Counselling and psychotherapy have grown up as largely secular, quasi-medical activities but religion, and especially spirituality and spiritual experiences, has not died away as was expected this century. If anything there is an increase in unorthodox forms of spirituality and therapy seems to play a part in this process. Indeed, it would be of even greater help to the clients involved if therapy was to drop its traditional hostility to spirituality and religion (further explored in West, 1998a, 1998b). If such were the case then the dilemmas faced by some of the Quaker therapists interviewed would disappear. Meanwhile they might be best served by making their supervisors aware of the increasing amount of work being undertaken, especially in the USA, on therapy, religion and spirituality, in particular the health-promoting possibilities inherent in spiritual beliefs, experiences and practices (for a useful summary see Richards and Bergin, 1997).

Implications

Supervision is only real supervision when it is true to the spirit rather than merely the letter of guidelines. To remain in a supervision relationship when you do not feel accepted and to hide information about your work from your supervisor is not to be in effective supervision, and consequently is dangerous for the therapist and especially dangerous for their clients. In my view the supervision relationship should be based on Rogers' (1951) core conditions of empathy, congruence and positive unconditional regard by the supervisor of the supervisee, within the remit of protecting and caring for the clients involved. These conditions will apply only if the taboo on healing is broken and if spirituality comes to be seen as a valid, indeed central, aspect of human experience that therapy should address.

The supervision relationship is probably the main forum in which unresolved issues relating to the therapist's practice should be explored. The future development of counselling and psychotherapy, particularly in the key area of healing and spirituality, depends on effective supervision and effective training of therapists and supervisors.

Supervision is not and should not be the only place where these issues can be addressed. Therapists can lay the blame for all their professional anxieties and shortcomings on their supervisors, which is clearly inappropriate. A greater acceptance of healing and spirituality within the largely secular world of therapy is required, which would be reflected by more research and the publication of papers devoted to these issues and conferences at which they could be debated. Developmental models for therapists also need to take account of the spiritual (discussed in West, 1995a). It also needs to be acknowledged that healing and spirituality have a profound impact on the individual therapist and may well need to be explored psychotherapeutically. These phenomena are powerful. Modern psychotherapy and counselling have tended to ignore their spiritual roots (McLeod, 1993) and have followed psychology in adopting a secular, scientific world view.

Considering now the question of integration of spiritual or healing interventions within the therapeutic relationship, questions arise. One of the difficulties faced by psychotherapy and counselling today is the demand to work in ways that have been shown to be effective. This had led, especially in the USA, to a focus on manualised forms of therapy in which the therapist delivers a set treatment package that research has shown delivers favourable results with the particular client group receiving the treatment. From such a viewpoint any use of innovative therapeutic work could be seen as unethical.

Yet there is little research evidence that any one school of therapy can deliver the best outcomes across a broad range of clients and their problems. This has been one factor in the growth of integrative and eclectic schools of psychotherapy and counselling which use techniques drawn from more than one school of therapy. However, there is as yet insufficient research evidence to justify confidence in the effectiveness of such integration (Hollanders, 1997).

The use of spiritual interventions within therapy is being increasingly researched, with sufficient positive results for their use to be justified with appropriate clients (Richards and Bergin, 1997). Healing, particularly within a therapeutic relationship, remains more problematic in research terms even though there is plenty of evidence of its effectiveness (Benor, 1993, 1994).

There now seems to be a movement back to the spiritual, or maybe a movement forward to a new integration of the spiritual into therapy, perhaps aided by an experientially based approach to spirituality. It seems that more people than the 48 participants in these two studies are integrating spirituality into their work; indeed it appears to be a phenomenon not restricted to the relatively small world of psychotherapy and counselling. The headache for the therapists and their supervisors will remain until these issues are honestly faced.

Acknowledgements

The two research projects mentioned above would not have been possible without the part played by my respondents and also the financial support of the Alec Van Berchem Charitable Trust and the Quaker Higher Education Trust for the first, and the Nuffield Foundation, British Academy, and Westward Trust for the second. Likewise the academic supervision and much more from Professor John McLeod for the first, and consultative supervision from Dr Henry Hollanders for the second. The faith and encouragement of both my editors, Barbara Lawton and Dr Colin Feltham, was a great help. Finally the part played by my wife Gay Morton is immeasurable.

References

Benor, D. J. (1993) *Healing Research, Holistic Energy Medicine and Spirituality*, Vol. 1. Deddington, Oxford: Helix Editions.

Benor, D. J. (1994) *Healing Research, Holistic Energy Medicine and Spirituality*, Vol. 2. Deddington, Oxford: Helix Editions.

British Association for Counselling (1996) *Code of Ethics and Practice for the Supervision of Counsellors*, Rugby: BAC.

Buber, M. (1970) *I and Thou*. Edinburgh: T. and T. Clark.

Elkins, D. N., Hedstorm, L. J., Hughes, L. L., Leaf, J. A. and Saunders, C. (1988) 'Towards a humanistic-phenomenological spirituality', *Journal of Humanistic Psychology*, 28(4): 5–18.

Guest, H. (1989) 'The origins of transpersonal psychology', *British Journal of Psychology*, 6(1): 62–69.

Hawkins, P. and Shohet, R. (1989) *Supervision in the Caring Professions*. Milton Keynes: Open University Press.

Hollanders, H., (1997) 'Eclecticism/integration among counsellors in the UK in the light of Kuhn's concept of paradigm formation'. Doctoral thesis, Department of Applied Social Studies, Keele University.

Jung, C. G. (1967) *Memories, Dreams, Reflections*. London: Fontana.

Kirschenbaum, H. and Henderson, V. (1990) *The Carl Rogers Reader*. London: Constable.

McLeod, J. (1993) *An Introduction to Counselling*. Buckingham: Open University Press.

McNeill, D. and Williams, K. (1993) 'Supervision for healers', *Healing Review*, 52: 6–8.

Richards, P. S. and Bergin, A. E. (1997) *A Spiritual Strategy for Counseling and Psychotherapy*. Washington: American Psychological Association.

Rogers, C. (1951) *Client Centred Therapy*. Boston: Houghton Mifflin.

Thorne, B. (1991) *Person-centred Counselling: Therapeutic and Spiritual Dimensions.* London: Whurr.

West, W. S. (1995a) 'Integrating psychotherapy and healing: an inquiry into the experiences of counsellors and psychotherapists whose work includes healing'. Ph.D. thesis, University of Keele.

West, W. S. (1995b) 'Supervision difficulties for psychotherapists and counsellors whose work includes healing'. Paper presented at First Annual Research Conference of the British Association for Counselling, Birmingham University, 25 February.

West, W. S. (1997a) 'Integrating psychotherapy and healing', *British Journal of Guidance and Counselling,* 25(3): 291–312.

West, W. S. (1997b) 'Impact of therapists' spiritual beliefs on their work: first findings'. Paper presented at Third Annual Research Conference of the British Association for Counselling, Birmingham University, 14 June.

West, W. S. (1998a) 'Developing practice in a context of religious faith: a study of psychotherapists who are Quakers', *British Journal of Guidance and Counselling,* 26(3): 365–375.

West, W. S. (1998b) 'Therapy as a spiritual process', in C., Feltham, (ed.), *Witness and Vision of Therapists.* London: Sage. pp. 168–179.

8

CLINICAL SUPERVISION IN COGNITIVE BEHAVIOURAL PSYCHOTHERAPY

Tom Ricketts and Gill Donohoe

As with the other psychotherapies, clinical supervision plays a central part in the training of cognitive behavioural psychotherapists. Good quality supervision which enables the trainee to reflect upon his/her application of cognitive behavioural approaches, the therapeutic relationship and his/her own response to the client enables the skills taught within training institutions to be practised and internalised in a way which maximises learning. Clinical supervision is also essential for the maintenance and further development of professional competence by qualified cognitive behavioural psychotherapists. However, the effect of supervision itself has not been the focus of a significant amount of research within cognitive behavioural psychotherapy, and there is a continuing lack of clarity regarding approaches to be utilised in supervision within the literature. There are no texts which focus exclusively on clinical supervision within cognitive behavioural psychotherapy. Considering the central importance given to operational definition and evaluation within cognitive behavioural psychotherapy this is a surprising situation.

This chapter will seek to review pertinent literature regarding clinical supervision, contrasting cognitive behavioural and cognitive perspectives where they appear to differ. It will draw upon some relevant psycho-therapy supervision literature, and discuss how insights and models from non-model-bound supervisory literature may be relevant to cognitive behavioural psychotherapy. The current state of clinical supervision within Britain will be discussed, and some guidelines for clinical supervision proposed.

Finally the authors' perspectives on some key issues which need to be addressed for cognitive behavioural clinical supervision to develop further will be outlined.

Cognitive behavioural psychotherapy

Cognitive behavioural psychotherapy arose as a result of the co-existence and subsequent integration of behavioural and cognitive approaches which shared common underpinning philosophies. Behavioural approaches, deriving initially from classical and operant conditioning perspectives, included Wolpe's early work on systematic desensitisation of fear (Wolpe, 1958), and the application of operant conditioning concepts to humans through 'token economies' (Ayllon and Azrin, 1968). Evaluation and elaboration of these approaches led to the development of exposure therapy for phobic conditions (Marks, 1969, 1981), and the development of a social reinforcement approach to operant conditioning. At the same time, Beck, Ellis and Meichenbaum were developing cognitive interventions based on the centrality of cognition in the maintenance of emotional disorders (Beck, 1976; Beck et al., 1979; Ellis, 1962; Meichenbaum, 1977). These theories proposed that emotional disturbance was mediated by the way in which the individual made sense of the world, and that effective therapeutic techniques would be those which identified, reality-tested and corrected distorted thinking, and the dysfunctional beliefs underpinning that thinking (Beck et al., 1979).

The behavioural and cognitive approaches shared many underpinnings, which led naturally to a closer association between the approaches. These included the following:

- that the therapy should be problem focused, and applied to a specified and agreed area of current dysfunction, rather than attempting to enhance general well-being;
- the importance of aiming to operationalise and make explicit procedures being utilised;
- the link between theory and practice, psychological research being given equal weight with the need for empirical evaluation of the developing techniques;
- the focus on detailed assessment of the individual, leading to a case formulation as the basis for individualised treatment;
- the active, educational and collaborative nature of the therapies.

Differences rested on the extent to which introspection, rather than behavioural observation should be central, and the claimed mechanisms underpinning emotional change in individuals (Hawton et al., 1989; Rachman, 1997).

An overarching concept which the approaches came to share was that of the scientist practitioner (Barlow et al., 1984). The three principles of the approach are that

1 The practitioner is a consumer of research findings concerning assessment or treatment, which he or she attempts to put into practice.

2 The practitioner evaluates his or her own interventions, where possible using measurement approaches, enabling a continual refining of practice with each individual.
3 The practitioner collects new data in his or her setting, which may be reported to other practitioners and researchers.

The emergence of cognitive behaviour therapy was assisted by the increasing importance of cognitive psychology within psychology generally, and the incorporation of cognitive models and techniques into the range of strategies utilised by behavioural psychotherapists. Specifically the effectiveness of the cognitive approach to panic disorder (Clark, 1986) led many clinicians to take a greater interest in the wider clinical application of cognitive approaches (Rachman, 1997).

Cognitive and behavioural approaches share an emphasis on the issue of individualised formulation. This involves the reframing of the individual's presentation within a cognitive behavioural model of the development and maintenance of their difficulties, drawing upon psychological and clinical research to make sense of their individual presentation (Kirk, 1989).

Approaches which are utilised by cognitive behavioural psychotherapists include:

exposure therapy (Marks, 1981; Rachman and Hodgson, 1980);
techniques for changing arousal levels such as applied relaxation (Ost, 1987);
skills training approaches such as social skills training (Trower et al., 1978) and problem-solving training (Hawton and Kirk, 1989);
operant conditioning approaches;
cognitive approaches such as Beck's cognitive therapy for depression (Beck et al., 1979).

Training of cognitive behavioural psychotherapists

In Britain, the British Association for Behavioural and Cognitive Psychotherapies (BABCP) is the professional body which accredits behavioural and cognitive psychotherapists. The BABCP began, as the British Association for Behavioural Psychotherapy, as an interest group in 1972, promoting behavioural approaches. Membership expanded slowly to include a wide range of professional groups, and by the mid-1990s membership had exceeded 2,000. As an interest group the BABCP was involved in the process of developing standards for registration of psychotherapists with the United Kingdom Council for Psychotherapy. In 1993, the BABCP became a member organisation of UKCP, and was recognised as the accrediting body for behavioural and cognitive psychotherapists.

A wide range of professionals in Britain undertake cognitive behavioural psychotherapy, including clinical psychologists, psychiatrists, nurses and counsellors. However, only approximately 19 per cent of the membership of the BABCP have chosen to become accredited as behavioural or cognitive psychotherapists (Williams and Garland, 1998).

Training in cognitive behavioural approaches has a long history in Britain, with the pioneering work undertaken by the Institute of Psychiatry in London providing the model for much early behavioural training for clinical psychologists, psychiatrists and mental health nurses. These training courses utilised the behavioural tradition of operationalising approaches, to define specifically the skills which trainees were to be taught, and to develop observation and feedback on live clinical practice as central to the training (Marks et al., 1977; Milne 1986). Another strand which ran throughout these training initiatives was the theoretical congruence of treatment models and supervisory approaches, with the directive, educational aspects of therapy providing a model for supervisory interventions.

In parallel, training and supervision models deriving from cognitive approaches also focused on the need to operationalise, observe and give feedback on the clinical practice of cognitive therapy trainees (Padesky, 1996), with the Cognitive Therapy Competency Scale (Young and Beck, 1980) providing an example of this process.

More recent writing on cognitive therapy training has emphasised the need for the congruence of therapy and supervisory methods, but with increasing emphasis on the operationalising of process aspects in supervision (Liese and Beck, 1997; Padesky, 1996). This will be discussed further below.

Supervision models and approaches

Many counsellors and psychotherapists, once they have attained an acceptable level of experience and competence, gravitate towards a training role or at least the role of supervisor. The development of these skills may begin within the therapist's initial psychotherapy training. For example, in a recently established training programme, the skills of educator, supervisor and consultant are developed under supervision (Sheffield Hallam University, 1997). The training and standards required for supervision are addressed in the following section. Such issues are also raised in the context of therapeutic and supervisory models. An example of such a parallel is the common assumption that a skilled practitioner equates with a skilled supervisor. If it is assumed that the model for supervision closely parallels the model or school of therapy, then this could be seen as strengthening the argument. In other words, if the skills required for the therapeutic encounter and the framework or theoretical stance are equally applicable to supervision, then there should be little need for further specialist training or a distinct body of knowledge. This is obviously a rather simplistic view and although one should consider the need for a therapy-congruent approach to supervision, it is also important to isolate the skills, methods and knowledge base specifically relevant to the highly complex process of supervision (Holloway, 1995).

Within this section we outline and discuss the characteristics, theoretical bases and methods of a cognitive behavioural approach to supervision and also the more specific but related field of cognitive therapy. Although there is no one identified cognitive behavioural psychotherapy specific supervisory model it is our aim to bring together the methods and structure which represent current practice. Models and approaches less allied to a particular field of counselling or theoretical approach will then be discussed along with their potential use within clinical supervision as a whole but more specifically cognitive behavioural psychotherapy supervision.

Rather than focusing exclusively upon supervisory models developed for training purposes, the authors intend to address the needs of all types of supervisory context, namely the three groups outlined below. This is not to say that training models have no relevance out of a training context or that one particular model or method should be adopted for a specific worker or context. At this point in time it is debatable whether a singular model for cognitive behavioural psychotherapy supervision can or does exist. Issues relevant to this will be addressed later in the chapter.

Professional groups who may require or seek cognitive behavioural supervision are:

- mental health professionals (for example nurses, social workers, doctors);
- trainee cognitive behavioural psychotherapists (again may include a range of professionals);
- qualified cognitive behavioural psychotherapists.

Cognitive behavioural specific models

The hallmarks of supervision within a cognitive behavioural approach include the following:

- emphasis on skills development;
- structured approach and goal orientation;
- considerable educative function;
- preference for live supervision (or use of video);
- focus on the clinical and professional, for example case management skills;
- skills practice and demonstration (modelling by supervisor).

The methods used and the level or intensity of supervision will vary according to need, but it is apparent that many of the features resemble approaches adopted within the therapeutic approach itself. This may be even more apparent when we consider a cognitive therapy approach to supervision. There are many similarities, for example cognitive therapy supervision is also structured, educative and focused upon therapeutic skill and knowledge. However, generally speaking, cognitive therapy supervision can seem to more closely resemble an actual therapy session. Liese and Beck (1997) directly compare the structure of a supervision and a therapy session, revealing the similarity at each stage of the process. They also advocate the management of supervisee problems when these interfere with the effective delivery of therapy. The supervisor would achieve this in the manner of therapy, conceptualising the problem with the supervisee, focusing on the supervisee as therapist, the supervisor or supervisory relationship and problem solving together. Helping the supervisee to identify their own beliefs as they arise and impact on the delivery of therapy would be a necessary and key component of supervision.

Liese and Beck (1997) advocate the use of a supervisory approach as outlined above with qualified and experienced therapists in addition to those in training. They argue that without supervision, even if the therapist has in the past undertaken specialist training, they are likely to become deskilled or 'drift' from their original expertise.

The congruence of the supervisory approach with the clinical method and the use of therapeutic strategies within supervision can lead to concern regarding the similarity between therapy and supervision and the need to distinguish the two. Both cognitive behavioural psychotherapy and cognitive therapy are goal oriented, as indeed are the supervisory approaches. Perhaps the greatest distinction is the difference between a personal goal and one which focuses upon the therapeutic process and the client. For example, the supervisee and their cognitive processes should only become the focus if it has been established that these interfere with the delivery of therapy and the clients' well-being. Traditionally it has not been a requisite for therapists to seek therapy themselves in order to practise cognitive behavioural psychotherapy or cognitive therapy. However, the advantage in practising strategies first-hand has been suggested (Padesky, 1996) and in the case of behaviour therapy it would clearly be an advantage to overcome a personal phobia before treating a client with a similar difficulty.

Linehan and McGee (1994) outline a cognitive behavioural approach to supervision designed principally for therapists treating severely dysfunctional clients who are suicidal and meet criteria for borderline personality disorder. Both individual and group methods are utilised and the approach is based upon Linehan's (1993) specific form of therapy developed for this client population, 'dialectical behaviour therapy'. Indeed the definition of therapy incorporates the 'treatment' of the therapist by the consultation-supervision team. Unfortunately there are few dedicated texts on cognitive behavioural models of supervision and although the authors do address cognitive behavioural supervision methods in general, the dialectical behaviour therapy model was developed with the specific client group and therapy team in mind.

Training models

A systems approach

Holloway (1995) identified the need for a supervisory model which could be applied to counsellors and psychotherapists across a range of therapeutic bases, rather than a 'counselling-bound' model which in her view placed limitations on the research and development of the body of knowledge in the field. Her approach is based therefore upon a scientist-practitioner model, drawing upon her own and others' experience in practising, teaching and researching supervision. This approach is consistent with cognitive behavioural principles, using empirical data to inform practice and enabling the development of a model upon which further research can be based. The author describes the model as a 'Systems Approach Model' incorporating seven dimensions representing the key components of any supervisory process. The seven dimensions include as the core factor the supervision relationship. The model is depicted in graphic dimensions to illustrate the interrelationship of all dimensions. The other dimensions include the client, the institution, the trainee and the supervisor, all as contextual factors with the tasks and functions of supervision in the forefront of the model. The tasks and functions are as follows:

TASKS This refers to the body of knowledge or skill requirements of the counsellor, which are categorised into five areas:

Counselling skill
Case conceptualisation
Professional role
Emotional awareness
Self-evaluation

FUNCTIONS The five functions depicted in the model refer to the supervisor's actions and form of communication with the supervisee:

Monitoring/evaluating
Instructing/advising
Modelling
Consulting
Supporting/sharing

The supervisory process incorporates the combination of any particular task and function at any given time and within any particular context. These combinations can be plotted on a matrix in order for the process to be analysed. The model can be usefully applied to all supervisory contexts and is illustrated within the text by analysing excerpts from taped supervision sessions. This model provides a useful framework for the analysis and development of supervisor skill and for use in research studies into the effectiveness of supervision and its components.

Developmental models

Other non-psychotherapy-specific models include developmental models and again much of this work has its origins in the United States. Within training in behavioural psychotherapy, the need to gear supervision requirements to the stage of training, phasing out the level and intensity of supervision towards the end of training, has always been recognised. An example of this is the English National Board training for mental health nurses (ENBCC 650). This eighteen month full-time behavioural psychotherapy training includes clinical supervision from qualified behavioural psychotherapists throughout the training. As well as a gradual reduction in the frequency of supervision, methods are varied as training progresses. For example the initial emphasis on live supervision with direct feedback and extensive use of modelling may reduce in favour of increased indirect methods such as case discussion and a focus on case formulation and therapeutic relationship issues.

Developmental approaches such as those outlined by Stoltenberg and Delworth (1987) describe the key characteristics and range of behaviours at various levels so that supervision can be more appropriately geared to the needs of the supervisee. Three levels can be identified (although other authors have identified four: see Hawkins and Shohet, 1989). Level one is characterised by the new trainee or novice and level three or four as that of a highly skilled or 'master' practitioner. The degree of independence or autonomy, self-awareness and focus of concern, stability and degree of anxiety, skill and confidence are all characteristics of trainee development through the stages. The highest-level practitioners will often be in a supervisory role.

The developmental approaches were established with a training context in mind and allow the supervisor to modify the supervision according to the needs of the trainee and to assist them through the stages of development. However, it appears equally applicable to all three of the supervisee groups noted above. Perris (1997), in a survey of cognitive psychotherapists as supervisees, identified a clear preference for less didactic, and more process-oriented approaches among the more experienced compared to the less experienced therapists.

Hawkins and Shohet (1989) highlight a danger of too rigidly assuming that supervisory needs and approaches to be utilised can be determined by the apparent level of supervisee development. There is a need to constantly evaluate all aspects of the supervisory context, and to recognise that supervisee needs may change significantly through the course of the supervisory relationship. In addition the supervisor will be going through a developmental process themself in moving into this challenging role, and should expect to receive supervision for their own development in this area.

Despite the difficulties or 'health warnings' associated with developmental models, one of the key requirements of the supervisor is the constant need to identify and adjust to the changing needs of supervisees. The systems approach enables the supervisor to operationalise and track the changing methods (functions) in line with the supervisees' needs (for example 'advising' may occur more frequently than 'consulting' in a new trainee). These models are complementary and have much to offer the cognitive behavioural approach to supervision.

The supervisory experiences and expectations of UKCP registered cognitive behavioural psychotherapists were surveyed by O'Carroll and Wesson (1997). They identified a preference for observational methods, such as the use of videotapes and live supervision, as contrasted with verbal methods. They also proposed that, given the centrality of competence assessments in cognitive behavioural psychotherapy training, the utilisation of some rating of competence in qualified therapists should be considered central to supervisory methods to be used.

Key components and methods

The key components and methods for cognitive behavioural psychotherapy supervision are outlined below. These reflect current practice with recommendations based on an integration of the above models and the limited research in this specialism.

- CBP supervision is mainly focused upon the supervisee acquiring and maintaining the necessary skill and knowledge to deliver effective therapy.
- Supervisory methods encourage self-assessment and autonomy and aim to balance validation of existing skills with the acquisition of new ones.
- Although there is an obvious educative role, supervision should be distinguished from training.
- Live supervision methods are utilised in order to provide accurate and prompt feedback. These may involve the supervisor being present at the therapy session, observing through a two-way mirror or with the use of a video camera and monitor. Audiotape recordings may be appropriate depending upon the level of experience and are frequently utilised in cognitive therapy supervision.
- Assessment and case conceptualisation skills are particularly important and may require more supervision time, particularly in the case of

inexperienced or newly qualified therapists (see Telford and Farrington, 1996).

- Basic counselling skills and therapeutic relationship issues need to be addressed within supervision. Models which incorporate these as well as the supervisory relationship are necessary within cognitive behavioural psychotherapy supervision.
- The process of supervision should be monitored by the supervisor taking account of the changing needs of the supervisee (for example using the systems approach: Holloway, 1995).
- Individual (one to one) supervision lends itself to the majority of methods although group supervision, for example with a number of peers, can allow for case discussion or case management supervision. The latter is limited, however, if no form of direct supervision (tapes, etc.) is incorporated.
- The content and method of supervision should take account of the supervisee's level of experience in line with developmental approaches. This appears to be the case regardless of theoretical orientation (see Perris, 1997).

Supervisor training

In the context of accreditation and registration of behavioural and cognitive psychotherapists, the BABCP has placed as a requirement for registration, that psychotherapists should have ongoing supervision. This is defined as a minimum of one hour per month for full-time clinicians, where their own clinical practice is the focus of the supervision (BABCP, 1998). Even this minimal requirement has created some difficulties, as the development of a register of cognitive behavioural psychotherapists has not been accompanied by a register of supervisors. The literature on supervision within cognitive behavioural psychotherapy focuses upon training supervision, and qualified therapists and others are faced with finding a supervisor in the absence of any means of making a judgement as to their quality.

In the context of the development of a new multidisciplinary training for cognitive behavioural psychotherapists at Sheffield Hallam University, the authors were faced with this issue. To address it, we developed a training for clinical supervisors, with the express purpose of training supervisors who could supervise qualified cognitive behavioural psychotherapists, course trainees, and other mental health professionals utilising cognitive behavioural approaches (Donohoe and Ricketts, 1997).

Course content included:

- reflection on own experience of being a supervisee;
- supervisory models and how they relate to cognitive behavioural psychotherapy;
- managing the supervisory relationship;

- the supervision contract and structure of supervision;
- tasks and functions of supervision;
- use of problem solving to develop supervisor skills and manage difficulties within supervision;
- supervisory methods;
- ethical, legal and professional issues.

Teaching methods included lectures to ensure grounding in the theoretical and practical aspects of supervision, group discussion and group exercises, presentation of research literature and case material, role play, and group member presentation of audiotaped supervision sessions for feedback and discussion.

Central to the training was the view that skills as a cognitive behavioural psychotherapist were necessary but not sufficient to undertake the role of clinical supervisor. The skills inherent within supervision were viewed as additional to those necessary for practice as a cognitive behavioural psychotherapist.

Given the limited availability of training for cognitive behavioural psychotherapy supervisors, it is appropriate to consider other psychotherapy and counselling supervisor training. The courses are likely to be appropriate if they allow the cognitive behavioural psychotherapist to integrate his/her therapeutic perspective with the models, research and approaches to the supervisory relationship which are being addressed. The general insights discussed above with regard to process and developmental models of supervision (Holloway, 1995; Stoltenberg and Delworth, 1987) are clearly helpful, even if the supervisor is utilising a therapy-specific model of supervision.

Supervisory practice guidelines

To date the BABCP has not responded to proposals that a register of supervisors be developed (Donohoe and Ricketts, 1997). This situation contrasts with that pertaining within the British Association for Counselling (BAC), which has an accreditation scheme for supervisors, with clear criteria, and assessment of competence (BAC, 1997).

As all professionals have a responsibility to work within their competence (BABCP, undated; BAC, 1996a; UKCC, 1992), there appears to be an urgent need for the BABCP to follow the BAC in developing guidelines for good practice in cognitive behavioural supervision. The BABCP has clear guidelines for practice with clients (BABCP, undated), and similar principles underpin good practice within supervision. Drawing on BABCP practice guidelines and the BAC *Code of Ethics and Practice for Supervisors of Counsellors* (BAC, 1996b), the following brief supervision guidelines are proposed:

Competence: Supervisors should take all reasonable steps to monitor and develop their competence, and to work within the limits of their own competence. They should be expected to receive supervision for their supervision work.

Confidentiality: As a general rule supervisors should not reveal confidential material shared with them within supervision, without the express permission of all parties concerned. Limits of confidentiality will apply.

Responsibility: Supervisors are responsible for the establishment of an explicit contract between themselves and the supervisee. This will include issues of confidentiality, appropriate behaviour, style and content of supervision, and the limits of confidentiality. The supervisor has responsibility towards public protection if they become aware of behaviours or omissions on the part of the supervisee which may be harmful to the client or others. More generally, the supervisor is responsible for maximising the supervisee's opportunity to utilise the supervision to enhance clinical effectiveness.

Safety: All reasonable steps should be taken to ensure the safety of the supervisee and their clients during their work together.

Effectiveness: The supervisor is responsible for attempting to maximise the effectiveness of the supervisee's practice, and to encourage use of appropriate outcome monitoring strategies by the supervisee.

Contracts: As noted above, an explicit contract regarding the structure and purpose of supervision should be agreed. This should make explicit the purpose, focus and style of supervision, together with issues relating to confidentiality, and the divulging of information to any third party such as members of a course team.

Use of live supervision: The direct observation of the supervisee's practice should form part of the supervisory contract. This allows for direct feedback on skills, rather than supervision relying exclusively on practitioner report.

As with other areas of cognitive behavioural psychotherapy, it is to be expected that the practice of supervision will be the subject of research to inform clinicians of methods that will maximise the benefit to supervisees and their clients from supervision. Whatever methods are utilised within supervision should be congruent with cognitive behavioural theories.

Summary and recommendations

Clinical supervision within cognitive behavioural psychotherapy is at an interesting stage. There is still little empirical evidence regarding the impact of clinical supervision on clinical outcomes (Lambert and Ogles, 1997), and difficulties with definition of the area. At the same time, cognitive behavioural psychotherapists have extensive experience of undertaking clinical supervision within training courses. The development of registration of cognitive behavioural psychotherapists within the UKCP has led to calls to strengthen the supervisory requirements placed on registered therapists, while at the same time there is an almost complete absence of training in cognitive behavioural clinical supervision for suitably experienced therapists.

The development of a registration scheme for supervisors, with a grand-parenting route to allow already experienced and competent supervisors to sidestep the requirement for further training, is one means by which we would propose developing the standard and availability of clinical supervision. As part of this process, there needs to be debate regarding the central features of clinical supervision within cognitive behavioural psychotherapy. A number of authors have developed supervisory models that appear to be applicable (Holloway, 1995; Padesky, 1996), and we have summarised in this chapter the principal methods and foci of cognitive behavioural psychotherapy supervision. In addition we put forward our supervisory guidelines as additional material to inform that discussion. One impact of a registration scheme for supervisors is likely to be the development of supervisory training appropriate to the needs of cognitive behavioural psychotherapists.

A further area requiring urgent attention is the application of the scientist-practitioner concept to the area of clinical supervision in cognitive behavioural psychotherapy. Research into the effects of supervision is underdeveloped, and there is appropriate scepticism amongst therapists regarding this lack of an evidence base (Rogers, 1998). Initial steps in describing supervisory models and approaches have been taken, and these indicate a degree of overlap with psychotherapy supervision research more generally (Holloway, 1995). Specifically, supervisee perspectives and preferences regarding clinical supervision are beginning to be defined (O'Carroll and Wesson, 1997; Perris, 1997). Lambert and Ogles (1997) provide a useful review of psychotherapy supervision research, including an analysis of the wide range of instruments which have been utilised to analyse the effects of supervision. Evaluations which seek to establish the effects of clinical supervision are required, in addition to small scale or single case studies. Whilst the effect of training on clinical outcomes has been well documented (Marks et al., 1977; Duggan et al., 1993; Newell and Gournay, 1994), the specific effects of clinical supervision have not.

Finally, the strengths of the cognitive behavioural supervisory approach are worth highlighting. There is a strong emphasis in all the texts reviewed on theoretical congruence, with the models being utilised by supervisor and supervisee matching, and the approach to supervision being informed by the approach to therapy. This shared and communicated theoretical perspective is a clear strength of the approach. In addition, behavioural and cognitive approaches to clinical supervision have long shared the emphasis on observation and feedback on the supervisee's actual, rather than reported practice. This provides powerful and effective opportunities to assist the supervisee in identifying difficulties and changing behaviour, and ensures that the supervisor's role in protecting the public from ineffective therapists is fulfilled. It is likely that other schools of psychotherapy could benefit from such a focus on behaviour.

References

Ayllon, T. and Azrin, N. (1968) *The Token Economy*. New York: Wiley.

Barlow, D.H., Hayes, S.C. and Nelson, R.O. (1984) *The Scientist Practitioner*. Oxford: Pergamon.

Beck, A.T. (1976) *Cognitive Therapy and the Emotional Disorders*. New York: International Universities Press.

Beck, A.T., Rush, A.J., Shaw, B.F. and Emery, G. (1979) *Cognitive Therapy of Depression*. New York: Guilford Press.

British Association for Behavioural and Cognitive Psychotherapies (undated) *Guidelines for Good Practice of Behavioural and Cognitive Psychotherapy*. Accrington: BABCP.

British Association for Behavioural and Cognitive Psychotherapies (1998) *Accreditation of Psychotherapists. Criteria and Guidelines for Applicants*. Accrington: BABCP.

British Association for Counselling (1996a) *Code of Ethics and Practice for Counsellors*. Rugby: BAC.

British Association for Counselling (1996b) *Code of Ethics and Practice for Supervisors of Counsellors*. Rugby: BAC.

British Association for Counselling (1997) *Counselling Supervisor Accreditation Scheme*. Rugby: BAC.

Clark, D.M. (1986) 'A cognitive approach to panic', *Behaviour Research and Therapy*, 24: 461–470.

Donohoe, G. and Ricketts, T. (1997) 'Prepared to practice, prepared to supervise?' Poster presented at the BABCP Conference, Canterbury.

Duggan, C., Marks, I. and Richards, D. (1993) 'Clinical audit of behaviour therapy training of nurses', *Health Trends*, 25: 25–30.

Ellis, A. (1962) *Reason and Emotion in Psychotherapy*. New York: Lyle Stuart.

Hawkins, P. and Shohet, R. (1989) *Supervision in the Helping Professions*. Milton Keynes: Open University Press.

Hawton, K. and Kirk, J. (1989) 'Problem-solving', in K. Hawton, P.M. Salkovskis, J. Kirk and D.M. Clark, *Cognitive Behaviour Therapy for Psychiatric Problems*. Oxford: Oxford University Press.

Hawton, K., Salkovskis, P.M., Kirk, J. and Clark, D.M. (1989) 'The development and principles of cognitive-behavioural treatments', in K. Hawton, P.M. Salkovskis, J. Kirk and D.M. Clark, *Cognitive Behaviour Therapy for Psychiatric Problems*. Oxford: Oxford University Press.

Holloway, E. (1995). *Clinical Supervision: A Systems Approach*. Thousand Oaks, CA: Sage Publications.

Kirk, J. (1989) 'Cognitive-behavioural assessment', in K. Hawton, P.M. Salkovskis, J. Kirk and D.M. Clark, *Cognitive Behaviour Therapy for Psychiatric Problems*. Oxford: Oxford University Press.

Lambert, M.J. and Ogles, B.M. (1997) 'The effectiveness of psychotherapy supervision', in C.E. Watkins (ed.), *Handbook of Psychotherapy Supervision*. New York: Wiley.

Liese, B. and Beck, J.S. (1997) 'Cognitive therapy supervision', in C.E. Watkins (ed.), *Handbook of Psychotherapy Supervision*. New York: Wiley.

Linehan, M.M. (1993) *Cognitive Behavioural Treatment of Borderline Personality Disorder*. New York: Guilford Press.

Linehan, M.M. and Mchee, D.E. (1994) 'A cognitive behavioural model of supervision with individual and group components', in S.E. Greben and R. Ruskin (eds), *Clinical Perspectives on Pychotherapy Supervision*. Washington, DC: American Psychiatric Press.

Marks, I.M. (1969) *Fears and Phobias*. New York: Academic Press.

Marks, I.M. (1981) *Cure and Care of Neurosis*. New York: Wiley.

Marks I.M., Hallam, R.S., Connolly, J. and Philpott, R. (1977) *Nursing in Behavioural Psychotherapy*. London: Royal College of Nursing.

Meichenbaum, D. (1977) *Cognitive Behavior Modification: An Integrative Approach*. New York: Plenum Press.

Milne, D. (1986) *Training Behaviour Therapists*. London: Croom Helm.

Newell, R. and Gournay, K. (1994) 'British nurses in behavioural psychotherapy: a 20-year follow-up', *Journal of Advanced Nursing*, 20: 53–60.

O'Carroll, P.J. and Wesson, M. (1997) 'UK survey of supervision in cognitive-behavioural therapy over the last 12 months'. Poster presented at the BABCP Conference, Canterbury.

Ost, L.G. (1987) 'Applied relaxation: description of coping techniques and review of controlled studies', *Behaviour Research and Therapy*, 25: 397–410.

Padesky, C.A. (1996) 'Developing cognitive therapist competency: teaching and supervision models', in P.M. Salkovskis (ed.), *Frontiers of Cognitive Therapy*. New York: Guilford Press.

Perris, C. (1997) 'Supervision of cognitive psychotherapy: expectations of the supervisees', *Clinical Psychology and Psychotherapy*, 4: 25–31.

Rachman, S. (1997) 'The evolution of cognitive behaviour therapy', in D.M. Clark and C.G. Fairburn (eds), *Science and Practice of Cognitive Behaviour Therapy*. Oxford: Oxford University Press.

Rachman, S.J. and Hodgson, R. (1980) *Obsessions and Compulsions*. Englewood Cliffs, NJ: Prentice-Hall.

Rogers, P. (1998) 'Hype that is hard to swallow', *Mental Health Practice*, 1: 18.

Sheffield Hallam University (1997) *BA (Hons) Adult Behavioural Psychotherapy ENB650 Definitive Document*. Sheffield: Sheffield Hallam University.

Stoltenberg, C.D. and Delworth, U. (1987) *Supervising Counselors and Therapists: A Developmental Approach*, San Francisco: Jossey-Bass.

Telford, A. and Farrington, A. (1996) 'Applying principles in practice', in S. Marshall and J. Turnbull (eds), *Cognitive Behaviour Therapy: An Introduction to Theory and Practice*. London: Ballière Tindall.

Trower, P., Bryant, B. and Argyle, M. (1978) *Social Skills and Mental Health*. London: Methuen.

United Kingdom Central Council for Nursing, Midwifery and Health Visiting (1992) *Code of Professional Conduct*. London: UKCC.

Williams, C. and Garland, A. (1998) 'UKCP – advantages and disadvantages', *BABCP News*, May: 9–10.

Wolpe, J. (1958) *Psychotherapy by Reciprocal Inhibition*. Stanford, CA: Stanford University Press.

Young, J. and Beck, A.T. (1980) 'Cognitive therapy scale: Rating manual'. Unpublished manuscript, University of Pennsylvania, Philadelphia.

9

SUPERVISING PRACTITIONERS WORKING WITH PEOPLE WITH ANTI-SOCIAL PERSONALITY DISORDER

Geoff Haines

I work as a lecturer practitioner in a medium secure unit for the care and treatment of mentally disordered offenders in a deprived inner city area. Patients have typically been convicted of robbery, arson, grievous bodily harm and manslaughter. Although most counsellors and therapists will not generally meet many people diagnosed as suffering from anti-social personality disorder, they may occasionally come into contact with such clients or sense such tendencies in some clients (and possibly even occasionally in some colleagues). Additionally, residential work of this kind necessarily challenges many traditional assumptions about boundaries. All supervisors need to be aware of the danger factors and opportunities which may arise when working with such difficult clients (Norton and McGauley, 1998). Throughout this chapter I hope to identify factors that may be of interest and use in generic counselling and supervision practice. Since there is a potential trend towards generic supervisors providing 'external supervision' it is in the interests of *all* supervisors working freelance to understand different working contexts. Readers should note that terms such as 'patient' are used in keeping with the context.

There appears to be considerable ambivalence shown by society about the care and treatment of mentally disordered offenders and especially about those identified as exhibiting anti-social personality or psychopathic disorders. On the one hand, people want protection from those they consider will do them harm, whilst on the other there appears to be a fascination with the myth of the uncontrollable sadistic killer. One reason for such preoccupations, besides a possible unconscious identification with both the victim and the perpetrator, may be a deeper wish to come to terms with the horror of the offence. At times it nonetheless seems difficult to separate fact from fantasy in the descriptions of such people in newspapers, films, videos, books and plays.

In exploring the myth further it can be argued that offenders may carry out the violence many people consider, even momentarily, inflicting on others. Furthermore there may be an element of unconscious envy of the psychopath's power to carry out anti-social acts. Nevertheless, some of the anti-social aspects of psychopathic behaviour such as engaging in high risk activities, adopting a dramatic personality and/or being in constant conflict with authority may be unwittingly reinforced by the transmission of various beliefs and forms of behaviour; again, through films, videos, plays, books and so on.

Mental health practitioners are also involved, to varying degrees, in generating, processing and destroying such myths. They are part of the mental health care system that collaborates in identifying and attempting to normalise behaviour through regulation, surveillance and confession (Foucault, 1979). Through such processes the individual identities of both patients and staff are created, fragmented and reconstituted in relation to the institutions which regulate and supervise this group of patients.

Many forms of supervision can be viewed negatively as a mechanism for disciplining employees through regulation and psychological manipulation (Rose, 1989). Supervision, however, may also be regarded more positively as a process for giving the practitioner time to examine and improve their practice and relationships with patients, with each other and with members of other disciplines and agencies.

A tradition of erratic clinical supervision, derived mainly from psychodynamic and behavioural models, has existed in some areas of mental health nursing since at least the Second World War. The supportive aspects of supervision however have only recently begun to be formally identified in parts of general nursing (UKCC, 1996) as seemingly important factors in the creation of good practice (Butterworth and Faugier, 1992).

Identification of possible psychopathic, borderline and narcissistic behaviours

As a counsellor and supervisor of counsellors it may be useful to identify some of the frameworks used by the medical profession in the identification of psychopathic and anti-social personality disorders. Before proceeding, however, it is important to re-emphasise the social stigma that is strongly associated with labelling people as offenders or diagnosing them as suffering from mental illness or disorder (Goffman, 1963). Walker and McCabe (1973) argue that the term 'psychopath' may serve as a label that obliterates more information than it conveys. The label may be used to justify a doctor's unwillingness to treat an uncooperative patient (Howells, 1976) or as a 'pseudo diagnosis' for offenders regarded as abnormal but not mentally ill. Immediately the diagnosis is recognised staff may automatically begin to put up their defences rather than looking for areas of trust to develop.

The diagnosis of psychopath or anti-social personality disorder may help, however, in predicting what type of treatment or therapy needs to be prescribed. Defining such terms might also help in estimating the number of the people with the diagnosis in a population. This in turn may assist future decision making in relation to the allocation of resources: for example, has a particular agency the resources to work with a particular patient?

Coid (1995) cites the work of Kendall (1989) who argues that, unlike physical disorders, few psychiatric disorders, among them psychopathic disorder, can be as adequately validated. Coid argues that reliable diagnostic approaches in relation to this particular group remain in their early stages. In the UK the term 'psychopath' is used more as a legal than a diagnostic category. The term allows for detention and treatment of the patient in a hospital setting, under the Mental Health Act 1983, as long as the patient's condition can be alleviated or further deterioration prevented. There is, however, little explanation of the term in law and it is left for the courts to interpret its definition.

In spite of this a number of often overlapping frameworks exist for the assessment of psychopathic and 'borderline' personalities including *DSM III (IV)* (APA, 1994) and *ICD 10* (WHO, 1992). For the purposes of this chapter it may be useful to describe one framework to aid practitioners in their assessment and ongoing work with patients.

From a medical perspective Hare (1980) presented a 20-item psychopathic checklist:

1 Glibness/superficial charm;
2 Grandiose sense of self-worth;
3 Need for stimulation/proneness to boredom;
4 Pathological lying;
5 Cunning/manipulative;
6 Lack of remorse/guilt;
7 Shallow affect;
8 Callous/lack of empathy;
9 Parasitic lifestyle;
10 Poor behaviour control;
11 Promiscuous sexual behaviour;
12 Early behavioural problems;
13 Lack of realistic long-term goals;
14 Impassivity;
15 Irresponsibility;
16 Failure to accept responsibility for own actions;
17 Many short term marital relationships;
18 Juvenile delinquency;
19 Revocation of conditional release;
20 Criminal versatility.

Other authors such as Davies and Fieldman (1981) and Coid (1993) have described psychopathic behaviour using these terms: selfishness, aggressiveness, no guilt or remorse for their behaviour, lack of shame, lack of empathy, callousness, a fundamental incapacity for love or making true friendships, lack of insight, inability to control impulses or delay gratification, demonstrations of pathological lying, seeking thrills, poor judgement, disregard for social conventions, social and sexual relationships that are superficial but demanding and manipulative, ability to extricate themselves from difficult situations by producing intricate and at times contradictory lies, producing theatrically convincing explanations and promises, and presenting as two-dimensional people able to simulate emotions and emotional attachment when it is advantageous to do so.

Gunderson (1984) considers that people diagnosed as psychopathic lack internal inhibition, which results in them experiencing brief psychotic episodes, panic states and impulsive episodes to avoid panic. Such patients are frequently involved in fights and promiscuity often assisted by drugs and alcohol. Such incidents reflect a desperate effort to make contact and revive the illusion of control over *something*. Alternatively the individual can react to anxiety-provoking situations by experiencing altered states of consciousness where they may loosen their sense of identity, feel detached from experiencing their emotions or feel that the world around them has become unreal, lifeless or two dimensional. Patients can also experience severe depression to the point where they believe phenomena within their environment convey special meanings to them, influence their behaviour, and that dramatic changes have occurred or are occurring within their bodies.

People with narcissistic personalities, which may be a component of an anti-social or psychopathic personality, are thought to possess a concept of self which is pathologically grandiose yet constantly envies others whilst also seeking attention from them. They often form exploitative and parasitic relationships through the use of a superficially charming exterior that hides a cold ruthless and sometimes sadistic interior. At the most extreme end of this spectrum such people relate to others primarily through aggression. They find it difficult to love others and to differentiate the love given by others from exploitation and manipulation. They can sometimes be found in occupations, such as working in abattoirs, that allow them to express their primitive cruelty (Kernberg, 1984).

From this analysis it can be seen that individuals who might be classified as suffering from a psychopathic disorder may not only exhibit exploitative and aggressive tendencies. They can also experience a full range of mental disorders that mask the underlying personality or may result in the individual receiving more than one diagnosis. The following case highlights the features of anti-social personality disorder and illustrates some of the difficulties that can arise in relation to such patients' care from both supervisees' and supervisors' points of view.

Case Outline

Paul has recently qualified as a mental health nurse and has been working with enthusiasm as a staff nurse for the last six months in an acute admission ward within a high security hospital. Over this period of time he has been supervised by Julia, a deputy ward manager working in another part of the hospital, who has no formal contact with Paul's colleagues or the patients he works with. Paul has been regularly attending supervision sessions for an hour every two weeks and has found it very useful.

In one particular session Paul describes his relationship with Carl, a patient experiencing hallucinations and delusions, with whom he has been developing a strong working relationship. Julia senses some incongruent aspects between Paul's positive account of this relationship and his agitated body language. She asks him if he is aware of this contradiction. After an initial tense silence, Paul begins to describe difficulties with a new patient, Dave. Highly sociable, Dave had quickly struck up a friendship with Kevin, a quiet compliant patient. On one occasion Paul had reminded Kevin that it was time for him to attend a session in the occupational therapy department. Dave had intervened, saying, 'Kevin doesn't have to go if he doesn't want to.' Dave continued to remonstrate, apparently on Kevin's behalf against Paul. Although this incident, in itself, was perhaps not highly significant, Paul reported to Julia that Dave seemed to be gradually befriending several of the more senior nursing staff in the ward, thus leading Paul to feel isolated.

Later, after the initial incident involving Kevin, Dave, in an aggressive outburst which almost resulted in physical violence, told Paul that he thought he had only come into the job to victimise weak patients and that underneath he was a coward. Julia asked Paul how he had felt about this. 'Very weak and scared,' Paul had replied. It transpired that Dave, a well-built man, known to have had some military training, had a number of convictions for grievous and actual bodily harm, including stabbing another person when under the influence of alcohol. During one prison sentence he had taken another inmate hostage and almost killed him. Paul and other staff had been warned not to be left alone with Dave in secluded areas of the ward. In spite of such concerns, it was hoped that some useful work could be done with Dave to reduce his level of suspiciousness and aggressive behaviour.

Julia went on to ask Paul if he had told any of the other ward staff about Dave's behaviour towards him. Paul said that he hadn't because they all seemed to get on so well with Dave. To add to Paul's discomfort, Dave had told him that he wasn't tough enough to work in a male ward and that he should work in a female ward. He also made fun of Paul's appearance and became directly threatening towards him. Paul had avoided reporting this to his colleagues because he was afraid that they would think that he was not 'up to the job'. Whilst being mindful of Paul's personal predicament, Julia impressed on him the need to keep his colleagues informed about Dave's threatening behaviour.

Further exploration revealed that Paul believed that it was necessary for him always to stand up to the threatening behaviour of others. He also admitted a need to be liked and almost to seek out the most demanding patients to test and prove himself. It was apparent to Julia that many long-standing personality traits could be explored but she believed the more urgent task in this session was to help Paul reflect on and change aspects of his relationship with Dave. She had also noticed her own protective feelings towards Paul.

One of Paul's most significant concerns was that Dave could easily play on his vulnerability. Julia acknowledged this and discussed with Paul the advantages of exploring this either in personal therapy or in other suitable ways. She suggested that they might concentrate on Dave's need to undermine and isolate Paul. In fact, on investigation, it became clear that Dave did not get on as well with as many of the senior members of the ward staff as Paul had initially reported. Julia encouraged Paul to put himself in Dave's position, in an attempt to subsequently help the patient develop insight into his own fears and inadequacies. For example, Dave might be apprehensive about finding himself in a high security hospital and, due to his level of anxiety, act out a need to control others. Julia went on to consider if Dave might despise the vulnerable part of Paul that he was unable to acknowledge in himself.

While on one level Paul could acknowledge Julia's insightfulness, he began to feel irritated at her seemingly 'facile' interpretations and lack of practical advice, and told her as much. Although momentarily thrown by this, Julia ventured to suggest that possibly Paul was using hostility towards her in the same way that Dave was throwing Paul off balance by his use of hostility. Paul hesitantly accepted that this parallel process might be occurring but still felt unclear as to how he could work effectively with Dave on a day to day basis. Unfortunately the session came to an end with Paul remaining frustrated. Insights had been gained but with no new strategies formulated.

Julia discussed this aspect of her session with Paul, in her own supervision, the next day. She realised that she felt quite powerless during her session with Paul and had perhaps resorted to too many interpretations to cope with her anxiety. Nevertheless, she believed that she had done some useful work with Paul on safety issues, allowing him time and space to ventilate his anxieties and to consider his problematic interactions with Dave from a different perspective. Norton and McGauley (1998) advise, especially when working with difficult patients, on the importance of monitoring relationships with colleagues, maintaining effective channels of communication with colleagues and creating a safe, intellectually and emotionally supportive environment through the use of appropriate supervision.

In institutions such as high security hospitals the clinical supervision of staff is essential, though it cannot realistically address and resolve every problem brought by the practitioner. Ultimately supervision may also provide an environment for addressing and working with the fears and anxieties associated with caring for this particular group of patients, rather than suppressing and avoiding such feelings. Issues from this case will be discussed in the following sections.

Aspects of caring for and working with people experiencing psychopathic disorder and anti-social personality disorder

This section outlines common phenomena experienced on wards and is presented as an aid to understanding the challenges and stresses experienced by practitioners working with such patients.

Ambiguities have often been associated with the role of the forensic mental health nurse. On the one hand they are expected to provide support, care and therapy for patients whilst on the other they are expected to maintain security and take part in the assessment of the patients' level of risk (Burrow, 1993; Tarbuck, 1994). Similarly, social workers, probation officers and other forensic practitioners have traditionally been faced with the dilemmas of care and control (Williams, 1996).

In a controlled environment, patients are compelled to be with nurses through legal processes rather than having any real choice in the matter. This puts a custodial dynamic into play in relation to the nurse–patient relationship, where the patient may be suspicious of the nurse's motivations for asking certain questions. Accordingly the patient might not always feel that the nursing staff are acting in patients' best interests. Such difficulties are illustrated in the relationship between Paul and Dave, where Dave appears to reject Paul's role as a carer while also setting him up as an oppressive yet cowardly authority figure.

Schultz and Darker (1986), nevertheless, identify trust as providing the cornerstone of the nurse–patient relationship, even within the forensic context, and see this as developing through four phases: introductory, testing, working and termination. They add that many people diagnosed as having psychopathic or anti-social personality disorder, like Dave, seem to get stuck at the testing or 'manipulative' phase.

This is not to say that staff do not manipulate patients and that they do not use the word 'manipulative' to dismiss sometimes valid aspects of patients' behaviour. Stuart and Sundeen (1992) argue that those who experience difficulties with emotional closeness often resort to using manipulation as a way of getting what they need or want. It can be seen as a tactic to keep others at arm's length. 'Manipulative' behaviour, however, such as self-harm, can often leave staff feeling alienated from colleagues and hostile towards the patient. The behaviour may gain the initiative for the patient in the short term but is usually self-defeating and prevents therapeutic progress.

Barnes and Frisby (1992) advise setting clear limits with patients exhibiting such behaviour, so that they will learn the disadvantages of manipulative behaviour and more satisfying, rewarding ways of relating. McCune (1987) also argues that confrontation can be a useful intervention for both parties but adds that at times this can be extremely emotionally stressful for staff.

Patients like Dave appear to be happiest when they are also causing chaos (McCord and McCord, 1963). Situations are often instigated by the patient's rapid changes of mood, attitude and behaviour, from being pleasant and compliant at one moment to aggressive and hostile the next. Moran and Mason (1996) suggest that staff can cope with such events by not second-guessing what the patient is going to attempt next; never being surprised or showing surprise; accepting the behaviour on face value as the 'behaviour of a psychopath' instead of showing disgust or anger and by discussing the rights and wrongs of the situation at a later, more appropriate time.

Furthermore they advise staff to be non-judgmental and non-moralistic in their attitudes towards the patient, thus denying the reinforcement the patient seeks. However, they fail to acknowledge the judgements that can arise out of using terms such as 'manipulative' to describe behaviour and they also don't acknowledge the tensions that can arise between members of staff and the patient when both exist in the same environment, possibly for years. Staff, therefore, need to learn from the actual behaviour of patients as well as keeping up to date with current research in the area.

As in the case of Dave, patients are likely to see nurses as just another group to attempt to dominate. To counteract this the staff need to be fluid and equitable in their dealings with patients so members of the overall group can learn to be in both dominant and submissive roles without feeling they have to resort to coercion. Leadership by the nursing staff also needs to allow the patient opportunities to experience leadership roles. Thus the staff lead more through example than through an autocratic management style (Moran and Mason, 1996).

Finally, patients like Dave are prone to quickly locate and manipulate staff whom they perceive as vulnerable, whilst deferring to more senior ward and medical staff. Moran and Mason (1996) say little about how staff in lower positions in the ward hierarchy might be helped and supported in enduring the possible discomfort of their position. They also say little about the general support and supervision of staff working within environments accommodating these kinds of patient. Ironically, front-line staff, usually lower in the professional hierarchy, bear the brunt of threat and manipulation, yet their supervisory needs are rarely adequately met.

Nursing and supervision: working in controlled environments

Insecure supervisors conducting clinical supervision may foster dependency by all too readily giving advice and information to new supervisees such as Paul. Much of Julia's work, as Paul's supervisor, will involve helping him to cope with the fear, anxiety and uncertainty of working with Dave. This will not only be about helping Paul to cope with unpredictable and potentially violent situations. In supervision Paul will also need to reflect on which aspects of Dave's behaviour could be better controlled by the patient himself. It is often difficult to identify the right answers in relation to how such behaviour 'should' be handled. Patients, and sometimes their representative, may pick up on this lack of clarity and use it against the nurse, which may in turn create feelings of inadequacy. Paul and his colleagues will also have to consider what aspects of Dave's behaviour can and cannot be tolerated, and what action to take if his behaviour becomes intolerable. Members of staff like Paul often have guidelines on how to work with behaviour such as that exhibited by Dave. Like most guidelines, however, they are subject to individual interpretations and, due to the individual characteristics of each patient, do not always have the desired effect.

A number of issues arise for nurses working in secure settings. Amongst these is an emphasis on maintaining the safety of the public and there are still sometimes harsh consequences for staff involved in breaches of security. With environmental control also comes an overcontrol of emotions and a reluctance to disclose areas of vulnerability such as fears of violence and of being perceived as weak by other staff and patients. Nurses can also have difficulties in openly discussing their approach to and feelings about patients and other members of staff. Due to the increasing levels of change within the health service, nurses can become cynical about managerial initiatives. They also have to be increasingly aware of patient rights and local and institutional, gender and racial discrimination (DoH/HO, 1992). Nurses are still confronted by the anxieties arising from inadequate staffing levels in some areas and inadequate education and training, especially of unregistered staff.

The predominantly masculine culture in many secure settings may arise because they are among the few areas of nursing where a male nurse can maintain the stereotypical masculine identity that he feels comfortable with. Secure settings also adopt many custodial and dehumanising aspects of prison culture, for example patients who become violent are described as 'kicking off' and patients passes are referred to as 'parole'. In some secure settings, nursing staff might find themselves in conflict, rather than co-operating with, other disciplines and agencies, especially in relation to initiating interventions and gaining fresh information about patients. Furthermore, clinical supervision may be perceived more as a process to regulate staff than as a mechanism for growth and support (Faugier, 1992).

In relation to recent problems at Ashworth Hospital, where there were alleged lapses in security in a ward treating patients with personality disorder, John Fillis, representing the health workers' union UNISON, argued that if staff are in a ward for four or five years they become so used to the patients that they consider their abnormal behaviour as normal. Tom Sandford (at that time the Royal College of Nursing Mental Health Advisor) replied, 'That is why you need to have effective clinical supervision' (Combes, 1997).

Managers may be wary of providing resources for supervision due to a lack of firm evidence that supervision will improve the organisation's morale and mental health and improve the quality of patient care (Porter,

1998). The United Kingdom Central Council for Nursing, Midwifery and Health Visiting (1996) has however endorsed the establishment of clinical supervision as an important part of strategies to promote high standards of care.

Dexter and Russell (1990) have created a model of clinical supervision, based on the work of Gerard Egan, for mental health nurses, arguing that clinical supervision has advantages for patients, practitioners and organisations. For the patient it ensures best quality of services, protection, confidence, systematic care and skilled practice. For practitioners, supervision provides a context for feedback; opportunities to clarify issues, to be informed and stimulated; help for nurses to remain patient centred and simultaneously to enable achievement of organisational and personal goals; opportunities to identify areas for development and training needs.

Supervision, if it is to be successfully implemented in a secure environment, needs to be well structured. Ideally processes need to be established where the supervisee would have some choice in selecting their supervisor (Rogers and Topping Morris, 1997). When given choice, however, supervisees may opt to select their friends as supervisors, which can lead to collusion between the supervisor and supervisee and a lack of rigour in confronting uncomfortable issues. Conversely it can be destructive and possibly unethical to attempt to compel a member of staff to engage in clinical supervision, especially if the supervisee has little respect for the supervisor.

Proctor (1991) argues that the supervision process can be enhanced by both parties engaging in contracting, establishing boundaries, acknowledging gender and cultural differences and forward planning (duration, times and reviewing of dates). Finding a suitably quiet, conducive environment within a secure setting can be difficult due to lack of space, pressure of time, shift systems and both parties possibly being more preoccupied with what might be happening outside the room rather than with what is taking place within it. In attempting to overcome such difficulties the supervisor needs to remain vigilant in containing the supervisee's anxieties while also supporting and encouraging them (Feltham and Dryden, 1994). The organisation of nursing within institutional settings may involve emergency situations and an ever-changing shift system. It can be easy for both parties, especially if a difficult issue has arisen, to avoid attending supervision sessions. Staff might also avoid supervision sessions because they think their work will be criticised or through fear of being forced to disclose aspects of themselves that they would prefer to keep concealed.

Due to the difficulties of maintaining confidentiality and trust within institutional settings it may be more beneficial to receive supervision from outside the organisation. Lack of resources, however, makes this difficult to achieve. If supervisors are drawn from within the organisation, then problems may arise over what material may be taken by the supervisor to *their* supervisor and whether the supervisee should be informed of this. The supervisor may have considerable difficulties if the supervisee has disclosed to them a plan of care with which they strongly disagree. They may be obliged to consider at what point the safety of patients and other members of staff may be put at risk if the particular information is not passed on to managers. The supervisor, in the first instance, may ask the supervisee to sort the situation out for themselves, in the name of developing assertiveness, but there may be entrenched problems within the organisation that would take more than a supervisee, at a lower level of the hierarchy, to sort out. The supervisor may also learn of issues concerning the supervisee's or other nurses' professional misconduct. The supervisor has to consider what strategies they would use in such a situation. If a supervisee were considered in breach of professional conduct then the supervisor, if a nurse, would have to make the supervisee aware of the gravity of the situation, and report it to the supervisee's line manager. If the nurse had witnessed other nurses in breach of professional conduct then they might advise the supervisee to report the incident to the relevant manager. Supervisors from within the organisation might also experience difficulties associated with breaches of confidentiality and trust, especially working within a closed community where so much power can be conveyed through the informal exchange of information. Conversely, supervisees may feel frustrated that they cannot have a fully confidential relationship with the patients they work with since it is traditionally stated that this could be a road to potential disaster.

Hawkins and Shohet (1991), in their model of supervision, emphasise the significance of the supervisor and supervisee reflecting on the interventions, strategies and reports used and made by staff in relation to the organisation of nursing practice. Such approaches need to be assessed in conjunction with their application to meeting patient needs. They also consider it of value to explore the metaphors, images, worries and concerns supervisees have in relation to the patients they are caring for.

In the second half of their model, Hawkins and Shohet (1991) focus on the supervisory process and concentrate on elements such as the emotions the supervisee brings to the supervisory process from their interactions with patients. This can take the form of personal material the client has re-stimulated in the supervisee that may be unconsciously repressed by the supervisee to avoid acknowledging uncomfortable feelings from the past. The supervisee might also wish to examine projected material from the client that may have been 'taken in' somatically or mentally.

From a forensic perspective, Cox (1996) argues that interchanges in this context always take place against a background of the presence or lack of trust and security. He regards supervision as being analogous to gardening: it involves a considerable amount of waiting and growing through apprenticeship, and facilitating appropriate attitudes.

Challenging issues in the supervision of staff

Although only a limited number of mental health nurses are trained as psychotherapists, some understanding of psychoanalytic theory and processes can be of use in helping to lower the nurse's level of anxiety. Such an understanding may help them stand back and possibly make sense of the often irrational and chaotic behaviour they witness around them. If such behaviour is brought into supervision then the supervisor may need to focus on their own and the supervisee's motives for wanting to discuss a particular patient's care. Will the discussion help the supervisee come to terms with the behaviour or might the discussion degenerate into a form of voyeurism? The supervisee may like describing bizarre behaviour due to their own lack of self-esteem in that it may give them a false sense of their sanity and power over the patient.

Given the hierarchical nature of the nursing profession it is sometimes difficult for both the supervisor and the supervisee to acknowledge how much the supervisor can learn from the supervisee. Furthermore, having worked in a mental health setting, a new supervisor may have gained a false sense of confidence from their work with patients and feel that they can work with any member of staff, at any level of intimacy, no matter what the problem. Such all-powerful feelings need to be addressed in the supervisor's own supervision. Furthermore the supervisor will also need to establish, possibly through the contracting process with their supervisee, as well as with their own supervisor, what the boundaries are of their level of competence. If the supervisee has significant personal problems they may need to seek specific counselling or therapy outside the supervisor–supervisee relationship. Similarly if a patient has physically assaulted the supervisee then there may be a need for specialist post-traumatic stress counselling.

Russell (1993) describes how power relationships exist between clients and therapists where power can be ascribed as well as taken. Such relationships can also be said to exist between supervisees and supervisors where some supervisors exercise inappropriate power over their supervisee and some supervisees abuse power in relation to their clients. Russell adds that it is difficult to identify where an abuse of power has taken place but suggests that it is useful to distinguish between authority, influence and force.

Added to this, supervisors need to be warned against complacency in relation to their understanding of supervisee problems, especially in relation to what they believe to be going on 'under the surface'. Such 'knowing' could well provide the supervisor with the illusion of being in control in a world that is constantly changing and being bombarded by new configurations of meaning and understanding (Plant, 1992). There is a need to begin to establish trust in order to try to confirm that both parties have a similar idea of the meaning of a particular word or series of events.

The supervisor also needs direct experience of the supervisee's work in order that they can attempt to understand the situations the supervisee is placed in. Supervisors must maintain some degree of objectivity; working in a different environment from that of the supervisee may prevent the supervisor colluding with them in particularly difficult working relationships. The supervisor needs to be aware of their own subtle responses to the situations supervisees describe to them. Before responding they must remember that they were not actually present at the time and that a number of subtle and significant variables could well have been present. Similarly supervisors need to be aware of inappropriately attempting to solve or come to terms with their own past management difficulties and indiscretions by projecting them on to the supervisee's current presenting problem.

The supervisor needs to be aware of class, race, gender, sexual orientation or other differences in relation to the supervisee and be sensitive to any tensions which might arise out of such relationships. Thompson et al. (1994) argue that there appears to be limited acknowledgement of racial issues existing in client–supervisee and supervisee–supervisor relationships. They point out that supervisees and supervisors often *don't know what they don't know*, which can create conflict and discomfort, and that they lack training in racial issues. Thompson et al. advise that supervisors need to develop empathy with the supervisee's culture and race, review where their own stereotypes are coming from and acknowledge power issues related to colonial history.

These are important issues, especially in secure environments where there is a higher than usual representation of African and Caribbean patients than in the overall population and staff are drawn from a variety of different racial groups (DoH/HO, 1992).

As patients can be involved in different forms of denial, that is consciously or unconsciously not wishing to know (Fairbairn, 1951), so too can supervisees by, for example, not realising that a paedophile who says they 'really like children' is reversing their denial of the severity of their actions. Or the paedophile who says that the child 'wanted me to do it' is placing responsibility on the child for their own unacceptable behaviour. Similarly staff, especially if they have spent considerable time working with a patient or because they are afraid of a patient's potential aggression, may reject the idea that a patient is becoming mentally unwell again even after warnings from a more detached position. Staff can similarly deny a patient's potential level of risk, especially after they have got to know the patient over a long period of time. Supervisees may have considerable difficulties in admitting they are afraid, especially of patients who have previously used threats of injury and death to get what they want. Cox (1996) points out that there is a thin dividing line between a difficult yet safely managed patient and a patient who really worries a supervisee.

There can also be denial of what is occurring in the supervision sessions, especially in the way supervisors use their power, for example when the supervisor is using the session to indicate their wealth of knowledge to the supervisee, or attempting to catch the supervisee out over an issue. Denial can also arise if, for example, a supervisee has difficulties acknowledging any anger with the supervisor or through the supervisor failing to acknowledge age, gender, socio-economic or cultural differences and tensions.

Many of the interpersonal aspects of past mental health nurse training have been underpinned by Rogers' (1951) humanistic principles of empathy, acceptance and genuineness. In forensic work, however, there are problems associated with 'entering the other's world without prejudice' (Rogers, 1975). Staff can easily become angry and nauseated by patients' present behaviour and past offences. Irritation can arise in relation to patients' level of denial over their offence and the existence of mental illness. There are, nevertheless, pressures on nurses, sometimes from other professional groups, to monitor the level of patients' insight into their mental illness, level of remorse over their offending behaviour and empathy with their victims. It is difficult for staff not to be judgmental in such situations. Even if they do not verbalise their judgements they may show non-verbal approval or disapproval. Patients considered to be suffering from anti-social personality disorder are often considered not to be 'ill' like patients with psychosis. Staff will sometimes express their frustration with such patients by saying that they are malingering in hospital and should be returned to prison. Conversely staff can express their anger with patients by dehumanising them by, for example, referring to them by their diagnostic category instead of their names, or describing behaviour in a judgmental way as 'acting out' (Cordess and Williams, 1996) or 'manipulative' rather than examining the tensions that may have led to such behaviour.

Successful outcomes from the supervisee's perspective, rather than focusing on the patient gradually becoming more amenable to therapy, may have more to do with the supervisee's ability to emotionally come to terms with the grosser crimes that the patient has committed (Cox, 1996). Cox adds that the patient's offence not only becomes etched into the lives of people around the patient but can also have a significant effect on supervisees' and supervisors' lives.

Richman (1992) indicates that criminals in reality often look far less aggressive than they are portrayed in the media, and can be seductive (Cordess and Williams, 1996). The perception that the patient appears less aggressive than initially perceived may lead to a feeling of relief in the supervisee followed by unwitting feelings of wanting emotional closeness with the patient. A considerable amount of work carried out between patients and staff may involve an element of seduction at varying levels that might also be replicated in the supervisor–supervisee relationship. The supervisee may then begin to act out a scenario that the patient has instigated previously. If the supervisor doesn't acknowledge the warning signs that the pair are beginning to develop an intimate relationship, this could be destructive to the supervisee's career and to the patient's future development. Other staff might fear that their lives will be put at risk through loss of confidentiality. Such a situation might also increase childlike feelings in the patient of power over everyone in the organisation and create similar feelings in other patients. Other patients, however, might fear information getting to the nursing staff that they would prefer to remain concealed. The establishment of intimate relationships between staff and patients may also rob the patient of the opportunity to examine and possibly reconstruct their lives with the aid of a neutral party. Alternatively the supervisee may overreact to the patient's seductive behaviour by finding the tensions too much to bear and aggressively rejecting the patient or breaking down outside the relationship. Or the supervisee may become emotionally cut off from the patient and ignore the patient's propensity towards dangerous behaviour. The supervisee may begin to believe the patient when they say they have 'turned over a new leaf', and this may result in putting others at risk (Cordess and Williams, 1996). Some patients may allow their past behaviour to dominate sessions with the nurse/supervisee, thus placing themselves beyond redemption and recovery.

Anger from the trauma that the patient has experienced in the past may be unwittingly reawakened by the nurse/supervisee. The patient may verbally attack the supervisee due to intolerable inner tensions, or resort to self-harm as a form of attempting to cope with what has occurred (Temple, 1996). Similarly, after the verbal attack the patient may begin to identify with the supervisee as a victim. The supervisee, in turn, may unwittingly find themselves acting in a similarly aggressive way towards the supervisor.

As previously indicated, due to their diminished feelings of self-worth or a lack of feelings of self, the only way the patient may know of gaining attention is through setting up situations that provoke anger in the nurse/supervisee which might then be projected on to the supervisor. The supervisee may begin to act out the patient's anger in supervision through, for example, turning up late, abusing their relationship with the patient, engaging in anti-social behaviour or being aggressive to others whilst idealising the supervisor. Such self-defeating behaviour, which may be a way of coping with intolerable internal tensions, is often associated with patients (Cordess and Williams, 1996) but can also be interpreted as rejection, within the supervisory relationship, of the supervisor.

Alternatively the supervisee may find that the patient has begun to strongly identify with her or him, especially at the beginning of the relationship. This may happen to the extent that the supervisee feels overwhelmed and taken over by the patient. Similarly this may happen in supervision where the supervisee identifies so strongly with the supervisor that the supervisor begins to be overwhelmed by the whole range of the supervisee's feelings. In turn such forms of identification might lead the supervisee to feel bereft of feelings. Temple (1996) points out that some patients use a combination of different defence mechanisms, forming a strong defensive system. They can take the form of omnipotence, projective identification, denial, idealisation and splitting.

Sometimes supervisees view the supervisor as a cruel, unfair authority figure. This may lead the supervisee to go as far creating self-defeating situations for them in an attempt to control the supervisor by exaggerating the advice offered, for example by being unnecessarily harsh or lenient when being advised to establish boundaries with patients.

Bateman (1996) identifies mentally healthy behaviour as operating when the supervisee is engaged in creative acts. He also considers the use of humour as an important health mechanism, which helps integrate interpersonal relations and private feelings into a balanced reality. Feelings are thus modified towards significant goals rather than being dammed or diverted. Humour can also be used to explore boundaries and sometimes say what otherwise might be unsayable.

For these reasons it is essential that those working with such patients and supervisees receive appropriate training and supervision so they are aware when they might be placating the supervisee in order to avoid criticism, which in turn might be directed towards the supervisee's manager. The supervisor must be aware of who the supervisee may represent for them in their own inner world and how their inner world might contaminate that of the supervisee.

Supervisees such as Paul may also fear describing their negative emotions about patients such as Dave in supervision for fear of conveying to the supervisor that they are out of control of themselves and thus not a 'good nurse'. Supervisees may also find it difficult to express their frustration and pessimism about a patient, believing that their behaviour will never change. It is important that such frustrations are discussed in supervision however, to prevent such feelings being directed back at the patient.

Conclusions

There are many significant aspects to the supervision of staff who work in secure mental health services. It may appear from the various types of institution such staff work in and the behaviours of the patient group that the voice of supportive supervision could easily be lost in a tide of verbal abuse, apathy and managerial change. It is important that supervisors themselves don't become complacent, maintain their self-awareness and receive supervision in this rapidly changing culture. It is also important to go out and examine support and supervision systems used in other environments, taking into account that what works in one culture or environment might not work so well in another.

In the writer's experience it is useful to have gained knowledge in a comprehensive range of theoretical perspectives when engaging in supervision (Jacobs, 1996). This can have the effect of helping the supervisor provide the supervisee with a wide range of options to view in relation to particular situations and a broad repertoire of skills and interventions for both the supervisor and supervisee to use.

It can be limiting and possibly damaging to the supervisee if a supervisor adheres dogmatically to one particular model or conceptual framework of supervision. This can inhibit creativity and spontaneity, which may go against the spirit in which such models were initially conceived. An example of this occurred to me. I had been trained and gained experience in one specific approach to counselling and supervision and found it difficult not to feel irritated in subsequent training workshops when other participants didn't strictly conform to the approaches I had learned. I attempted to resolve my irritation by constantly reflecting on how much my feelings were a product of past experience and inner rigidities and how much they were perhaps due to the lack of what I considered to be 'skilled' behaviour adopted by the other participants. As Cox (1996) argues, however, hiding behind theory will not provide protection from the emotional storms the supervisee is liable to bring to supervision.

It is difficult when working as a supervisor, with supervisees in a secure environment, not to feel at times emotionally mauled by supervisees. To overcome the possibility of the supervisor, in such situations, becoming hostile towards the supervisee and to come to terms with such emotional dents and bruises it is, again, essential that the supervisor have some form of supervision. The purpose of this is for support, as well as to unravel what is located within themselves that they would like to change and what is more to do with the supervisee's own emotional state. Similarly, conducting supervision sessions can increase the supervisor's feelings of aloneness in the world. This can occur especially when considering questions such as: which party is involved in projecting what? How do I know what I am projecting on to the supervisee? And is this feeling a projection from the supervisee or something more to do with my own past experience? Finally, as Cox (1996) points out, it is essential, especially for staff working within the sometimes emotionally highly charged atmosphere of a secure psychiatric setting, for both supervisors and supervisees to strike a balance between their working life and their personal lives outside work. If staff become over-committed and preoccupied by work then they are likely to overlook the importance of time away to relax and revitalise themselves. Conversely, if staff are preoccupied at work by activities taking place in their personal lives then the quality of attention paid to the patients will suffer, which may have a deleterious effect on the quality of their care. Supervisors must help supervisees achieve this balance when attempting to meet the needs of such challenging patients.

References

APA (1994) *Diagnostic and Statistical Manual of Mental Disorders*, 4th edn. Washington, DC: American Psychiatric Press.

Barnes, C. A. and Frisby, R. (1992) 'Personality Disorder' in T. Brooking, S. A. H. Ritter and B. L. Thomas (eds), *A Textbook of Psychiatric Mental Health Nursing*. London: Churchill Livingstone.

Bateman, A. (1996) 'Defence mechanisms', in C. Cordess and M. Cox (eds), *Forensic Psychotherapy: Crime Psychodynamics and the Offender Patient*. London: Jessica Kingsley.

Burrow, S. (1993) 'The role conflict of the forensic nurse', *Senior Nurse*, 13 (5): 20–25.

Butterworth, T. and Faugier, J. (eds) (1992) *Clinical Supervision and Mentorship in Nursing*. London: Chapman and Hall.

Coid, J. W. (1993) 'Current concepts and classifications of psychopathic disorder', in P. Tyler and G. Stein (eds), *Personality Disorder Review*, London: Gaskell, Royal College of Psychiatrists.

Coid, J.W. (1995) in B. Dolan and J.W. Coid (1995) *Psychopathic and Anti-Social Personality Disorders: Treatment and Research*. London: Gaskell.

Combes, R. (1997) 'Total breakdown', *Nursing Times*, 93 (8): 17.

Cordess, C. and Williams, A.H. (1996) 'The criminal act and acting out', in C. Cordess and M. Cox, *Forensic Psychotherapy: Crime Psychodynamics and the Offender Patient*. London: Jessica Kingsley.

Cox, M. (1996) 'A supervisor's view', in C. Cordess and M. Cox, *Forensic Psychotherapy: Crime Psychodynamics and the Offender Patient*. London: Jessica Kingsley.

Davies, W. and Fieldman, P. (1981) 'The diagnosis of psychopathy by forensic specialists', *British Journal of Psychiatry*, 138: 329–331.

Department of Health/Home Office (1992) *Review of Health and Social Services for Mentally Disordered Offenders and Others Requiring Similar Services* (Chair, J. Reed). London: HMSO.

Dexter, D. and Russell, J. (1990) in D. Dexter and M. Walsh (1996) *Psychiatric Nursing Skills: a Patient-centred approach*. London: Chapman and Hall.

Dexter, D. and Walsh, M. (1996) *Psychiatric Nursing Skills: A Patient-centred Approach*. London: Chapman and Hall.

Dolan, B. and Coid, J. W. (1993) *Psychopathic and Antisocial Personality Disorders Treatment and Research*. London: Gaskell, Royal College of Psychiatrists.

Fairbairn, W.R.D. (1951) 'A synopsis of the development of the author's view regarding the structure of their personality', in W.R.D. Fairbairn, *Psychoanalytic Studies of the Personality*. London: Routledge and Kegan Paul.

Faugier, J. (1992) 'The supervisory relationship', in C.A. Butterworth and J. Faugier (eds), *Clinical Supervision and Mentorship in Nursing*. London: Chapman and Hall.

Feltham, C. and Dryden, W. (1994) *Developing Counsellor Supervision*. London: Sage.

Foucault, M. (1979) *Discipline and Punish: The Birth of the Prison*. Harmondsworth: Peregrine Books.

Goffman, E. (1963) *Stigma: Notes on the Management of Spoiled Identity*. Englewood Cliffs, NJ: Prentice-Hall.

Gunderson, J. G. (1984) *Borderline Personality Disorder*. Washington, DC: American Psychiatric Press.

Hare, R.D. (1980) 'A research scale for the assessment of psychopathy in criminal populations', *Personality and Individual Differences*, 1: 111–117.

Hawkins, P. and Shohet, R. (1991) 'Approaches to the supervision of counsellors:

the supervisory relationship', in W. Dryden and B. Thorne (eds), *Training and Supervision for Counselling in Action*. London: Sage.

Howells, K. (1976) 'Interpersonal aggression', *International Criminology and Penology*, 4: 319–330.

Jacobs, M. (ed.) (1996) *In Search of Supervision*. Buckingham: Open University Press.

Kendall, R.E. (1989) 'Clinical Validity', *Journal of Psychological Medicine*, 19: 45–56.

Kernberg, K. (1984) *Severe Personality Disorder: Psychotherapeutic Strategies*. New Haven, CT: Yale University Press.

McCord, W. and McCord, J. (1963) *The Psychopath: An Essay on the Criminal Mind*. Princeton, NJ: Van Nostrand Books.

McCune, N. (1987) 'In someone else's shoes', *Bulletin of the Royal College of Psychiatrists*, 11 (6): 196.

Moran, T. and Mason, T. (1996) 'Revisiting the nursing management of the psychopath', *Journal of Psychiatric and Mental Health Nursing* (Blackwell Science), 3, (3): 189–194.

Norton, K. and McGauley, G. (1998) *Counselling Difficult Clients*. London: Sage.

Plant, S. (1992) *The Most Radical Gesture*. London: Routledge.

Porter, N. (1998) 'Providing effective clinical supervision', *Nursing Management*, 5 (2): 22–23.

Proctor, B. (1991) 'On being a trainer', in W. Dryden and B. Thorne (eds), *Training and Supervision for Counselling in Action*. London: Sage.

Richman, J. (1992) *Selected Contributions of Psycho-Analysis*. London: Hogarth Press and the Institute of Psycho-Analysis.

Rogers, C. (1951) *Client Centered Therapy*. New York: Houghton Mifflin.

Rogers, C. (1975) 'Empathic: an unappreciated way of being', *Counseling Psychology*, 5: 2–10.

Rogers, P. and Topping Morris, B. (1997) 'Clinical supervision for forensic mental health nurses', *Nursing Management*, 4 (5): 13–15.

Rose, N. (1989) *Governing the Soul: The Shaping of the Private Self*. London: Routledge.

Russell, J. (1993) *Out of Bounds: Sexual Exploitation in Counselling and Therapy*. London: Sage.

Schultz, J. M. and Darker, S. L. (1986) *Manual of Psychiatric Care Plans*, 2nd edn. Canada, Toronto: Little, Brown.

Stuart, G. W. and Sundeen, S. J. (1992) *Principles and Practice Psychiatric Nursing*, 3rd edn. St Louis: Mosby.

Tarbuck, P. (1994) 'The therapeutic use of security: a model for forensic nursing', in T. Thompson and P. Mathias, *Lyttles Mental Health and Disorder*, 2nd edn. London: Baillière Tindall.

Temple, N. (1996) 'Transference and countertransference: general and forensic aspects', in C. Cordess and M. Cox, *Forensic Psychotherapy: Crime Psychodynamics and the Offender Patient*. London: Jessica Kingsley.

Thompson, J., Lago, C. and Proctor, B. (1994) *Race, Culture and Counselling Supervision*. London: Institute of Integrative Psychotherapy.

United Kingdom Central Council for Nursing, Midwifery and Health Visiting (1996) *Position Statement on Clinical Supervision for Nursing and Health Visiting*. London: UKCC.

Walker, M. and McCabe, S. (1973) *Crime and Insanity in England*, Vol. 2. Edinburgh: Edinburgh University Press.

Williams A. H. (1996) *Counselling in the Criminal Justice System*. Buckingham: Open University Press.

WHO (1992) *International Classification of Diseases*, 10th edn. Geneva: World Health Organisation.

10

NEW CHALLENGES FOR SUPERVISING IN ORGANISATIONAL CONTEXTS

Sue Copeland

The supervisor–worker relationship is the key encounter where the influence of the organisational authority and professional identity collide, collude or connect. (Hughes and Pengelly, 1997: 24)

Over the last decade considerable change has taken place in the field of counselling supervision. Carroll, writing in 1988, likened counselling supervision to the beginning stages of a jigsaw puzzle with all the pieces being around somewhere but difficult to put together. The roots of the counselling supervisory process are in private practice but now many more counselling services are being set up in organisational contexts. In educational, industrial, medical and service settings counsellors are being employed either by the organisation itself or by the growing number of employee assistance programmes (EAPs). The growth of counselling services within these diverse organisational contexts has been largely in response to perceived stress in the workplace and the need for managers to have a policy with regard to their 'duty of care' towards employees. However, in many instances theoretical orientation and the mode of delivery of the counsellor may not match the culture of the organisation (McMahon Moughtin, 1997). Counselling and supervision are very often set up in an *ad hoc* manner, frequently in haste as a response to media hype about stress in the workplace. Consequently it is not surprising that little attention is paid to the counselling supervisor, who they are, their qualifications, experience and general suitability for the work within an organisational context.

Counselling supervision within such diverse organisational contexts such as health, education, counselling agencies and industry is a complex process. Organisational culture needs to be understood in order to make sense of the counselling process and the issues that the employees bring, issues that can be directly related to the organisational structure, culture and ongoing change within the organisation. However, many supervisors will not be disposed to working with their supervisees on these contextual issues. This may be because they lack interest in them or do not have the necessary knowledge and skills needed to work with them. Additionally a supervisor's theoretical orientation will influence their attitude towards short term solution-focused therapy, which is one of the favoured models of counselling within organisational contexts. Mander (1998) maintains that different counselling populations demand different supervisory styles and she goes on to describe short term psychodynamic work that appears to be a contradiction in terms. Some counsellors and supervisors who work psychodynamically may not be disposed or even able to work in this short term way. Yet in counselling and supervision the market place demands that supervisors and counsellors work in settings other than private practice. They have the choice to work in organisational contexts and many may do so for economic reasons, with or without the knowledge and skills needed or the theoretical orientation that dovetails with the counselling being offered in that context.

This chapter will begin to address the complexity of working in such settings in relation to the *Code of Ethics and Practice for Supervisors of Counsellors* (BAC, 1996) and the need for supervisors and organisational managers to have a shared understanding of the supervisory process. Supervision will be clearly contextualised and the effect of organisational culture on the counselling and supervisory process will be debated. The role of the supervisor in different organisational contexts highlights dilemmas, responsibilities and tasks that a supervisor must face including that of change agent. The increasingly complex role of the supervisor in such settings will present new challenges to those who may have had very little training for this dimension of their work. Some supervisors choose to reject this type of work and remain in the relatively uncomplicated world of private practice, a world where they do not have to compromise their position when working at the interface between the organisation, the supervsiee and their manager.

The growth of workplace counselling: putting supervision in context

Workplace counselling has mushroomed, but many counsellors and supervisors have continued to work as though they were engaged in private practice. The 50 minute hour remains the norm for counsellors and tight boundaries mean that information about the organisation is shared only by the client, counsellor and supervisor and no one else. It is as if the counselling service exists in a vacuum. Yet organisations fund counselling services for their own benefit. If employees are psychologically fit then productivity is likely to be buoyant. So the counsellor and supervisor need to work with, not against the organisation. They have to tread a fine line between serving the client and the organisation. With this position come benefits, but also responsibilities. The extent of these responsibilities will depend on the organisational context and the extent to which counsellor and supervisor are prepared to communicate directly with the line managers. Counsellors and supervisors have information about the organisation that may not be available to others (Walton, 1997) and so they need to find a way of releasing that information ethically, for the benefit of all concerned.

Julia was working as a counsellor with five employees from the same department. They all talked about the bullying behaviour of their common line manager. When this issue was brought to supervision the supervisor did not become directly involved but helped the counsellors to be assertive and find the appropriate method of communicating this information to their line manager. This example illustrates the responsibility that the counsellor and supervisor have towards the organisation that employs them. It does mean though that they also acted in the interests of the clients and within the bounds of the agreed contract on confidentiality. The extent of this confidentiality is laid down in the *Code of Ethics and Practice for Supervisors of Counsellors* (BAC, 1996).

A shared understanding of supervision

Increasingly BAC has recognised the need to develop their *Code of Ethics and Practice* to include the organisational dimension of the supervisor's role. The *Code* published in 1996 recognises the complexity of this role. The purpose of the *Code* remains to 'establish and maintain standards for supervisors who are members of BAC and to inform and protect counsellors seeking supervision' (1996: 2.2.1). Nevertheless it is explicit that the supervisor must take into account the setting in which the counsellor practises. There should be clarity about lines of accountability and responsibility between 'supervisee/client, supervisor/supervisee, supervisor/client, organisation/supervisor, organisation/supervisee and organisation/client' (3.3.6). The *Code* indicates a clear distinction between line management supervision and counselling supervision. It acknowledges that best practice should be that the supervisor does not act as line manager but that where this is unavoidable then the supervisee does have access to independent counselling supervision. Yet best practice will not always be possible in a financial climate that is restrictive and where internal supervision allied to the managerial function is more economically viable than splitting the role. A dual role will not be impossible to manage ethically if contracts are clear and boundaries are adhered to. Martha found herself in this position, as line manager and supervisor of four counsellors in a large psychology department of a hospital. The dual role was not a comfortable one but she managed it ethically by monitoring her work carefully in line with the BAC's 1996 *Code of Ethics and Practice*. She was not afraid to confront her own managers when they pressed her to breach confidentiality about a counsellor's work with a client . They did not understand her supervisory role within the counselling service. Therefore, there is a need for all managers, especially if they are not counsellors, to understand the supervisory process.

The word 'supervisor' in organisations refers to someone who has hierarchical and managerial authority over others. There is a structured power differential and often an appraisal function that accompanies the role. If this is what the counsellor's line manager understands by supervision, it will lead to a great deal of misunderstanding. Supervision in the context of counselling is very different: it is a collaborative process with, in theory at least, very little power differential. The aim is to create a psychological space for the exploration of work with clients. A supportive learning environment is built where the counsellor reflects on their work and grows in ethical competence, confidence and creativity (Proctor, 1994). It is easy to see why supervision can be confusing within an organisational setting, yet a clear distinction can be made between a line manager, who is production orientated and concerned with the financial success of the organisation, and a counselling supervisor, who is process orientated and involved with how the employee works within the organisation and remains psychologically healthy both within and outside it (Cooper, 1989).

The potential for misunderstanding is there in all types of organisation; those whose function it is to deliver counselling services to the public and those in which the counselling services are provided as a part of a duty of care to employees, e.g. in industry, health, education, social and public services. However, it would seem sensible to predict that supervisors in counselling agencies will have less difficulty in helping their managers to understand the supervision process than supervisors working in other organisational settings. This will not always be the case, as managers in counselling agencies are not always counsellors and are often employed for other skills such as accountancy and administration. Increasingly there is the need for counsellors and supervisors in whatever setting to educate their managers about the supervisory process. The differences between managerial and counselling supervision need to be explored in terms of the non-hierarchical nature of the process within a managerial model. It is important in all types of organisation for line managers to understand that, unlike themselves, counselling supervisors will be looking at casework and how organisational issues impact on that. The latter will not expect to be involved with disciplinary matters or any allied managerial function. This three-way educative process with manager, supervisor and counsellor needs to take place in all organisational settings but will be easier where the culture is one which encourages growth both in the individual and the organisation.

Organisations and their cultures

All employees shape the culture of an organisation by the way they behave and the way they communicate with one another. Anecdotes, stories and jokes represent a rich vein of information about culture. It may be tempting to talk as if an organisation has one consistent culture, taking much the same form throughout, but this is seldom the case. In organisations there are often many different and competing value systems that create a mosaic of organisational realities rather than a uniform corporate culture (Morgan, 1986). Separate departments will identify with their profession or particular client group and have a different view of the world and the nature of their organisation's business (McMahon Moughtin, 1997; Morgan, 1986). This may result in a set of professional subcultures that are diametrically opposed. For example in a large health trust the counselling service has a learning and development culture whilst within the remaining part of the organisation there is a bureaucratic culture. The counselling service is the 'caring' or human face of the organisation (Carroll, 1997) which is split off, forming a subculture within the organisation (Harwood, 1993). By providing a counselling service the organisation is reflecting a *caring* image to the public but one that does not permeate the culture of the organisation as a whole (Sugarman, 1992). The incompatibility of the two cultures will lead to communication difficulties between counselling service personnel and managers in other parts of the organisation. The supportive and educative role that supervision plays for the counsellor is not valued and supervision is seen as an indulgence rather than a necessity in this context, making communication difficult and leaving the counsellor and supervisor undervalued.

In situations such as these the supervisor's role is vital in enabling the counsellor to recognise the different cultures and not collude with the client to the detriment of the organisation, or vice versa. So the fit between the counsellor's values and the organisation's priorities needs to be examined (Lee and Rosen, 1984) and the place for this is in supervision. The supervisor may have direct or indirect knowledge of the organisational culture depending on whether they are employed in-house or externally. However, it is necessary for them to have some understanding of the organisation's business. This may come from working in a similar setting as a counsellor themselves or it may come from supervising several counsellors in similar settings. Opinion differs as to whether it is necessary to have direct experience of working in the same type of organisation. Research into counselling supervision in primary care suggests that supervisors for this work should have at least some experience of the GP surgery setting and be aware of the unique problems faced by counsellors in primary care (Burton et al., 1998). When interviewed, supervisors in a variety of settings agreed that to have some knowledge of their supervisee's work setting was beneficial. It is important to consider whether the dilemmas of supervision are similar across differing settings such as education, health and industry, including service industries and counselling agencies. What is clear is that there is a need for a move away from the prevailing individualistic philosophy that dominates counselling theory (McLeod, 1994).

Understanding diverse organisational settings

The prevailing individualistic philosophy that dominates counselling theory does not translate well into an organisational context. Certainly the client is the centre of the supervisory process yet they do not exist in a vacuum but live and work within a system that has a culture of its own. These organisational settings are in education, health, social service , industry or counselling agencies, both local and national.

Firstly let us look at supervision within an educational context. As educational institutions expand and reorganise for financial efficiency, competition and insecurity become the norm. In one instance both an in-house counsellor and her external supervisor found themselves redundant when the counselling service in a small college of further education was closed for reasons of financial efficiency. It is within this environment that counsellors and supervisors have to work, dealing with the casualties of institutional defence mechanisms (Harwood, 1993). Counsellors employed within a university for example are faced with a situation where 'rationality and achievement are valued and emotional distress is swept under the carpet' (McLeod and Machin, 1998: 328). Both counsellors and supervisors, whether in-house or external to the organisation, need to decide if they are willing or able to involve themselves in the political arena in these institutions. In one educational setting a counsellor and her supervisor found themselves in a situation where the manager of the service had instigated a policy about students who missed counselling session appointments. If they missed two then they were not allowed to use the service again. The counsellor felt this was an unsuitable way of dealing with students who did not turn up for appointments and so needed to decide whether she would challenge the policy. She decided to go ahead but needed her supervisor's support for this action which, in an insecure environment, could have severe repercussions for her continued employment in that organisation.

Secondly, supervision within a health service setting can be complicated when traditionally the counsellor also has the role of nurse. This is invariably a cost-cutting exercise by the organisation and it can lead to difficulties for the supervisor who will need to help the counsellor to separate the different roles and distinguish when she is engaged in either counselling or nursing. The boundaries are complicated and this can mean that ethical codes are broken if both roles are not clear to the counsellor and her client. Inherent in circumstances such as these is a culture that undervalues and ignores the counsellor and the supervisory role (McLeod and Machin, 1998).

Thirdly let us look at counselling agencies both local and national. Supervision, usually internally, in such organisations appears to be uncomplicated. All these agencies, whether large or small, will have their own historical, cultural and economic history into which the supervision process fits. For example Sarah manages a small counselling agency for people with eating disorders. As the agency has grown her role is increasingly split between that of counsellor, supervisor and manager. This has created tension between her and the other counsellors. They resent what they see as her gradual isolation from them as she bids for more funds and balances a tight budget, making difficult staffing decisions. Sarah knows that her managerial tasks will increase as the agency grows and that although she continues to counsel and supervise she now also needs to think organisationally. She has never lost her clinical expertise, and her understanding of the necessity for adequate supervision enables the counsellors to be certain that this will remain a priority even when money is scarce. However, balancing her dual role becomes more difficult even in the learning and development culture which has grown within the organisation.

Supervisors with a dual role in an organisational context

The dual role of supervisors working in an organisational context is an interesting one. The assumption is made that the dual role will be problematic regardless of the context or the nature of the dual role itself and that the sole role relationship, certainly in counselling, 'allows both parties freedom to work towards the benefit of clients without complications from other roles' (Nixon and Carroll, 1994: 12). However, this has not been confirmed by supervisors who have talked about their dual role as supervisor/counsellor, supervisor/trainer and supervisor/line manager. In general the most problematic dual role was found to be that of supervisor/line manager. As McLeod (1994) notes, the clinician–manager relationship is a source of difficulty in many counselling and human service agencies. This is in agreement with BAC's *Code of Ethics and Practice for Supervisors of Counsellors* which says 'there is a distinction between line management supervision and counselling supervision' (BAC, 1996: 3.3.6). The dual role of supervisor/trainer was seen as an advantage by many supervisors who were interviewed for research into supervision in organisational contexts. Initially this appears to be logical because of the compatibility of the educator role with the supervisory process. But the managerial role is based on a more unequal power differential, incompatible with the counselling process (Nixon and Carroll, 1994). Another important distinction is that the manager is production orientated while the supervisor is process orientated, as noted previously (Cooper, 1989). The dual role supervisor and line manager is more likely to be found in a health or social services setting where there may be an economically driven solution to the need for professional counselling supervision. To begin with, the dual role of supervisor/trainer will be considered here.

Within voluntary counselling organisations the dual role position of supervisor/trainer is common and seen as an advantage in many ways. For some supervisors there are benefits in being able to see the results of their training when engaged in subsequent supervision sessions. There is also the notion that education and training has always been part of the supervisory process and so is a justification for the dual supervisor/trainer role. It can provide a bonding experience for supervisors and their supervisees as they interact in a different capacity during the training sessions. There may be a hidden agenda for some supervisors, who enjoy training and so are reluctant to relinquish it. In a similar context counsellor trainers have a supervisory role with their trainees, often in group supervision. This is an integral part of a tutor's role and gives them the advantage of having a greater knowledge of all aspects of the trainee's work. However, the trainee counsellor will sometimes have an external supervisor to whom they can take issues that they are uncomfortable bringing to a tutor/supervisor who also has an assessment role. On balance then this type of dual role is seen by the tutors and supervisors as being advantageous. The dual role of supervisor/line manager can be more problematic.

A supervisor within a health services setting found that when he relinquished the line manager role he could be clear about the supervisory process and focus on the client without being distracted by managerial issues. The power differential between line manager and supervisee and the line manager's priorities was the source from which the difficulties arose. BAC (1990) anticipates this when it says that 'choosing a line manager as a supervisor can lead to difficulties, since a conflict of interests may arise between the needs of the unit or institution (the priority of the line manager) and the needs of the counsellor'. However, in this case the counsellor was not able to choose their own supervisor but was allocated one by the organisation. The inability to have a free choice of supervisor within an organisation context indicates where the power will lie within that relationship.

Norma experienced this when she joined a counselling team in a large health trust setting. She was asked whether she would have any objections to her line manager also being her counselling supervisor. She did feel some disquiet about this decision but felt she could not object in her first week of office. She also knew that this decision was made for sound financial reasons and feared her hours would be cut if she insisted on external supervision. So she resolved not to bring any contentious clients to her line manager until she was sure that her interests as a counsellor were being respected. Where there is a conflict of roles a manager cannot be in 'a state of neutral concern over outcomes' (Nixon and Carroll, 1994: 14), whatever dual role position they hold. Some line managers also need to supervise the internal counsellors because of the financial implications of employing a supervisor from outside the organisation. This may be a pragmatic choice for organisations, especially service industries where budgets are small. The financial constraints on voluntary counselling organisations may also make dual roles an economic necessity. Therefore it is evident that the dual role of supervisor/trainer is more acceptable to both supervisor and supervisee than supervisor/line manager. However problematic the dual role position is, working as an external supervisor with very little or no communication with the organisation, except through their supervisee, can be just as difficult.

The supervisor who is external to the organisation

When a supervisor is external to the organisation, paid only for counselling supervision, then a wide spectrum of relationships can occur. At one end of the spectrum they may be employed directly by the organisation with a well thought out contract which stipulates clear lines of responsibility. The organisation will expect the supervisor to take some responsibility for reporting on the competence of the counsellor and oversight of the well-being of the employees using the service (Tehrani, 1996). This may seem a large responsibility and is one that some supervisors choose not to take. Alternatively the supervisor may have been chosen by their supervisee and have no contact at all with the organisation. This will come as a relief to managers who have a fear of the emotional aspects of the organisation (Gray, 1993). It is difficult to imagine any similar job where there would not be a contract of employment with responsibilities clearly stated and lines of communication outlined. Supervisors who do not have these safeguards may feel disempowered.

Marion was a supervisor who had no contact with her supervisee's organisation but felt that she needed a pay rise. Her supervisee had to ask for the increase on her behalf. She was refused. This left Marion feeling powerless. Lack of communication then may safeguard confidentiality for the client and counsellor but it will leave the supervisor with no rights *vis-à-vis* the organisation. The supervisor will also probably feel under-valued when the organisation takes their competence for granted and when they are not interested in the supervisee's progress. Malpractice by the supervisee may go undetected by the organisation if the supervisor has no avenues of communication with the management. Yet the *Code of Ethics and Practice* (BAC, 1996) says that 'supervisors are responsible for setting and maintaining the boundaries between the counselling super-vision relationship and other professional relationships e.g. training and management' (BAC, 1996: B.1.4). These boundaries need to be clear and unambiguous for the benefit of supervisee, client and organisation. Yet it may suit the supervisor to remain anonymous in relation to the organisation. There is no danger then of collusion between supervisor and manager to the detriment of the supervisor's relationship with their supervisee.

So there are obvious dangers for the supervisor, the supervisee and the organisation when the supervisor is external and there is no contact between the supervisor and the organisation for whom they are working. There are no channels of communication to alert managers to malpractice and neither is there any way of knowing whether the supervisor is competent to do their job. The position of the in-house supervisor is different but equally challenging.

The in-house counselling supervisor

A supervisor who is in-house within a counselling agency is less ambiguously placed. The organisation appoints and monitors their work and there is a feedback system that allows them to have communication with the management. The management however may not always understand the nature of the work of the agency. They may be accountants, solicitors, etc. who have agreed to give their time and skills to help the agency function effectively as a business but they will not necessarily understand the counselling process. Financial constraints will drive their work and counselling supervision may appear to be a luxury that the agency cannot afford. But if the agency is small and has grown, possibly from self-help beginnings, then the manager is more likely to be a counsellor and supervisor. This will aid communication between workers but it can also cause frustration for a manager who will have to juggle both agency and worker needs, which may often conflict. In the two types of agency, large and small, an in-house supervisor will have different dilemmas. In the larger, national counselling agencies, with the internal channels of communication already established, the supervisor will be in a strong position. They will have regular meetings with the management team, who will value their professional expertise. There may be heated discussion about the financial constraints needed to balance the books when the priorities of managers and counsellors differ. Technically, the supervisors are in a strong position to advise managers, who will learn about ethical codes and the need for professionalism. They will be heard.

Similarly in smaller counselling agencies where the manager also has a dual or triple role as counsellor, supervisor and manager, the channels of communication will be open even if the manager's position is still in its formative stages as the organisation develops. Therefore an in-house supervisor is in a strong position to influence policy and to play a more active role in the organisation from within. Whether in-house or external, part of the role of the supervisor is to educate and act as an agent of change for the organisation.

The supervisor as an agent of change within the organisation

Fulfilling a role as an agent of change in an organisation is not one that all counsellors and supervisors are willing to undertake (Copeland, 1998). For some it will be outside their remit and others will not have the necessary contextual experience to be effective. Sugarman maintains that 'the skill requirements for a work based counsellor are a combination of those of the personal and political change agent' (1992: 28) and if this is so the supervisor will need to be similarly equipped. These skills and experience, often gained in fields outside counselling, are an ideal basis for influencing organisational policy. A supervisor working for a large counselling agency was surprised to find that his line manager did not fully grasp what counselling supervision was all about. He wrote a paper on the subject and found it was useful in educating his manager and indeed the whole of the organisation. Counsellors and supervisors also have information about the organisation which may not be available to others (Walton, 1997). Harwood (1993: 54) says about counsellors in educational institutions that 'they are usually in touch with some of the effects of institutional practice, which otherwise remain hidden from the full scrutiny of management'.

So both counsellor and supervisor need to find ways of releasing that information, within the boundaries of agreed confidentiality, for the benefit of the organisation. For example a group of counsellors being supervised together will hold information about the shadow side of their organisation's culture, the shadow side that deals with 'the covert, the undiscussed, the undiscussable and the unmentionable' (Egan, 1994: 4). This shadow side activity can affect productivity and the quality of working life and yet be outside the reach of ordinary managerial interventions unless the activity is brought to the manager's notice. A group of counsellors, with the support and encouragement of their supervisor, could be in a position to release such information gathered in the course of their counselling sessions. They could talk about issues and not individual cases, so keeping client confidentiality whilst working for the benefit of the organisation as an agent of change.

Conclusion

Supervision in organisational contexts is a complex issue. Supervisors who undertake this work face ethical and professional dilemmas that arise from working at the interface between the client, counsellor and the organisation. They have an important role in helping the organisation to understand the counselling and supervisory process and how this impacts on the organisation. However, they will not be effective if they continue to work as though they were supervising in private practice, taking no account of the organisation as a changing system with its own distinctive set of cultures. What is needed is a continual dialogue with the counsellor and their line manager to negotiate ethical boundaries. This involves the counsellor and supervisor working in partnership to be proactive rather than reactive. *The Code of Ethics and Practice for Supervisors of Counsellors* (BAC, 1996) provides guidelines for ethical practice but they need to be interpreted according to the context. The nature of the business, the culture, management style and interlocking systems in each organisation are different but it will be useful for all supervisors working in or for organisations to:

- negotiate a contract that outlines the roles and responsibilities of all parties including the counsellor's line manager;
- have an agreed line of communication, plus payment for any work outside the supervisory sessions, including meetings with the counsellor's line manager to discuss any issues of conflict including salary changes;
- have an understanding of the organisation's culture and how it affects the counselling service;
- have an understanding of organisational change in order to help the counsellor work with, not against that change.

These guidelines are not exhaustive but will form the beginning of a working relationship between the counsellor, supervisor and organisation. In a time of rapid change in the nature of counselling supervision there is a need to be aware of the organisational context in which it takes place and the restraints that such contexts put on the counselling and supervisory process. These restraints will cause ethical and professional dilemmas for all parties concerned and may lead to changes in the *Code of Ethics and Practice for Supervisors of Counsellors* (BAC, 1996) advocated by King and Wheeler (1998). Changes in such a code may be needed, but more realistically there is a need for supervisors to be trained in supervising in diverse organisational settings, a training that helps prospective supervisors to think strategically rather than individualistically. This is a real shift away from current practice but one which must take place if supervision is to survive and be meaningful in the twenty-first century.

References

British Association for Counselling (1990) *Information sheet, 8*. Rugby: BAC.
British Association for Counselling (1996) *Code of Ethics and Practice for Supervisors of Counsellors*. Rugby: BAC.
Burton, M., Henderson, P. and Curtis-Jenkins, G. (1998) 'Primary care counsellors' experience of supervision', *Counselling*, 9 (2): 122–130.
Carroll, M. (1988) 'Counselling supervision: the British context', *Counselling Psychology Quarterly*, 1 (4): 387–396.
Carroll, C. (1997) 'Building bridges: a study of employee counsellors in the private

sector', in M. Carroll and M. Walton (eds), *Handbook of Counselling in Organisations*. London: Sage.

Cooper, M.G. (1989) 'Clinical supervision in the EAP', *Employee Assistance Quarterley*, 4 (3): 65–77.

Copeland, S. (1998) 'Counselling supervision in organisational contexts: new challenges and perspectives', *British Journal of Guidance and Counselling*, 26, (3): 377–386.

Egan, G. (1994) *Working the Shadow Side*. San Francisco, CA: Jossey-Bass.

Gray, H. (1993) 'Unscrambling the B-picture: counselling, consultancy and strategic management', *British Journal of Guidance and Counselling*, 21 (2): 156–160.

Harwood, D. (1993) 'Organisational consultancy, institutional dynamics and the role of the student counsellor', *British Journal of Guidance and Counselling*, 21 (1): 53–63.

Hughes, L. and Pengelly, P. (1997) *Staff Supervision in a Turbulent Environment: Managing Process and Task in Front Line Services*. London: Jessica Kingsley.

King, D. and Wheeler, S. (1998) 'Counselling supervision: to regulate or not to regulate?', *Counselling*, 9 (4): 306–310.

Lee, S.S. and Rosen, E.A. (1984) 'Employee counselling services: ethical dilemmas', *The Personal Guidance Journal*, January: 276–280.

Mander, G. (1998) 'Supervising short term psychodynamic work', *Counselling*, 9 (4): 301–305.

McLeod, J. (1994) 'Issues in the organisation of counselling : learning from the NMGC', *British Journal of Guidance and Counselling*, 22 (2): 163–174.

McLeod, J. and Machin, L. (1998) 'The context of counselling: a neglected dimension of training, research and practice', *British Journal of Guidance and Counselling*, 26 (3): 325–336.

McMahon Moughtin, M. (1997) *Focused Therapy for Organisations and Individuals*. London: Minerva Press.

Morgan, G. (1986) *Images of Organisations*. Newbury Park, CA: Sage.

Nixon, J. and Carroll, M. (1994) 'Can a line manger also be a counsellor?', *Employee Counselling Today*, 6 (1): 10–15.

Proctor, B. (1994) 'Supervision – competence, confidence, accountability', *British Journal of Guidance and Counselling*, 22 (3): 309–319.

Sugarman, L. (1992) 'Ethical issues in counselling at work', *Employee Counselling Today*, (4) 4: 23–30.

Tehrani, N. (1996) 'Counselling in the Post Office: facing up to the legal and ethical dilemmas', *British Journal of Guidance and Counselling*, 24 (2): 265–275.

Walton, M. (1997) 'Counselling as a form of organisational change', in M. Carroll and M. Walton (eds), *Handbook of Counselling in Organisations*. London: Sage. pp. 129–145.

11

A SUPERVISORY REVOLUTION? THE IMPACT OF NEW TECHNOLOGY

Stephen Goss

The spread of new technology, particularly computing technology, in very many areas of our lives has been widely commented on. While new technologies have been eagerly embraced in some quarters they have also been viewed with great caution elsewhere. It has even been noted that many people have a certain degree of negative reaction to that technology in the form of 'technostress' (Weil and Rosen, 1997) or 'technophobia' (Brosnan, 1998) which has been found to improve only when they become sufficiently familiar with it to begin to feel at ease once more (Mueller, 1997).

It is interesting to note that all changes in communication technology seem to be accompanied by similarly contradictory reactions. Despite Church suppression of the free development of mass printing in the mid-fifteenth century (McLuhan, 1962) there was also a papal edict describing print as 'a divinely inspired invention' (cited in Rosenthal, 1998). The then revolutionary technology was exploited by the same people who were anxiously trying to prevent what seemed to them to be its dangerously disorganised proliferation (Chartier, 1994; Eisenstein, 1983; Febvre and Martin, 1976). Another communications revolution came with the intro-duction of the telegraph in the 1790s and was greeted with an equally mixed response, so perhaps it should be no surprise that we find that the same is true of the internet today (Johnson, 1998).

Unlike the application of new technology in the medical field, where tele-medicine as a means of consultation with expert practitioners has been recognised for some time, supervision of counselling via any form of new technology is less frequently considered. It is only in quite recent years that articles have begun to appear considering the use of new technology in any aspect of the therapeutic milieu (e.g. Lago, 1996). However, their number seems to increase at about the same rate as the controversy surrounding their use (Adams, 1998; American Psychological Association, 1998; Bloom 1997, 1998; Goss et al., 1999; Grohol, 1997; Johnson, 1998; Kling,

1996; Marino, 1996; Marks et al., 1998; Morrissey, 1997; Sanders and Rosenfield, 1998) which is itself fuelled by the bewildering array of options, the sometimes breathtaking pace of change and the relative dearth of good quality research.

Some authors urge a cautious approach (e.g. Lee, 1998; Robson and Robson, 1998). Even to issue guidance on the use of computers in counselling (National Board for Certified Counselors, 1997) has courted the loud disapprobation of some sections of the profession on the ground that doing so appears to dignify such activities with a premature and, as yet, unjustified impression of acceptability (Morrissey, 1997). Other authors are willing, even enthusiastic, to embrace the new possibilities and get on with making the most of them as rapidly as possible without letting terminology get in the way (Ainsworth, 1997).

Some of the possible uses of new technology in supervising counselling and psychotherapy discussed in this chapter are already familiar to a number of practitioners while others are yet to be explored. It seems futile to attempt to ascertain their outright effectiveness at this early stage in their development and the discussion will, for the most part, be restricted to describing the options, outlining some of their uses and the potential pitfalls known at this point. Neither does this chapter attempt to cover all the issues exhaustively. To do so would require an entire rather lengthy book so the following discussion will be restricted to an exploration of the issues that are most pertinent or that act as examples drawn from the wider range of possibilities.

E-mail: two different kinds

This section will discuss two kinds of electronic mail, or e-mail. The first and most widely known is that type of exchange which relies on messages written on a computer and sent to a specified electronic address either via the internet or a local network of computers (known as an *intranet*). Just like ordinary post, these messages can be read and responded to at any time. Messages are generally delivered within a matter of minutes or even seconds, although there is no guarantee as to when the recipient will switch on their machine in order to read and respond to what has been sent.

The second form of e-mail is the instant type which is given various names by different internet service providers and software manufacturers. What all the systems have in common is that when two (or more) people are at their machines simultaneously messages are exchanged so fast that speed of communication is limited primarily by typing ability.

At first glance, the slower, more basic form of e-mail seems to be little more than the electronic equivalent of a letter sent through the post in the normal way and it can indeed be considered analogous for some of the issues involved. However, there are some important differences, largely of convention, in their use and the effects of communicating, however rapidly, via a machine (Robson and Robson, 1998). The written style in either kind of e-mail is frequently extremely informal, for example. The ease with which they can be sent and received seems to encourage rapid composing and little of the usual formal and stylistic considerations expected in most forms of writing. Even spelling, grammar and basic punctuation are frequently left unchecked. This may lead to a greater freedom and immediacy of expression, making e-mail communication much closer to everyday conversations than that which can be achieved through letters in what has been termed a 'secondary orality' to emphasise its verbal qualities (Ong, 1982). The more rapid version of e-mail typically consists of exchanges of very short phrases, single words or even non-verbal prompts in a manner very close indeed to the tone and content of everyday speech. The obvious exception is that everything is 'said' via the computer keyboard and screen, but it is telling that terminology appropriate to speech, rather than writing, is commonplace (Brice, 1998).

It is sometimes asserted that e-mail is, or may prove to be, inadequate for building the kind of relationships required for therapy or counselling to take place (Robson and Robson, 1998) and the same may be true of counselling supervision. The loss of visual and even audible cues, the lack of immediacy in responding and the potentially dehumanising effects of replacing a face with a screen have all been used to suggest that a sufficiently reliable, trustworthy and deep relationship simply cannot be established. Certainly, however imitative of speech the style may become, there is an inevitable shift from verbal to literary skills. How, for example, could supervisor and supervisee relate at a deeply empathic level? How can the full subtlety of emotional processes be expressed? How would a supervisor gain any accurate sense of how a counsellor feels towards their client if they are only reporting, or are only aware of, part of the therapeutic relationship?

However, balancing these legitimate questions is the suggestion that deep, lasting and highly emotionally charged relationships can be and are built through e-mail correspondence. Indeed, deep relationships sustained through exchanges of letters are a literary form with centuries of tradition. Furthermore, letters are a recognised, if infrequently used, medium for carrying out counselling itself. That too has a long history, dating back at least to Freud, while today, CRUSE Bereavement Care issues guidelines on counselling by letter (Wallbank, 1994) and e-mail counselling services are already up and running and recognised in the current literature (e.g. Murphy and Mitchell, 1998).

The rapid growth in the use of e-mail has led to something of a rediscovery of the possibilities of written exchanges. Even without resorting to 'emoticons'[1] the depth of feeling that can be both expressed and experienced and the felt quality of relationship can be impressive. Consider the following anonymised extracts from e-mails, all of which are taken from exchanges with a counselling supervisor carefully exploring the possibilities of e-mail communication for the purposes of supervision.[2]

You may find this hard to believe but you are one of the very few who really is privy to what goes on in my thoughts, (scary huh?)Quite why we should have developed this raport[3] defies explanation.

It must be unusual to find this sort of connection. I certainly have never experienced anything that could even come close (now I am really taking risks!) . . . I really feel that this relationship is certainly producing the most open, warm, truthful, deep understanding . . . that I have been allowed into in my lifetime.

You wonder how our exchanges would have been different had we met first face to face, well I think that with all visual and sensory aids out of the way this is much more open and I know that in the past I never would have conversed with a man on this level without being affected by body language, voice, tone, eye contact, smell and so on, in this way I feel complete abandonment in my self expression. So in some ways you have got to the more important part, the part which in reality you would probably have got to know last of all!

You know in some ways I feel more secure about our relationship than those around me in my everyday existence. That could be because I have time to carefully consider (well most of the time lol) my replies which not always being a confident person I find reassuring. Also I know that we trust each other implicitly . . . and I can totally be myself without the masculine/feminine thing getting in the way.

If these feelings can be expressed, understood and reflected upon through e-mail, it must be worth at least giving serious consideration to the question of whether the supervisory relationship could be sufficiently strong to constitute a near equivalent to ordinary face to face work, at least when carried out under the right conditions. Certainly, these examples suggest that e-mail is capable of freeing up certain constraints, allowing supervisees to be more open in some ways than they might expect to be in a face to face encounter.

While there may be clear advantages to this, it must be acknowledged that potential problems in trying to create such relationships, and the sufficiently reliable conditions needed to sustain them, abound. Knowledge of even the most simple identifying information is denied by the use of e-mail, for example. The lack of visual information alone means that there is great scope for e-mail to facilitate the growth of fantasy relationships with largely fantasy-based perceptions of the people involved. The scope for unacknowledged and untestable transference, projection and parallel processes is vast and unpredictable.

It would also seem that the stripping down of most normal affective information in such communication is capable of provoking very strong, perhaps even exaggerated, affective responses. It may be that we have a tendency to compensate for not being able to see our correspondent by feeling our own responses to what they 'say' all the more strongly.

'Flaming', as such incendiary events are sometimes known when begun deliberately, is all too easy to precipitate accidentally when comments, especially if intended humorously, are bereft of the context which would, in everyday speech, have made their content clearly understood by both parties.

The issue about the degree to which written communications are trustworthy, whatever medium is used, is even harder to deal with. E-mail counselling and supervision must both struggle with issues of whether the participants are who they say they are. There have been notorious examples of people using e-mail in less than entirely transparent ways. There are even well documented cases in which a mental health professional, or perhaps someone posing as one, took on a highly convincing false persona and successfully encouraged people to trust them (e.g. Van Gelder, 1996), although no complaints have yet come to the attention of the relevant professional and regulatory bodies of these pretences being used in a professionally abusive manner, according to any of the leading professional bodies in either Europe or the USA.

While in direct supervision of counselling the degree to which a supervisee reveals the true nature of themselves or their work can still remain problematic and, at the very least, there are real difficulties in fully representing the experience of working with a particular client (Mearns, 1995) there is the opportunity for supervisors to come to a judgement about the honesty, openness and the degree of insight and awareness of the person in front of them. This may be no simple matter of biographical fact checking but concerns the detail of effective and ethical practice which a supervisee might, naturally, prefer not to reveal in full. Supervisors must then rely on the myriad of subtle changes in communication, discrepancies in tone of voice, demeanour and so forth in the constant flow and flux of a spoken session.

E-mail allows both participants the opportunity to review their words before sending them. While the ease of sending an e-mail encourages its typical informality, and all too easily a distinct lack of proper consideration, if one is being careful there is an absolute ability to take back one's words before the other person is aware that anything has been expressed. Empathy with an e-mail correspondent is possible, as demonstrated above, but it seems very likely that there must be a greater chance for supervisees to hide anything that might betray substandard aspects of their counselling work or anything they might prefer to keep hidden. The 'ethical watchdog' role of supervision is therefore strictly limited if this form of e-mail is relied upon exclusively.

However, positive functions have been ascribed to e-mail specifically because of the relative anonymity it offers. The ease with which the whole and unexpurgated truth can be hidden, especially one's identity, affects all exclusively electronically mediated relationships. Turkle (1995) has suggested that it offers the opportunity to express aspects of our lives that are too risky to expose elsewhere. If the essential 'policing role' of supervision is severely curtailed, the opportunities for safely exploring issues that might not otherwise see the light of day may be dramatically increased.

It is worth noting that, at least in the British Association for Counselling (BAC) scheme of things, 'the primary responsibility of the supervisor is to the counsellor rather than to the employer' (Mearns, 1997: 83). The supervision experience most sought by counsellors is one of support in which 'the counsellor would feel able to explore her areas of greatest difficulty in the knowledge that the purpose of the work is to assist her in her development rather than to oversee her work and judge her competence' (1997: 84) especially for those whose work relies on a person-centred framework (Dryden and Thorne, 1991; Mearns, 1995).

With this in mind the advantages of having the safety in which to expose one's darkest professional secrets or most embarrassing errors and *faux pas* might be seen as offering a different, and perhaps more productive, mechanism for protecting clients. Given the anecdotal evidence that 'people are often more open with their real feelings when they don't seem as directly accountable for them' (Klug, 1998: 3) a certain amount of credence can be given to the suggestion that we might begin to generalize to the supervision arena and explore whether counsellors actually gain support for more areas of their work when detailed discussion can remain entirely anonymous in this way. There are already a few documented cases demonstrating that some individuals do seem enabled to express intimate, personal and highly sensitive details via e-mail even when unable even to broach the subjects with the same person face to face (e.g. Ridden, 1998). These are more and more frequently being added to by anecdotal evidence such as that quoted above.

There is also the general question of the effectiveness of e-mail-based relationships in achieving personally meaningful goals but as yet there appears to be no more than anecdotal evidence regarding this. Combined with the potential for miscommunication, or even the misrepresentation in Van Gelder's (1996) account of a male therapist successfully posing as female, it is certainly important that we install adequate safeguards, many of which are not required in other forms of communication.

The first of these must certainly be that the e-mail exchanges should not be the only form of supervision used by the supervisee because of the inherent limitations of the medium. A second might be that at least one face to face meeting should be arranged between the prospective supervisor and supervisee or, better, a series of meetings until sufficient relationship has been established for some sessions to be undertaken by e-mail. Clearly, this has significant implications for supervision carried out over great distances. However, if inclusion of face to face meetings was shown to be a fundamental mechanism for quality control or for ensuring the effectiveness of the supervision, some of the possibilities for international supervision work would necessarily be severely curtailed.

It is significant that the BAC Individual Counsellor Accreditation Management Group (ICAMG) takes the view that telephone counselling can be accepted as valid experience for accreditation purposes only if it forms part of the work carried out with a particular client; the bulk of the work must be in a face to face setting (ICAMG, 1997). Although it has never been tested, the logic behind this requirement (loss of verbal communication, the indirect and distant nature of the communication, etc.) might be thought to operate in just the same way for any other electronically mediated form of communication, including e-mail. The same principle might also apply to the adequate supervision required for the ethical practice of counselling (BAC, 1998). This highly qualified and partial acceptance of any means of electronic communication gives a good indication of its current status in the counselling profession as a whole and it may be that such caution will remain prudent for some time to come, while further research is carried out.

At the very least, good practice might require some additional tasks of both supervisee and supervisor for the sake of verifying each other's identities through registration with, or membership of, the relevant professional bodies local to them. Sharing details of past and present education and employment would also make the identity of both parties more transparent and reliable despite such matters rarely, if ever, being enquired into prior to face to face supervision work.

For supervisors there are also a great many practical issues to consider before embarking on a career as an e-mail supervisor. The length of time spent reading and responding to a single e-mail message from a supervisee will depend entirely on its length and contents. It is not analogous to the consulting room hour in which the time boundaries can easily be kept in mind by both participants. It may not be possible to respond to every important issue raised in a lengthy e-mail from a supervisee. A supervisor contracting to work with a supervisee in this way will also have to consider the issues of confidentiality considered further below, responsibility for maintaining secure records and ownership of the written record of supervision that is produced.

Video links

The technology required to have live video links between remote sites is becoming more and more widespread. Although at the time of writing the required hard- and software are considered quite high grade, the history of this sector has been one of constant technological advances accompanied by rapidly reducing prices and consequently greater availability of the equipment no longer quite at the cutting edge. Video telephones will also become more and more common over the next few years and it is not inconceivable that video links will eventually become as common as the telephone is today.

Napier University in Edinburgh and the University of the Highlands and Islands in northern Scotland are already offering experimental video-counselling services to students too far from the main facilities to make any face to face consultations feasible. Napier University has been carrying out research into the possible uses of video consultations for supervision of counselling with some success, albeit qualified as noted below.

There are numerous advantages of this kind of technology over any of the written media considered above. Location and visual appearance are much more certain while the flexibility of consulting colleagues with equal ease over any distance is retained. Few people now question the use of the telephone as a means of communication and video consultation may eventually be seen as sitting part way between that and face to face work.

However, video technology is still rather far from a perfect substitute for the consulting room and not all the problems and limitations associated with other forms of computer-mediated communication are removed. Firstly, there is the question of the quality of connection that can be achieved. Products currently on the market, which may be perfectly adequate for other tasks, vary in quality from very good indeed (near broadcast television quality pictures and sound) through to being unacceptable for complex emotional communication. Pictures may be very small, fuzzy or highly pixellated; they may blur, especially if either person makes large or rapid movements, and it can be very difficult to read with certainty the expression on the other person's face.

A further common technical difficulty at present is a time delay between the image and sound being sent and being received, sometimes of several seconds. This has a quite profound effect on the pace and pattern of a conversation. The usual non-specific encouragers (Ivey, 1998) like 'uh-huh', 'mn-hmmn' and so on are nearly impossible to use because although *uttered* at the point where they form part of the natural flow and turn-taking of conversation, they may be heard at the other end as an inappropriate interruption to the following phrase. To interrupt or seek clarification is also difficult for the same reason and participants may find themselves spending much more time than would otherwise be the case simply waiting for a very clear pause before speaking unless some specific response is requested of them. The result can often be that the conversation becomes somewhat slow, stilted and over-emphatic. The casual and incidental components of speech tend to be minimized and the deliberate turn-taking leads to a more declamatory style comprising whole statements separated by somewhat unnatural pauses from whole, still largely uninterrupted, responses.

All of these things can be more or less overcome or ignored when video links are used for most purposes in, say, business or management, but in counselling and counselling supervision the effect can be profound. There are enough barriers to easily flowing communication and the development of close working alliances for us to want to avoid additional ones where at all possible.

Even when all these limitations are, ultimately, resolved by improvements in the technology some other problems remain. The most common concerns relate to the introduction of the screen as both barrier and frame.

The participants are communicating as if through a partially opaque window and it is easy to pay insufficient attention to how one appears to the other person, and whether that is distracting or misleading, as one's attention is, naturally, drawn to the picture of the other person, not of oneself.

Having, and maintaining, an acceptable camera position is an additional burden and ensuring that the detail of one's face is visible while also allowing the screen image to include hand gestures can be difficult. Typically these things can be adjusted at either end but it is easy for both parties to have their main attention elsewhere. Given the greater level of disruption caused by, say, shifting in one's chair, which may necessitate changing the camera angle and then checking with the other person that one is still clearly visible, it is easy to see how both supervisor and supervisee may feel that the technology is coming between them in metaphorical as well as literal terms.

It is also not at all unheard of for people engaged in any kind of video conferencing to begin to lose the awareness of being in company as time goes by, and to behave more as if they are alone in a room, as they literally are, and unobserved, which they are not. The normal social graces need to be maintained somewhat more deliberately than usual in order to avoid the distraction of seeing someone grimacing a private response, looking away at something out of sight or even absentmindedly picking their nose.

Nonetheless, video links do seem to offer a real possibility of engaging in deep emotional relationships, at least to the extent required for supervision of counselling to be carried out. They also offer the possibility of recording the sessions either for training purposes or as an aid to reviewing their content for the participants themselves. If numerous caveats apply, such as ensuring that the technology is of adequate quality, that both parties are very familiar and comfortable with the whole process and how to handle it, they merely limit the occasions for which it is appropriate rather than ruling it out altogether.

Independent software and 'expert' systems

An increasing range of software tools are becoming available, many of them over the internet, that can be used either in direct therapeutic work with clients or to support counsellors. These have been reviewed elsewhere (e.g. Baldry, 1998; Grohol, 1997; Kelley-Milburn and Milburn, 1995; Marks et al., 1998) and space precludes a summary of the products currently available. Such programmes have increased in their sophistication rapidly over recent years. Although few yet exist that aim to act in anything that could be called a supervisory role for counsellors, there are those that seek to provide information to clients and clinicians alike in just the same way that an expert on the topic would do.

Some can provide valuable assistance to counsellors by offering a relatively quick and easy way in which to access information on particular topics and can even make recommendations regarding interventions to use in specific circumstances. The main problem is one of quality control, as discussed below.

Advertising, information and promotional possibilities

A further commonly commented upon aspect of information technology has been the use of web sites as ways of promoting services of all kinds. In some respects there are few differences between this form of advertising and any other and it may well be that no additional burdens apply for the electronic marketing of, say, routine face to face work while an additional way in which such things can be located is offered.

However, readers have complained for at least the past five centuries that there are just too many books out there to be helpful (Rosenthal, 1998) and there are certainly significant problems with identifying excellent, good or poor information on the internet. With no effective safeguards in place it can be difficult in the extreme to identify the arrogant, ignorant or unscrupulous offering supervision of dubious quality, or which they are ill equipped to give. Furthermore the task of identifying quality lies entirely with the consumer. There is undoubtedly a role for professional bodies in counselling and psychotherapy alike to take a strong and positive lead in laying down criteria by which services can be judged.

Ethical issues

Confidentiality is undoubtedly the most problematic ethical issue that any provider of information technology services handling sensitive information must consider. It is widely accepted, although not always acknowledged by the computer industry, that virtually any security system can be broken given a sufficiently skilled, experienced and determined 'hacker'. However, there is little public concern about the safety of exchanging information through the ordinary postal system or by telephone, and ordinary e-mail might be considered to be approximately as safe with only a few further considerations.

The first is that any company offering access to the internet is very likely to store all messages that pass through its system and may have legitimate reasons for viewing their contents. Secondly, it is easy for an e-mail address to be very slightly mistyped, with the result that the e-mail is delivered to an entirely different person and location. It is also much easier for any electronically held information to be duplicated and re-sent, so that any leaks of sensitive information could, in theory, be much more serious than any mislaid paper documentation or overheard verbal conversation. Indeed, it was in recognition of this that the Data Protection Act (Parliament, 1984) controlled the storage and dissemination of most electronic information relating to individuals in the UK.

With reasonable care it is quite possible to put in place at least some protections against the worst potential disasters. Once aware of the dangers each side can use encryption systems that will render the contents of an e-mail incomprehensible to anyone else without determined effort on their part. Further safety can be added with the use of more than one level of encryption, but that is often considered unnecessary. Care should be taken when entering e-mail addresses but most systems have automatic return addressing for replies to any message received. It is already evident that discussion of cases should not risk identifying the client to the supervisor so far as possible. If the same level of care is taken as in the provision of other forms of written case study material the chances of clients being directly harmed by the very rare errors in message delivery or 'hacking in' are slight. Rather harder to guarantee for either party in an e-mail exchange is the confidentiality of the setting in which it will be read. Not everyone has access to their e-mail in such a way that the screen cannot be seen by others but without such conditions any sensitive exchanges should certainly not be begun.

The legislation relating to the country in which information is held, including stored e-mails, must always be adhered to, of course. If the detail of the Data Protection Act is followed precisely, it may be that clients should give their fully informed consent before they are discussed in any written electronic medium.

A further ethical consideration is that although one of the great advantages of supervision via remote links of any kind is access to professionals in different parts of the world, there are serious potential problems raised by the provision of services across international boundaries. This makes the enforcement of ethical regulations much more complex and it is still uncertain which countries have legal jurisdiction. Either party may have cause to complain about the wrongdoings of the other and supervisors may even have legal and ethical concerns about a supervisee whose practice is governed by laws and regulatory bodies of a completely different nature making it very difficult for them to take effective action.

Conclusions

The widened access offered by most forms of electronic communication brings a great many problems and opportunities. The great advance in equality of access to expert supervision is significant. Not only can otherwise insurmountable geographical barriers be covered, but many people with certain disabilities can be enabled to work in a more equal way. An example is the use of video links for the deaf or hearing-impaired for whom sign language may be the preferred form of communication.

Furthermore, anyone who can operate a computer (whether by keyboard, voice commands or any other means) may be rendered indistinguishable from anyone else in many electronic encounters and thus can be judged on their words, with greatly reduced possibilities for prejudicial assumptions to be made about them.

Balancing such improvements to equality of access, it must also be remembered that a *reliance* on technology would necessarily disenfranchise all those without access to it whether for financial or any other reasons. Those to whom it is unfamiliar face a steep learning curve before tech-nostress and technophobia are overcome and it has been suggested that women may have a lesser predisposition towards use of technological aids (Brosnan, 1998). If this is the case it could, of course, be interpreted as a way of countering the commonplace finding that men are *under*-represented in counselling whether as counsellors or as clients (e.g. Bennet, 1995).

However, there are other advantages offered by the immediacy of access for all those who can make use of technologically mediated communication. Counsellors could, for example, e-mail their supervisor right after a difficult session when all the details are fresh in their mind with the emotional content never having to be recalled as in face to face supervision work. Future developments are likely to enhance the ease with which we can access technology even further by removing reliance on the currently familiar keyboard with increased use of voice commands or controls that are very nearly as simple as those of ordinary televisions.

Certainly, however, it is only sensible for anyone undertaking work with any new technology to ensure that all those involved are thoroughly familiar with the systems that are to be used and that all necessary consents are properly obtained.

How worried should we be about the advent of new technology in counselling supervision? A parallel might be drawn with printing once again. As Eisenstein (1983) has argued, the introduction of the new medium of communication was associated with many developments from the Renaissance, the scientific revolution, specific nationalisms and individualism. The technology itself is much less likely actually to cause such changes. Its role is much more likely to be no more than a mediating one. The forces for new content must be present already for the method by which they are communicated to have an impact. What we are faced with now is a range of more or less problematic opportunities from which we have the task of choosing those best fitted to our needs.

The Dearing Report (Dearing, 1997) has suggested that all students in higher education will, or should, expect to have their own laptop computers by 2005. If everyday use of technology will permeate the lives of even that relatively poorly funded section of society there seems little option but to address the issues presented by that looming prospect today. Despite any hesitations we may have, the counselling profession will be obliged to make some responses to developments in electronically mediated communication. It is certain that those responses will be all the better for being fully informed and based on direct examination of the possibilities new technologies offer us and full experimental exploration of their uses, their dangers and the lessons we will need to learn before they can be fully and most appropriately applied (Goss et al., 1999). Many areas warrant further exploration and at this relatively early stage in the development of technological applications in counselling and supervision much work clearly remains to be done.

Furthermore, it will not be very long before advances in technology and its applications render the preceding discussion, and any like it, more or less dated. Indeed, no description of the state of the art in these matters is likely to be able to claim to be definitive, let alone final. However, there has been sufficient progress in the uses of new technology in counselling, psychotherapy and in the supervision of them for the next step to be the development of a coherent strategic response from the counselling profession. Perhaps, most of all, that should be led by those who provide supervision. It is becoming essential that we are at least conversant with the opportunities and pitfalls presented to us.

Notes

1   These are semi-pictorial symbols for specific emotions, reactions or facial expressions. The best known is the simple 'smiley face' which comprises a colon, hyphen and close bracket thus :-). Other examples include ;-) for a wink, ?-o for confusion or 8-o for wide eyed amazement. Acronyms are also commonplace including LOL meaning 'Laughing Out Loud' or, for greater emphasis, ROFL for 'Rolling On Floor Laughing' among many others.

2   The setting was deliberately selected as being as closely analogous to actual supervision as possible while minimising any potential for harm from an exclusive reliance on this untested method (in much the same way as analogues for counselling situations are commonly used in counselling training and research).

3   These extracts also exemplify the relaxed attitude to spelling, punctuation and style typical of e-mail: many, perhaps most, users of e-mail become increasingly unlikely to correct errors such as this spelling of 'rapport' as they become sufficiently at ease to reduce their need for 'performance management' (McLeod, 2000).

References

Adams, S.C. (1998) 'Concerns about counselling online' (on-line) Available: http://www.counseling.org/ctonline/sr598/letter1_698.htm

Ainsworth, M. (1997) 'Terminology . . . is this therapy?' (on-line) Available: http://www.metanoia.org/imhs/isittx.htm

American Psychological Association (1998) 'Ethics committee issues statement on services by telephone, teleconferencing and internet', *American Psychological Association Monitor*, 29 (1): 38.

BAC (1998) *Code of Ethics and Practice for Counsellors*. Rugby: British Association for Counselling.

Baldry, S. (1998) 'Applications of information technology in counselling and psychotherapy'. M.Sc. thesis, Napier University, Edinburgh.

Bennet, M. (1995) 'Why don't men come to counselling? Some speculative theories', *Counselling: Journal of the British Association for Counselling*, 6 (4): 310–313.

Bloom, J.W. (1997) 'N.B.C.C. webcounseling standards', *Counselling Today Online*, Available: http://www.counseling.org/ctonline/sr598/nbcc_standards.htm

Bloom, J.W. (1998) 'The ethical practice of webcounseling', *British Journal of Guidance and Counselling*, 26 (1): 53–59.

Brice, A. (1998) 'A case study of therapeutic support using e-mail'. Unpublished paper prepared for the Association for University and College Counselling Working Group on e-mail, Sheffield.

Brosnan, M. (1998) *Technophobia: The Psychological Impact of Information Technology*. London: Routledge.

Chartier, R. (1994) *The Order of Books*. Cambridge: Polity Press.

Dearing, R. (1997) *The Dearing Report: Report of the National Committee of Inquiry into Higher Education. Report with Evidence. The Lord Phillips of Ellesmere (Chairman) Session 1997/98*. Norwich: HMSO.

Dryden, W. and Thorne, B. (eds.) (1991) *Training and Supervision for Counselling in Action*. London: Sage.

Eisenstein, E. (1983) *The Printing Revolution in Early Modern Europe*. Cambridge: Cambridge University Press.

Febvre, L. and Martin, H.-J. (1976) *The Coming of the Book: The Impact of Printing 1450–1800*, ed. D. Gerard, English edition London: NLB. Originally published (1958) *L'Apparition du livre*. Paris: Albin Michel.

Goss, S.P., Robson, D., Pelling, N.J. and Renard, D.E. (1999) 'The challenge of the Internet,' *Counselling: Journal of the British Association for Counselling*, 9 (1): 37–43.

Grohol, J.M. (1997) *The Insider's Guide to Mental Health Resources Online*. New York: Guilford.

ICAMG (1997) Extract of minutes from meeting of 5 December, item 97/64, by kind permission of Co-Chair of Individual Counsellor Accreditation Management Group.

Ivey, A.E. (1998) *Intentional Interviewing and Counseling: Facilitating Client Development*, 2nd edn. Pacific Grove, CA: Brooks/Cole.

Johnson, S. (1998) 'Therapy from long distance debated Internet, telephone and mail counseling expected to grow', *San Jose Mercury News*, 9 April: 1.

Kelley-Milburn, D. and Milburn, M.A. (1995) 'Cyberpsych: resources for psychologists on the Internet', *Psychological Science*, 6 (4): 203–211.

Kling, R. (ed.) (1996) *Computerisation and Controversy*. London: Academic Press.

Klug, E. (1998) e-mail to psych-couns@mailbase.ac.uk 16 March.

Lago, C. (1996) 'Computer therapeutics: a new challenge for counsellors and psychotherapists', *Counselling: Journal of the British Association for Counselling*, 7 (4): 287–289.

Lee, C. (1998) 'Counselling and the challenges of cyberspace', *Counselling Today Online*, April. Available: http://www.counseling.org/ctonline/sr598/lee498.htm.

Marino, T.W. (1996) 'Counselors in cyberspace debate whether client discussions are ethical', (on-line) Available: http://www.counseling.org/ctonline/archives/ct0196a1.htm.

Marks, I., Shaw, S. and Parkin, R. (1998) 'Computer-aided treatments of mental health problems', *Clinical Psychology: Science and Practice*, 5 (2): 151–170.

McLeod, J. (2000) 'The contribution of qualitative research to evidence-based counselling and psychotherapy,' in N. Rowland and S. Goss (eds), *Evidence Based Health Care in the Psychological Therapies*. London: Routledge.

McLuhan, M. (1962) *The Gutenberg Galaxy: The Making of Typographic Man*. Toronto: University of Toronto Press.

Mearns, D. (1995) 'Supervision: a tale of the missing client', *British Journal of Guidance and Counselling*, 23 (3): 421–427.

Mearns, D. (1997) *Person-Centred Counselling Training*. London: Sage.

Morrissey, M. (1997) 'NBCC webcounseling standards unleash intense debate', *Counseling Today Online*, 40 (5) (on-line) Available: http://www.counseling.org/ctonline.archives/ct1197/webcounseling.htm.

Mueller, J.H. (1997) 'Test anxiety, self efficacy and computer experiences'. Paper presented to the 50th Annual Meeting of the New Zealand Psychological Society, Massey, NZ, 1 September.

Murphy, L.J. and Mitchell, D.L. (1998) 'When writing helps to heal: e-mail as therapy', *British Journal of Guidance and Counselling*, 26 (1): 21–32.

National Board for Certified Counselors (1997) *Standards for the Ethical Practice of WebCounseling* (on-line). Available: http://www.nbcc.org/wcstandards.htm.

Ong, W.J. (1982) *Orality and Literacy: The Technologizing of the Word*. London: Methuen.

Parliament (1984) *Public General Act. The Data Protection Act. Ch. 35. An Act to Regulate the Use of Automatically Processed Information relating to Individuals and the Provision of Services in Respect of Such Information*. London: HMSO.

Ridden, G. (1998) 'Free in the Net: tutoring on e-mail'. Unpublished paper: University of Sheffield.

Robson, D. and Robson, M. (1998) 'Intimacy and computer communication', *British Journal of Guidance and Counselling*, 26 (1): 33–41.

Rosenthal, M. (1998) *Modern Times Bookstore: Futures and Histories of the Book*. Available on-line: http://www.mtbs.com/bklst1.html.

Sanders, P. and Rosenfield, M. (1998) 'Counselling at a distance: challenges and new initiatives', *British Journal of Guidance and Counselling*, 26 (1): 5–10.

Turkle, S. (1995) *Life on the Screen: Identity in the Age of the Internet*. New York: Simon and Schuster.

Van Gelder, L. (1996) 'The strange case of the electronic lover', in R. Kling (ed.), *Computerisation and Controversy*. London: Academic Press.

Wallbank, S. (1994) *Counselling by Letter*. Richmond: CRUSE Bereavement Care.

Weil, M.M. and Rosen, L.D. (1997) *Technostress*. New York: Wiley.

12

TAKING SUPERVISION FORWARD: A ROUNDTABLE OF VIEWS

Likely development of supervision of counsellors working in primary care

Penny Henderson

My assumptions are: that counselling in primary care will still exist after the year 2000; that it will have spread beyond the current 50 per cent of practices; that it may succeed in its current development into a distinct professional discipline contributing to more consciously multiskilled teams in primary care, and that it may operate increasingly as a part of managed psychological services. If it survives, supervision of counsellors in primary care will need to develop in form, function and practice.

Issues

Counsellors will have to become fuller members of the multidisciplinary team where medical views continue to dominate, and this must affect the management of confidentiality in the team.

A more grounded theory of supervision of counsellors in primary care may emerge as more of the counsellors who have trained specifically to work in this context become ready to become supervisors, and to apply their experience to the development of supervision practice. This will increase the choice of supervisors with clear expectations of working in this setting, who have themselves done short term work with this range of the population. This may redress difficulties arising because most supervisors of counsellors in primary care currently come from other disciplines: psychiatry, psychology, psychotherapy or social work. Many have not themselves ever worked as counsellors in primary care, or met the team or seen the conditions under which the counsellor practises.

Models of supervision

For this distinct medical context, models of supervision will need to be developed which:

– Address issues arising from the context as relevant and crucial. These include management of the service, of waiting lists and the referral process; liaison with medical colleagues and learning a sufficiently shared language to develop respect for each other's assessments. The supervisor's role in supporting the counsellor to assess effectively needs more discussion.

– Attend to the restorative/supportive function of supervision very explicitly, in acknowledgement of the number, range and difficulty of clients the counsellor will be holding; to create a still place for reflection in the busy and pressurised working world.

– Encourage both supervisor and counsellor to acknowledge their limits, and the limits of a public service role: what they do not know, whom they are not competent to work with , how to make a difference with a client rather than seek a cure. It is important that both counsellors and supervisors find ways to extend their understanding and develop shared strategies to supervise brief counselling, and appreciate the contribution that brief and timely interventions can make for people who would not otherwise have access to psychological services without stigma and a long wait.

Limits to expertise and brief counselling contracts require supervision to be a space of sufficient safety so that the counsellor will willingly bring their 'mistakes' and uncertainties freely, and where they are reviewed rigorously for learning. With complaints increasing, both will have to talk about how the supervisor will support a counsellor in these circumstances, and the supervisor will need to be clear what supervisory responsibility she has for her supervisees' work – if any.

Challenges

There are three major and predictable challenges, and all three provide opportunities to be grasped:

– If trainee placements continue in primary care, they must be managed and integrated into a service where there are already existing skilful counsellors who can mentor or even supervise the trainee. Possibly the least experienced trainees should contact a supervisor about *every* client after they have assessed them. It's worth noting that no one uses trainees in employee assistance programmes, another major organisational context with probably less diversity of client problems. This is a major challenge to the training organisations and to the employing GPs, but supervisors too need to be clear, if trainees request supervision for a placement in primary care, what needs to be in place for it to be safe enough for patients and trainees alike.

– Exploring the huge range of unfamiliar territories: there are still proportionately too many white, female and middle-class counsellors and supervisors, and trainings have not until recently sufficiently addressed the learning necessary to work respectfully with people from other cultures, classes, places and orientations. Supervisors must develop awareness, skill and knowledge about the consequences for the counsellor–client and counsellor–supervisor relationship of triangles of difference, particularly about differing models of health, illness and healing. Setting up regular reviews of how well the supervisory relationship is working could contribute to this openness.

– Collaborative work with GPs may focus on either somatising patients, who come with body pain but no pathology that can be identified, or 'heartsink' patients (it is the GP's heart which is said to 'sink') who are high utilisers, and often also somatisers. Counsellors need to develop their assessment skills, and be willing to 'hold' and work with the patient, attending to dual transferences and capitalising on them, or to provide support for the GP without necessarily seeing the patient at all. Supervisors have to understand the potential and difficulties of such arrangements, and support the counsellor to work with them.

Supervisory practice may develop in form, because more counsellors are likely to combine individual supervision and group supervision, in order to get the benefits of individual time and of a range of reactions to their work. Many may more freely seek consultation 'on the hoof' by phone or e-mail or in the corridor about patients who present problems the supervisor has no expertise about. Clearer contracts relating to frequency of supervision, who is accountable for the counselling work, whom to turn to if there are problems in the supervisory relationship, will be necessary.

The balance between the supervisory functions may shift for supervision of experienced counsellors, with more focus on assessment and focusing skills, contextual matters and counsellor support. For trainees the functions still need to be normative, developmental and supportive, and the frequency of supervision and ratio of client sessions to supervisory hours need to be high so that patients are protected. Monitoring, support and developmental functions are served best by a trusting relationship and regular and appropriate numbers of hours of supervision so that trainees are not just exploited as a cheap option.

In practice, it is essential to clarify the limits of supervisor responsibility for the counsellor's work. The likelihood of complaints from patients, and the need for supervisors to develop more clarity about what they are accountable for in relation to the counsellor, may usefully encourage them to reflect on and be explicit about their own limits, and make good supervisory contracts which are regularly reviewed. That will be clearer for all concerned.

The supervision needs of counsellors working in higher and further education

Steve Page

I shall focus specifically on the changing supervision needs of counsellors working in higher and further education (whom I shall refer to as 'student counsellors'), although I believe that some of the issues raised are relevant to supervisors of counsellors in other fields. Post-compulsory education is going through a period of rapid change, with a considerable increase in the number and range of students. Along with this we are seeing more varied and flexible course structures, greater use of technology-aided learning and an emphasis on the 'lifelong learning' agenda (Dearing, 1997).

One of the consequences of the widening range of students is that counsellors are faced with a growing number of clients with serious emotional and psychological difficulties. This requires supervisors to accompany student counsellors through complex clinical decisions and help them assess and develop their capacity to work therapeutically with a diverse and challenging range of client issues. Sometimes this involves assisting counsellors in deciding when to refer clients to other agencies and in finding effective ways of working in partnership with psychiatric, psychological, medical and voluntary services. There are clients for whom referral or collaborative working is the preferred option on clinical grounds but impracticable to effectively instigate because of the transitory lives many students lead. In such instances the counsellor may need support to deal with the resulting frustration and disappointment.

Supervisors of student counsellors, particularly those who work alone or head services, need to be willing to discuss the development and imple-mentation of strategies appropriate to the changes taking place within their supervisees' institutions. This may include supervisees deciding whether or not to become involved in areas of work that offer creative opportunities to use the skills and experience developed as counsellors in new ways that are not therapeutic counselling *per se*, for example developing ways of delivering educational guidance. It may also mean determining the therapeutic criteria for deciding which changes in their work to accept and which to challenge. Such decisions involve a balance of principle and pragmatism. To do this effectively supervisors need to have quite a sophisticated understanding of the context within which their supervisees are working (Bell, 1996).

The third and final consequence for supervisors of the changing environment within which student counsellors are operating that I want to consider relates to gathering evidence through audit, evaluation and research. The increased emphasis on quality audit (Ross and Lago, 1998) and evidence-based practice (Goss and Rowland, 1999) means that counsellors must become involved in these activities or risk being sidelined. It follows that supervisors need to encourage their supervisees to undertake these tasks and help them do so in ways that enhance rather than undermine their therapeutic work. This requires supervisors to be conversant with the issues involved in such methodologies and be willing to challenge resistance should it emerge (Page et al., 1999), recognising that to some counsellors these activities will seem quite alien. Where they do not have the necessary knowledge supervisors may need to assist their supervisees to access others who do.

In short, supervisors need to be prepared to assist student counsellors to continually refine and develop their therapeutic, professional, organisational and evidence-gathering skills while monitoring the impact of any changes upon the integrity of client work. This takes the supervisors of student counsellors beyond the traditional definitions of this role, bringing significant managerial and practice development issues within the ambit of clinical supervision.

References

Bell, E. (1996) *Counselling in Further and Higher Education*. Buckingham: Open University Press.

Dearing, R. (1997) *Higher Education in the Learning Society (Summary Report, ref: NCIHE/97/849)*. London: National Committee of Inquiry into Higher Education, Crown Publications.

Goss, S. and Rowland, N. (1999) *Evidence-Based Health Care in the Psychological Therapies*. London: Routledge.

Page, S., McMahon, G. and Goss, S. (1999) 'Practitioner research', in S. Goss and N. Rowland, *Evidence-Based Health Care in the Psychological Therapies*. London: Routledge.

Ross, P. and Lago, C. (1998) *Benchmarks for Quality Standards in University Counselling Services*. Sheffield: Universities' and Colleges' Staff Development Agency.

Taking supervision forward to embrace innovative roles for counsellors in organisational settings

Elizabeth Holloway

Counsellors are increasingly being recognised for their ability to work effectively within complex organisational structures (Carroll, 1996; Carroll and Holloway, 1999). Are supervisors prepared to participate in the development of innovative roles for counsellors in organisational settings? Do supervisors have the specific knowledge and expertise germane to the new organisational settings?

Counsellors are often establishing the first programme of counselling in organisations and frequently there are no other counsellors on the staff with whom to consult. Thus, in many situations counsellors are being supervised outside of the organisation in which they work because supervisors with specific knowledge of the setting are not available. Without supervision that guides these pioneering roles to honour both the fundamental skills and the identity of counsellors, our profession could be compromised rather than enhanced by these new opportunities. Thus, while protecting professional values and identity, supervisors need to nurture an openness to new ideas, venues for intervention, labels for communication of the work, and skills that heretofore have been peripheral to counsellors' roles.

A substantial number of counsellors and their supervisors have begun the process of adapting and stretching counsellors' skills to fit the organisational reality (Carroll, 1996). However, training programmes for supervisors have only recently incorporated skills such as systems analysis (Holloway, 1995), organisational culture (Carroll, 1996), policy-making procedures, counsellor-corporate contracting, accountability and report writing, and ethical decision making within a corporate structure (Carroll and Holloway, 1999). The advent of counsellors in corporations is forcing educators to reconsider what skills are necessary for effective practice, and subsequently the prerequisite knowledge and skills for supervisors. Although a number of different skills are relevant to the organisational counsellor (Carroll, 1996), in this brief comment I will focus on the issue of accountability in practice. This includes the use of evaluation criteria and procedures that evaluate outcomes of practice in a multifaceted system.

Traditional strategies for counsellor accountability have included charting of the counsellor's assessment and interventions with each client. These documentation procedures are largely descriptive and usually include intake summaries, progress notes, summary notes, psychological testing reports, and any additional information solicited from auxiliary professionals. Supervisors in training situations have full access to client files. In some cases they are required to sign each entry, and often give feedback to trainees regarding form, style and relevance of information contained. Many times it is the testimony or suggestion of the client that they feel much better and are ready to end treatment that provides the counsellor with 'outcome information'. Although for supervisors this information is useful in helping the counsellor self-evaluate the goal–intervention–outcome connections in their work, this type of case by case analysis does not fit a system that is primarily concerned with bottom-line efficiency and effectiveness.

Accountability of a service within the larger system of an organisation must document the goals, objectives, procedures and outcome of each service programme. The development of sound outcome measures that can be aggregated across many cases and services is critical to substantiate the effectiveness of counselling programmes and to justify continued financial support. Each of the potential interventions must be defined not only in terms of goals and target group, but also of outcome measures. The choice of outcome measures and procedures for the collection of information from service provider to recipient of the service is a critical part of the design of the programming. To date, counsellors have been well prepared to develop programmes that reach a variety of constituencies; however, 'outcome measures' have often been viewed as 'research measures' irrelevant to the actual delivery of care in real settings. Unfortunately, traditional researchers of psychology have earned this reputation amongst practitioners. However, there are recent innovations in the design of 'programme evaluation research' that is designed to fit the context of actual service delivery programmes (Heppner et al., 1998). Central to the role of the programme evaluation is evaluating the effectiveness of a particular programme with a defined group of participants (Benkofski, 1998). The programme evaluator, in this case the counsellor, selects measures that reflect the specific objectives of the programme and that produce the type of information that can be easily interpreted by decision makers unfamiliar with counselling terms, procedures and expected outcomes. Often this means the use of observational and more anthropological methods that collect information as a project unfolds as well as follow-up effects at selected points in time.

For example, let us take a counselling service within a for-profit organisation. The service has two professional counsellors on staff and they are required to provide programmes of service at three levels of intervention. These levels might be described as (a) developmental, for example retirement planning, career advancement, parental leave; (b) preventative, for example stress management, interpersonal skills for employees in supervisory roles; and (c) remedial, for example mediation and conflict resolution, direct counselling for employees who seek help for psychological and interpersonal concerns. Each of these programmes is targeted to promote the well-being of the employee at different stages of need and programmes are generally more costly as the care becomes more urgent. This conceptualisation presents a multi-pronged approach to programme planning that was developed in a college-counselling environment (Morrill and Hurst, 1971). The design of an evaluation programme that reflects the efficacy of this type of programming must consider the systemic effects of such programming. For example, preventative programmes delivered first as psychoeducational instruction to a group may in the short run increase the number of referrals for individual counselling related to stress. That is, individuals in the workshop discover that there are services available and that their condition can be treated effectively. In the long run, however, preventative programmes should enable employees to establish healthy living patterns that will prevent the development of more severe stress reactions. This is but one example of the complexity involved in designing programme evaluations that can accurately determine the impact of a programme.

Finally, counsellors must be prepared to subject the outcome data to a cost/benefit analysis critical to the survival of any programme in the business sector. The skills of programme evaluation and cost/benefit analysis could easily be taught in the supervisory curriculum. The supervisors, in particular, may find an important role in planning and overseeing such programme evaluation efforts in their work with counsellors in organisational settings. It behoves training programmes to teach the skills of programme evaluation, aggregate data collection at a local level, survey development and local mechanisms for gathering information on counselling services that are relevant to the nature of our work. If we do not do it within the profession, the organisation in which we work will apply its own cultural standards of data collection, privacy and accountability that often do not fit the service delivery systems of counselling.

Trainers and supervisors can open new avenues of service for counsellors' skills. Training programmes need to equip supervisors and counsellors with 'bottom line' accountability tools and reporting methods that maintain their credibility and substantiate their value to the organisation's productivity. To have the advantage of gradually shifting the corporate culture to enhance the well-being of human resources, we must learn the language of survival without jeopardising our ethics. As supervisors and educators of supervisors we can expand the skill base of counsellors' roles and ensure that the profession takes leadership in designing and evaluating new programming for corporate systems. The future of counselling is not in traditional roles alone. It is in the application of our skills in human relations and systems analysis to the many groups and organisations in which people live, work, and play.

References

Benkofski, M. H., C. C. (1998) 'Program evaluation', in P. P. Heppner, D. M. Kivlighan Jr. and B. E. Wampold (eds), *Research Design in Counseling*, 2nd edn. New York: Brooks/Cole. pp. 488–513.
Carroll, M. (1996). *Workplace Counselling*. London: Sage.
Carroll, M. and Holloway, E. (eds) (1999) *Supervision in Context*. London: Sage.
Heppner, P. P., Kivlighan, D. M. Jr. and Wampold, B. E. (1998) *Research Design in Counseling*, 2nd edn. New York: Brooks/Cole.
Holloway, E. (1995). *Clinical Supervision: A Systems Approach*. Thousand Oaks, CA: Sage.
Morrill, W. H. and Hurst, J. C. (1971) 'A preventative and developmental role for the college counselor', *The Counseling Psychologist*, 2(4): 90–95.

Studying tapes of sessions can be essential for practitioners to become better practitioners

Alvin R. Mahrer

Here is a tiny distillation of what is described elsewhere (Mahrer, 1996; Mahrer and Boulet, 1997).

Picture a teacher and about one to five trainees or professionals, studying audiotapes of actual sessions. We meet regularly, perhaps once or twice a month. Picture our studying three kinds of audiotape: (a) We study prized tapes of the actual sessions of fine, exemplar, master practitioners. Thankfully, we have a library of these precious audiotapes. (b) We study tapes of our own therapy sessions with the people we work with, our patients, or whatever term seems best. (c) We study tapes of each member's own sessions with, by, and for ourselves. More about this later.

Study tapes to continuously improve the practitioner's in-session competencies and skills

Before the group meets, the practitioner decides which part of the audiotape is to be studied. Generally, the part is selected because (a) something exciting happened here. The practitioner is pleased, proud, happy, satisfied with something about this part. Or (b) right about here the practitioner felt bad. Something was not good, went wrong. This part was bothersome, troubling, worrisome, a real problem. It helps to be honest.

Studying the tape means trying to discover what the practitioner actually did that was so good, that worked so well, or that was so bad, made things worse, and what the practitioner might have done to make things much better. Once the concrete skill is identified, the practitioner can play the tape in actual training to practise the newfound skill over and over until the practitioner becomes genuinely competent in using that practised skill under those conditions. Here is solid skill training to increase actual competency.

Study tapes to discover the practitioner's own inner, deeper conceptual framework for psychotherapy

Most practitioners label themselves as belonging to some family. I do psychodynamic therapy. I do existential. I am a cognitive therapist, an Adlerian, a Gestalt therapist, an integrative-eclectic therapist. Some special practitioners are ready and willing to believe in and to study a mysteriously rich pool of their own, inner, deeper, partly formed core notions, ideas about what people are like, how and why people feel good or bad, do what they do, change. These practitioners are curious about discovering their own deeper, hidden conceptual frameworks for psychotherapy.

Start by identifying the liked and disliked parts of the tape. The key is to study these particular parts of the session in a careful, penetrative, probing, ever-deeper analysis of these core notions. The payoff is the gradual uncovering, clarification and discovery of your very own, inner, deeper, conceptual framework for psychotherapy.

Study tapes to have better sessions with, by, and for yourself

Most therapists do therapy unto others. Therapists administer treatment to clients. Instead, picture all sorts of people, even practitioners, having sessions with, by and for themselves. No therapist. And picture good teachers teaching interested others, one at a time or in small groups, how to go through and to become proficient in having their own experiential sessions. How can a person learn how to have their own experiential sessions?

Tape sessions of your teacher showing you how to go through your own sessions. This is the experiential version of what is called psychotherapy! Tape the experiential sessions that you carried out by yourself. Then study the tapes by yourself or with a fellow learner or with a teacher so that you get better and better at having your own experiential sessions (Mahrer, 1996; in press).

I consider the careful study of audiotapes, in these ways and for these purposes, to be the challengingly best way for practitioners to become better and better practitioners. I therefore challenge and invite all interested practitioners to study tapes of sessions to continuously improve their in-session competencies and skills; to discover their own inner, deeper conceptual frameworks for psychotherapy; and to become better and better at having their own psychotherapy sessions with, by, and for themselves.

References

Mahrer, A. R. (1996) *The Complete Guide to Experiential Psychotherapy*. New York: John Wiley and Sons.

Mahrer, A. R. (in press) 'How to use psychotherapy on, for, and by oneself', *Professional Psychology: Research and Practice*.

Mahrer, A. R. and Boulet, D. B. (1997) 'The experiential model of on-the-job teaching', in C. E. Watkins, Jr. (ed.), *Handbook of Psychotherapy Supervision*. New York: John Wiley and Sons. pp. 164–183.

Trends and developments in supervision in Europe

Jennie McNamara

> In some European countries counselling is an old tradition concerned with individual growth. In others it is a philosophical concept still to be confronted by experience, or it is an advice giving practice performed by specialised professional advisors, or, and not infrequently by fortune tellers. European counselling concepts and practices are struggling with differences. (*EAC Newsletter*, June 1994)

Just as within the profession of counselling and psychotherapy as a whole, supervision is a diverse practice. European countries have largely developed supervision in their own way and at their own pace. Within the past decade some countries have actively developed supervision, whilst within others it is still virtually unknown.

Currently there is no European-wide understanding of supervision. In some countries the word 'supervision' is synonymous with counselling and is taken to be the same activity. In others it is more strongly linked with a medical model in which supervision is only undertaken with students, qualified practitioners being seen as not needing to be supervised. Some countries, for example Germany and the UK, have an already well established knowledge and practice base, whilst in places such as Russia the profession is in an embryonic stage and training is being provided by practitioners from other countries.

Since the opening up of the East European borders, America, Germany and the UK have been active in introducing training and supervision within these countries. This situation has posed interesting debates amongst trainers and supervisors. Should we impose Western models on very different cultures or stimulate a two-way learning process as we are challenged to review our dogmas? As professional mobility across Europe increases, will this over time influence the models of supervision needed, as supervisors move across the cultural divide, leading to the development of new skills and awareness? It has become increasingly apparent that these questions need to be addressed.

Overall, within Europe there is a clear split between countries which support and favour an adaptation to the BAC model of supervision, including mandatory supervision for experienced practitioners and guidelines for the ratio of supervision hours. Directly opposed to this model other countries take the view that BAC requirements and guidelines are far too low for the profession to be taken seriously in their country. In line with this position they recommend a greater emphasis on mandatory personal therapy, a higher number of training hours and frequency of supervision. A third view is that of countries that support greater freedom for practitioners in determining the amount of supervision required. These countries tend to view counselling training as postgraduate and usually require practitioners to have qualifications and experience in one of the helping professions. In general, European countries hold the view that personal therapy should be mandatory, aiding reflexivity and complementing the supervision process.

Until recently, European-wide organisations that represent different modalities, such as the European Association for Transactional Analysis, have contributed a lot to the development of models of supervision that enable dialogue across country-culture boundaries. However, these organisations have also worked in isolation without the sharing of skills or experience across modalities. This picture is beginning to change and will be strongly influenced over the next few decades by the emerging umbrella organisations for the profession, the European Association for Counselling (EAC) and the European Association for Psychotherapy (EAP).

The EAP is already fairly well established and accepted in many countries. In June 1998 the EAP awarded its first European Certificates in Psychotherapy. It is working with national umbrella organisations and governments to establish criteria for training, qualification and ongoing professional development. Alongside there is an EAP committee for supervision that has established and continues to develop criteria for supervision. EAC is in an earlier phase of development. There is a lot of interest in this organisation as it has potential to represent a wide cross-section of professionals, from those using counselling skills in their work to those wishing to be accredited European counsellors. Many countries have expressed a strong need for EAC to lay down standards for training, qualification and supervision. Currently there are six countries with established National Associations for Counselling (NAC).

The EAC encourages supervisors to:

- constantly develop a multicultural awareness;
- recognise cultural differences between supervisor and supervisee at country/cultural level, and address these in a non-judgmental way;
- move their own communicative behaviour towards the country/cultural orientation of the supervisee.

Supervision in the twenty-first century will no doubt be influenced by these organisations as they develop and embody a European-wide definition of supervision. Their main focus is to establish European standards for the profession, thus enabling professional mobility across country-culture boundaries. Clearly supervision needs to be wide enough and broad enough to incorporate both context *and* centralisation. We need flexible standards that are changeable, realistic and achievable.

Note

The EAC has developed a draft definition of supervision:

Counselling supervision is a contracted professional relationship between two or more individuals engaged with counselling activities that leads to reflection on the counselling situation and its structure. It provides support and containment for the counsellor and the counselling work.

Supervision responsibly monitors the working process between counsellor and client. (EAC Newsletter, November 1998)

Supervision of supervision?

Michael Jacobs

Who created God? The question is not irrelevant to supervision, because a similar puzzle is constantly raised by those who begin to train as supervisors. We may need supervision of our supervision, but who supervises the supervisors who supervise the supervisors who supervise . . . *ad infinitum*?

The question also demands we ask whether there may not be obsessive aspects to supervision. Is supervision of supervision of supervision a check on whether we are doing it right? Is it a means of learning the skills of supervision? Is it about being a better supervisor? In this increasingly mad search for perfection – whether it be watertight protection of the public, or flawless practice, or the most perceptive insight – we run into all the dangers of over-kill. Who has it right? The British Association for Counselling, for example, which insists upon a minimum time for supervision every month? Or the UK Council for Psychotherapy, to take a different example, which requires members to be aware of the need for supervision at certain points in practice? I suggest that the latter organisation recognises the possibility of maturity, and that the mature therapist or counsellor has a good sense of when to ask for help.

Maturity also recognises that it is impossible to cover every eventuality, and that supervision cannot in the end protect anyone: only the therapeutic relationship can do that and even that can go wrong, even for the most careful of counsellors or therapists. Client and therapist have differing degrees of responsibility, and there are impossible situations where no one can do the right thing. Maturity also means appreciating the value of lifelong learning without there having to be lifelong schooling, and of self-regulation over the apparent necessity of imposed rules and regulations.

And if this maturity could be achieved, how much healthier we would be! For a start we would recognise that responsibility in the conduct of supervision and therapy and counselling is always in our own hands: supervision of supervision is icing on the cake, making practice look pretty, and adding to its flavour no doubt; but not everyone has a sweet tooth. And might not the same be said about supervision of therapy and counselling? Of course we need it when we start, but more because of our inability to contain autonomously the doubts and uncertainties that will, we learn in time, always be there. Experienced practitioners never lose their doubts, but learn to work with them and despite them. Furthermore, if we changed our rigid thinking about perpetual supervision, then voluntary agencies – often with a list of people waiting to become counsellors, but held back through lack of supervisors – could become flexible about how their experienced counsellors are supervised, so releasing existing supervisors for the newer counsellors.

It is a myth to think that supervision can prevent mistakes. We need to recognise that we can never be as gods: that the search for perfection, and the wish to avoid all error, is part of an obsessional culture which is in danger of losing not only its freedom, but also the creativity that goes with it.

'In supervision with . . .'

Geraldine Shipton

I want to think about the role of supervision in creating a frame for clinical work in the mind of the supervisee. Robert Langs (1994) has written extensively about the need to maintain a boundary around supervision, much as we do in psychotherapy (see also Gray, 1994 for a discussion of the therapeutic frame). Langs' argument is persuasive but extreme: it seems as if he sees little difference between therapy and supervision and therefore strongly recommends that principles applied to the therapeutic frame be upheld for supervision.

I am concerned, in a more general way, with the framing effect of supervision. A history of supervision (see Edwards, 1997) shows that the frame has altered over time and has looked different in various locations, such as Vienna and Budapest: it is not a fixed entity. The concept of frame comes from the world of art, and there we also find that the framing of paintings has altered distinctly throughout history, and has served a range of functions (see Penny, 1996). At times the frame has served to harmonise the painting with the setting, making it fit with the décor; sometimes the frame has been designed to show to advantage the contents of the painting; on occasion the frame has been used to make a point about how we locate works of art in our lives, or whether or not art 'bleeds' out of its frame into the rest of the setting.

Thinking about supervision in these ways has helped me to understand some misgivings about the words 'in supervision with . . .' which I have become aware of recently, and which seem to represent a kind of false imprimatur of quality, as if the supervisee must thereby be endowed with some of the qualities of the supervisor. The ethical requirement to be 'in supervision' for trainees is essential and for qualified counsellors is probably a good thing, in principle. However, being 'in supervision' does not, of itself, ensure that clinical work is really being thought about creatively, much as our photographs in a clip-frame on the wall do not guarantee quality within the frame. Legislating supervision into ethical codes solves one problem but creates another one: responsibility subtly shifts to another site – the frame of the supervisor him- or herself. I think this is why, in psychotherapy, many experienced practitioners tend to use the term 'consultation' which implies that clinical responsibility lies with the person seeking consultation, and not with the consultant. I am not arguing for taking supervision out of ethical codes for counsellors, but am proposing that the healthy principle of consultation should be thought about, rather than the application of a 'rule' which stops the thinking process and furthermore, throws our regard upon the supervisor, rather than the supervisee as the locus of responsibility and quality. Whether or not this means a change of terminology is of less interest to me than the question of responsibility and quality, which can easily slip away under any nomenclature.

References

Edwards, D. (1997) 'Supervision today: the psychoanalytic legacy', in G. Shipton (ed.), *Supervision of Psychotherapy and Counselling: Making a Place to Think.* Buckingham and Philadelphia: Open University Press, pp. 11–23.

Gray, A. (1994) *An Introduction to the Therapeutic Frame.* London: Routledge.

Langs, R. (1994) *Doing Supervision and Being Supervised.* London: Karnac.

Penny, N. (1996) 'Back to the wall', in J. Hindle (ed.), *London Review of Books: An Anthology.* London and New York: Verso. pp. 173–180.

Supervision and mature professional counsellors

Sue Wheeler

Over the past twenty-two years the British Association for Counselling (BAC) has worked unerringly to develop high standards and ethical codes for the practice of counselling in Britain. The achievements of the organisation are not to be underestimated. The emphasis placed on the central role and function of supervision for counselling practice has been accepted and valued, although BAC has taken the requirement for supervision one step further than most other professions in Britain and North America, in making supervision a career-long requirement. Elsewhere, counselling supervision is a requirement for trainees and optional or desirable thereafter. In related professions such as clinical psychology, nursing, social work, psychotherapy, medicine and the clergy, post-qualification supervision may be part of continual professional development, but is not a condition for ethical practice. The UKCP *Ethical Guidelines* (1997: 3) make no mention of supervision but refer to 'the requirement [of psychotherapists] to maintain their ability to perform competently and to take necessary steps to do so'. UKCP member organisations have their own codes of ethics. The *Code of Practice* of the West Midlands Institute of Psychotherapy (1995: 3) states that 'It is recognised that continuing professional consultation whether in supervision and/or therapy and combining education, are consistent with maintaining oneself responsibly as a practitioner.'

As a new organisation seeking to develop a new profession, it is understandable that BAC has had trainees and 'young' professional counsellors in mind, when developing codes of practice. However, it has perhaps neglected to take account of the fact that some of its founder members are neither trainees nor 'young'. Yet despite many years of experience as counselling practitioners, supervisors, authors, trainers and members of professional committees, they are still in the same category of counsellors as those in training. To maintain accreditation they are still required to have 1.5 hours of supervision per month, as well as supervision of supervision and training (BAC, 1997b), to adhere to the *Code of Ethics* (BAC, 1997a). Furthermore, for mature counsellors whose training role takes up the majority of their time, who continue counselling to maintain individual accreditation and registration (and hence credibility with students), the number of hours of supervision is the same as the requirement for trainees! One hundred and fifty hours of counselling per year requires a minimum of eighteen hours of supervision, one supervision session for every 8.33 hours of counselling. BAC accredited training courses (BAC, 1996) recommend a minimum of one hour of supervision for every eight hours of counselling.

The mature, experienced practitioner is not taken into account by some of BAC's requirements, although a recent publication (BAC, 1998: 3) accedes that 'in the exceptional case of a well trained, highly experienced but *unaccredited* counsellor undertaking a light caseload . . . the assessment of sufficient supervision [might] dip below the baseline'. To other professions, the requirement for career-long obligatory supervision conveys the message that counselling is a profession that cannot be trusted, that has to be constantly under surveillance. Counsellors sometimes express irritation that their employers are reticent to pay for supervision. From the employer's perspective, they may wonder who they have taken on that the counsellor cannot be trusted to work independently.

Supervision requirements are tied into the current accreditation schemes as well as the *Codes of Ethics* (BAC, 1997a, 1997b), which also take no account of experience. Re-accreditation is required every five years in perpetuity. While this might be seen as a good way of ensuring that standards of competence are maintained, it also undermines principles of self-regulation and self-monitoring. It is possible that counsellors may decline in competence because of medical, psychological or personal or practical circumstances, but this could apply to any other professional person, who is not subject to the same regular scrutiny. It is true that peer monitoring is easier in organisational settings and many counsellors work alone, but the same applies to psychoanalysts and psychotherapists, some doctors and clergy, dentists and most para-medical professionals. For older, more experienced counselling practitioners, there are no means to validate their experience with senior professional status and exemption from the continued requirement to prove or defend themselves as competent therapists. The UKCP *Ethical Guidelines* (1997) expect psychotherapists to engage in continued professional development, which implies more trust than the requirement for lifelong supervision implicit in the BAC ethical codes. For this and many other reasons mature counsellors may begin to look elsewhere for professional allegiance, for an organisation that respects experience and does not infantilise its members with global supervision requirements. Without doubt most counsellors would continue to have appropriate supervision, but without the resentment at being required to do so. The counselling profession must address this issue in the twenty-first century, or it will risk losing many of its founder members who have contributed so much to its development.

References

British Association for Counselling (1996) *The Recognition of Counsellor Training Courses*. Rugby: BAC.

British Association for Counselling (1997a) *Code of Ethics and Practice for Counsellors*. Rugby: BAC.

British Association for Counselling (1997b) *Codes of Ethics and Practice for Supervisors of Counsellors*. Rugby: BAC.

British Association for Counselling (1998) *How Much Supervision Should You Have?* (Information sheet). Rugby: BAC.

United Kingdom Council for Psychotherapy (1997) *Ethical Guidelines*. London: UKCP.

West Midlands Institute of Psychotherapy (1995) *Code of Ethics and Code of Practice*. Birmingham: WMIP.

The interface between supervision and therapy in the supervision of experienced practitioners

Val Wosket

The personal and professional selves of many therapists become inseparable as they gain experience and seniority. Engaging in therapeutic work can, for the experienced practitioner, have a reciprocal quality that is life-changing for the therapist as well as for the client (Wosket, 1999). For those therapists for whom the practice of their craft reflects a growing personal authenticity, and particularly for those who elect to work in more personally determined ways as they get older and (hopefully) wiser, their supervision will need to accommodate such changes.

Just as the professions of counselling and psychotherapy are reaching maturity, so too are individual practitioners. A great number of therapists now practising will have received their initial training or apprenticeship several decades ago. As a supervisor of a few of these well seasoned therapists, it frequently strikes me how differently I work with them to when I work with trainees and newly qualified practitioners. Rarely during the supervision of therapists from this more senior generation do we discuss counselling strategies, specific therapeutic interventions or treatment plans. Instead, I find myself talking with them about their personal issues as they relate to significant life changes, including their experience of being in other roles (e.g. manager, parent, partner, carer) and the impact that these have on their therapeutic work. For these individuals their life issues are their supervision issues. To the extent that they draw on aspects of themselves in their therapeutic work, these practitioners need to bring to supervision those parts of the self that are touched and affected by their clients.

Sometimes I have known these individuals over a number of years and witnessed the life-changing events that come to impact on their therapeutic work: jobs and careers are lost and gained; a long term marriage or partnership breaks down and they become single again; a parent, sibling or child dies or suffers serious illness; their own ageing, illness or disability has to be faced and accommodated; early idealism, naivety and enthusiasm give way to dogged realism, ennui, even despair and burnout. It seems to me that all of these life events have a legitimate place in supervision. What is common to them all is the experience of loss and adjustment and, as Judith Viorst (1987) has so cogently argued, losses are necessary, unavoidable and increasingly frequent realities of life for all of us. As we get older our experiences of loss and change accumulate and need to be assimilated into the professional persona. Supervision is a place where these experiences may be acknowledged and explored for the ways in which they impact on both client *and* therapist.

A legitimate question arising in this context might be: 'Why not pack these people off to personal counselling or therapy to sort themselves out?' – as we so often do with trainees, whose personal issues then become fodder for their forty or so hours of required personal counselling. Granted, periods of personal counselling or therapy are often appropriate throughout a practitioner's career, yet emergent and intransigent aspects of self cannot always be 'worked through' and then laid by. It may be that they are going to be around for a long time, or even for the rest of our lives. A degenerative illness or an irrevocably stressful work environment are realities to be faced every day within the context of therapeutic work – not isolated issues or problems that can be cleared out of the system given sufficient doses of therapist-generated catharsis or the challenging of self-defeating patterns of thinking and behaviour.

In saying all this, I am not suggesting that it is all right for supervisors to counsel their supervisees – even where they are experienced practitioners who have ongoing personal dilemmas that affect their therapeutic work. What I am proposing is that as supervisors our principal function is to listen well and acceptantly to that which is most at the forefront of our supervisees' concerns about their work with clients. And if this involves personal material I think we need to listen to this too. This may mean that on occasion we extend our role to encompass those, for instance, of debriefer or problem management consultant. As I believe that supervision and counselling can sometimes accommodate dual roles and relationships (Wosket, 1999), I think we can do this without it necessarily meaning that the boundary between supervision and therapy stretches so far that it snaps, with the result that we tumble and disappear into the supervisee's inner world and lose all sight of the client.

To try to make this proposition more concrete, let me give a couple of examples where I have worked extensively at this interface between therapy and supervision with two supervisees. The first is a supervisee who was diagnosed with a degenerative illness that would inevitably begin to show itself to clients. Here we spent many hours monitoring the impact of the illness on both himself and his clients until the day arrived when we both faced the painful reality that he should stop counselling. I continued to supervise him for an extended period beyond the termination of his counselling role while he struggled to come to terms with the impact that this transition was making on his professional identity. Though we no longer discussed therapeutic work with clients in these sessions, they nevertheless maintained a professional focus as we covered such issues as exploring possibilities for other professional activities he might become involved with on a voluntary basis wherein he could draw upon his extensive experience as a counsellor; how he might deal with approaches from ex-clients who lived in the same rural community in which he was well known and who were concerned about his welfare; whether it remained appropriate for him to take on for supervision people who approached him from time to time and knew about his changed circumstances. Whilst continuing to attend supervision, he also took part in a support group of people suffering from the same illness as himself, where he was able to address some of the more directly personal aspects of his situation.

My second example concerns a therapist who, over the several years in which I supervised her, was increasingly required to take on management responsibilities within her workplace – a voluntary organisation that found itself undergoing externally imposed change at a dizzying velocity over a short period of time. During this period my supervisee experienced the death of both her elderly parents and the serious illness of her own child while simultaneously struggling to fend off sometimes insupportable amounts of work-generated stress. Of course, all of these experiences affected her therapeutic competence and part of the work undertaken in supervision involved helping her decide when she needed to reduce her caseload, when she needed to withdraw from therapeutic work entirely for a period of some months and when she was able, again, to pick up the reins of her counselling role. At one stage the situation reached a point of crisis and, while this meant that she stopped counselling for some time, she still attended supervision regularly so that I could listen and support her in exploring the impact this temporary loss of role had on her personal and professional identity. I believe that she experienced supervision during this period as a restorative and regenerative process which played its part in helping her eventually to return to the fray and re-engage in a more refreshed state with her clients.

To conclude, I would suggest that the professional bodies that construct definitions of clinical supervision and then design the codes of ethics and practice governing its conduct need to take more account than currently exists of the differing supervision needs of experienced practitioners. To split the exploration of personal issues off from the task of supervision brings a danger of encouraging the therapist to split the self off from the role of practitioner. The clear and immediate danger that then occurs is that supervision becomes a sterile and sanitised activity and one that accommodates only intellectual discussion or, worse still, a smug collegial blandness.

References

Viorst, J. (1987) *Necessary Losses*. New York: Ballantine.
Wosket, V. (1999) *The Therapeutic Use of Self: Counselling Practice, Research and Supervision*. London: Routledge.

Supervision for the twenty-first century

Brigid Proctor and Francesca Inskipp

This is the view of two women who have been engaged in the provision of counselling, supervision and training since the beginning of BAC. The inception of BAC marked the provision of a forum for people engaged with counselling. This led to a body of people with diverse ideas and interests co-operating successfully in the development of shared ethics and standards of practice. The past decade has seen a landslide towards the professionalisation of counselling and psychotherapy although some of the initial differences have not been addressed or resolved. We anticipate that the next decade will bring developments which, internally, arise out of that precipitous and, perhaps, premature professionalisation. Externally, they will be in response to social, economic, technical and political changes which are being widely prophesied for the millennium. Rather than join in the prophesying, we want to:

- spell out our aim for supervisors and the process of supervision;
- review where supervision stands in 1999;
- suggest what we think needs to happen if those aims are to be realised.

Our aim

We would like to see the process of supervision become more accountable, and integrated into the various professional bodies. This would support and challenge supervisors and supervisor trainers to recognise their responsibility to help the profession become increasingly centred in shared core values while being adaptive to client need in rapidly changing circumstances.

Supervisors are used as gatekeepers to the profession, as official monitors, as carriers of received wisdom and as holders of hope in times of despair. They are in a special position to be the channels between different limbs of professional bodies – committees, trainers, agencies, providers and counsellors. Unless or until the supervisor role is revised, practitioners who are also supervisors need to be thinking ahead, logging feedback from the field, and providing feedback to professional bodies. In the field, they need to be open to changing need and provision and lead in developing good practice. We believe that with proper support and challenge, the complex role is functional and a better choice than splitting off monitoring from support.

At present, supervisors have no regular networks. There is no clearing house where recurring issues in counselling and supervision can be identified nor any channel of communication through which these can be fed back. Professional codes of ethics stipulate that everyone needs to be in supervision but supervisor trainers have no meeting ground. Provision of supervision training can be (and possibly is) idiosyncratic since there are no guidelines. No one knows which trainings are linked to supervisor accreditation; whether there is selection or monitoring of applicants, or what are standards and criteria for appraisal or assessment. Although our impression is that supervisor training is developing quite pragmatically it is probably still more tribal and sectarian than is suitable for the dilemmas of many counsellors on the ground.

In the field we know that counsellors are increasingly:

- engaged in brief practice, geared to the needs of clients from EAPs and GP surgeries;
- requiring organisational, team and system skills;
- working with a wide range of clients, including those not catered for by 'community care';
- struggling with integrating old and new counselling ideas and practice;
- working with an informed and increasingly litigious public.

Meanwhile, supervisors are

- working with mixed groups of trainees from varied training courses;
- at the interface of the scrabble for trainee placements and the resulting decline of traditional 'volunteering';
- supervising mixed teams of related professionals needing interpersonal and counselling skill.

These circumstances call into question our honesty in saying we are an accountable and self-monitoring profession. They leave supervisors and the profession open to criticism and litigation. Our arrangements do not acknowledge the impossibility of policing. Neither do they honour our intention to do our best to safeguard clients and support and challenge counsellors to deliver an excellent service.

So what needs to happen if supervision and supervisors are well prepared for the millennium? Supervisors need to be either flexible specialists, or specialists in flexibility. They need to be aware of the consequences of their working contexts and clear about the roles and responsibilities which go with a range of supervision contracts. This requires both holding and testing core values.

In GP practices, for example, counsellors need to adapt to working in a medical team while holding their unique professional contribution. Supervisors may have to challenge ideas of confidentiality and assessment, and help counsellors educate the team about the possibilities and limitations of counselling.

Those working with counsellors who undertake a wide variety of counselling, training and consulting need to be aware of organisational as well as client issues. This will require them to be clear and grounded in their basic understanding of good practice. When working with other professionals who want consultative supervision, supervisors need to be flexible or specialised and clear about their roles and responsibilities.

The role of trainee supervisor should perhaps be bracketed from that of consultative supervision. It carries specific 'hard skill' responsibilities for appraisal and assessment which ally it with training. Supervisors, trainers and agency managers need to work as teams, and be required to do so by the profession.

System issues

Supervisor training should be geared to field requirements. We need a system for developing basic guidelines for supervisor training and co-ordinating 'levels' of practice. When counselling trainers were invited to produce an accreditation system for counsellor training courses, it changed the field. Practical endeavours require tribal myths and realities to be addressed. The development of the supervisor accreditation scheme has not, on its own, had that effect.

Professional bodies should initiate a supervisor forum. In our experience, supervisors, especially those who are new to the role, are hungry to meet, to exchange ideas and clarify anomalies of their complex tasks. Issues of training and co-accountability must be addressed. Short of supervision of supervision of supervision, how can we become truly self-monitoring and co-accountable? The profession(s) have to determine methods, but they must have systematic supervisor feedback from the field and seek to develop a body of research and anecdotal information which helps identify if supervision is the best answer to the purposes it is expected to satisfy.

In summary, individual supervisors take responsibility to carry 'parental' roles for the profession. They can do this best by helping practitioners develop as self-monitoring and self-reflective practitioners who are adaptive to changing need and provision. They themselves should model groundedness and flexibility and be supported and challenged to recognise their responsibility as developers of good practice and of the profession.

INDEX